Key Stage Three
English

No doubt about it — KS3 English is a tricky business. Need help? Then look no further...

This brilliant CGP book is packed with crystal-clear notes and examples to help you analyse texts and improve your writing — plus plenty of practice questions (with answers) to make sure you've got the hang of everything.

And as an extra treat, we've even included mixed-topic tests and a practice exam at the end of the book. You'll be a KS3 English expert by the time you've finished.

How to access your free Online Edition

This book includes a free Online Edition to read on your PC, Mac or tablet.
You'll just need to go to **cgpbooks.co.uk/extras** and enter this code:

4333 9401 7145 0904

By the way, this code only works for one person. If somebody else has used this book before you, they might have already claimed the Online Edition.

Complete
Revision & Practice

Everything you need for the whole course!

Contents

Published by CGP

Editors:
Chloe Anderson, Holly Robinson, Jack Tooth

With thanks to Paula Barnett and Heather Cowley for the proofreading.

With thanks to Emily Smith for the copyright research.

Extract on p41: Copyright Exodus Travels: exodus.co.uk.

Extract on p42: From *Spaghetti Pig Out* as published in *Uncanny!* by Paul Jennings
Text copyright © Paul Jennings, 1988
First published by Penguin Group Australia. Reprinted by permission of Penguin Random House Australia Pty Ltd.

Extract on p45: *Swim With The Fishes*, p26-27 , from *Extreme Encounters* by Greg Emmanuel © 2002, Quirk
Productions. Reprinted with the permission of Quirk Books, Philadelphia, Pennsylvania.

Extract on p81: Permission given by Viva! www.viva.org.uk.

Poem on p115: *For One Night Only* first appeared in *The All-Nite Café* (Faber, 1993). Copyright © Philip Gross.

Poem on p116: *First Ice* by Andrei Voznesensky.

Extract on p127-8: AN INSPECTOR CALLS by J.B. Priestley (Penguin Books, 2000). Copyright © J.B. Priestley, 1947.
Reproduced by permission of Penguin Books Ltd.

Extract on p129: DEATH OF A SALESMAN by Arthur Miller. Copyright © Arthur Miller, 1949, used by permission of
The Wylie Agency (UK) Limited.

Extract on p169: Print rights for THINGS FALL APART by Chinua Achebe (William Heinemann 1958, Penguin Classics
2001). Copyright © Chinua Achebe, 1958. Reproduced by permission of Penguin Books Ltd.
Digital Rights for THINGS FALL APART by Chinua Achebe Copyright © Chinua Achebe, 1958, used by permission of
The Wylie Agency (UK) Limited.

Letters on p173: With thanks to Mark Charles Dickens for permission to reproduce the letters of Charles Dickens.

Extract on p174: From CNN.com, 28th August 2013 © 2013 Turner Broadcast Systems. All rights reserved. Used
by permission and protected by the Copyright Laws of the United States. The printing, copying, redistribution, or
retransmission of this Content without express written permission is prohibited.

Poem on p178: Copyright Siegfried Sassoon by kind permission of the Estate of George Sassoon.

With thanks to Rex Features for permission to include the images on pages 112, 121, 122, 124, 131, 131, 132, 134,
137, 139, 140, 142, 143, 144, 145, 147, 148 and 149.

For copyright reasons, this book is not for sale in the USA, Canada and Philippines

Every effort has been made to locate copyright holders and obtain permission to reproduce sources. For those sources
where it has been difficult to trace the originator of the work, we would be grateful for information. If any copyright
holder would like us to make an amendment to the acknowledgements, please notify us and we will gladly update the
book at the next reprint. Thank you.

ISBN: 978 1 84762 156 6

Printed by Elanders Ltd, Newcastle upon Tyne.
Images & Clipart throughout the book from Corel ® and Clipart.com

Based on the classic CGP style created by Richard Parsons.

Basic Punctuation

This stuff is about as basic as it gets. People do get it wrong though — when they're <u>rushing</u> and not <u>thinking</u>. Learn it really well, and before long you won't even <u>need</u> to think about it.

Remember these Simple Sentence rules

You'll almost <u>certainly</u> know these two rules, but here's a <u>reminder</u>.

> 1) Every sentence <u>starts</u> with a <u>capital letter</u> and <u>ends</u> with either a <u>full stop</u>, a <u>question mark</u> or an <u>exclamation mark</u>.
> 2) Proper nouns (the names of <u>people</u>, <u>places</u>, <u>books</u>, <u>days</u> and <u>months</u>) all need capital letters.

Here are a couple of <u>examples</u> of the rules in action:

You need a capital letter at the <u>start</u>.

On Tuesday, my uncle went on holiday to Greece.

And of course, there's a <u>full stop</u> at the <u>end</u>.

<u>Days of the week</u> have capital letters.

Greece is a <u>place</u> so it needs a capital letter.

William Shakespeare wrote 'Macbeth'.

William Shakespeare is the <u>name</u> of a person so it needs capital letters.

'Macbeth' is the <u>name of a play</u>, so it starts with a capital letter.

Questions need Question Marks

If you're writing a question, make sure to use a <u>question mark</u>. It sounds obvious, but it's easy to forget.

Do you think that is fair?

Don't use loads of Exclamation Marks

1) Only ever use <u>one</u> exclamation mark at the end of a sentence.
2) When you're writing, think about whether you <u>need</u> to use exclamation marks <u>at all</u>. If you use them <u>too often</u>, they <u>won't</u> have the effect that they're supposed to.

I couldn't believe it! Today was finally the day! I was going to embark on a trip of a lifetime!

If you end every sentence with an exclamation mark, it <u>loses its impact</u>.

Without punctuation, your writing won't make sense

This stuff is very basic, so there's no excuse for getting it wrong. You should be able to do it <u>without even thinking about it</u> — that way you won't make <u>daft mistakes</u>. Go back over it again if you need to.

Sentences, Phrases and Clauses

Writing in <u>proper sentences</u> is another skill you really <u>can't</u> do without, so read this page <u>carefully</u>.

A **Sentence** has to have a **Verb**

Normally, every sentence you write has to be <u>about</u> something. It can only be <u>about</u> something <u>happening</u> if it's got a <u>verb</u>. (Remember, <u>verbs</u> are <u>doing</u> and <u>being</u> words.)

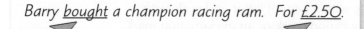

Barry <u>bought</u> a champion racing ram. For <u>£2.50</u>.

This is about him <u>buying</u> the ram — "bought" is the <u>verb</u>.

You can't do this. There's <u>no verb</u>, so this <u>isn't</u> a sentence. "<u>It cost £2.50.</u>" would be fine because "cost" is a verb.

In <u>creative writing</u>, you might notice that some writers <u>don't</u> always follow this rule. This can be very effective, but it's best to be <u>careful</u> and stick to what you know if you're not sure.

This part doesn't contain a verb.

<u>Windswept and forlorn.</u> The coastline looked like a tattered ribbon.

Use **Phrases** and **Clauses** to **Improve** your **Sentences**

<u>Varying</u> the <u>length</u> of your sentences can make your writing <u>more interesting</u>. You can make <u>simple</u> sentences <u>better</u> by <u>adding phrases</u> and <u>clauses</u>.

> There's more info about using different sentences to make your writing more interesting on p.22.

- A <u>clause</u> is a part of a sentence which has <u>a subject</u> and <u>a verb</u>.
- A <u>subject</u> is the person (or thing) that <u>performs</u> the action described by the <u>verb</u>.
- A <u>main clause</u> is a clause that makes sense <u>on its own</u> (so a main clause can be used as a sentence).
- A <u>phrase</u> is a part of a sentence which <u>doesn't</u> have <u>a subject</u>, or <u>doesn't</u> have <u>a verb</u> (some phrases might not have either).

You can <u>add</u> a <u>clause</u> to a sentence using a <u>conjunction</u> (joining word).

This is a <u>clause</u>. "The ram" is the <u>subject</u> and "likes" is a <u>verb</u>.

<u>The ram likes being outside</u> but <u>Barry lets him in the house</u>.

<u>Conjunctions</u>, like "but", <u>join clauses</u>.

This is also a <u>clause</u> because it has a <u>subject</u> ("Barry") and a <u>verb</u> ("lets").

You can also <u>add</u> a phrase to a <u>clause</u> to make a sentence more <u>interesting</u>:

This is a <u>clause</u> because it has a <u>subject</u> ("The ram") and a <u>verb</u> ("chews").

<u>The ram chews Barry's coat</u> in the dark.

This is a <u>phrase</u>. It doesn't have a verb.

Every sentence should have a verb...

... and some sentences will have more than one clause. Varying sentence length is a really great way to improve your writing, especially when you're doing some creative writing — have a look at p.22.

Commas

You'll definitely <u>need</u> commas in your writing, so make sure you know <u>how</u> to <u>use</u> them.

Use **Commas** in **Lists**...

Commas are used to keep the items in <u>lists</u> separate.

> *I went to the shop to buy bread, butter, soup and cheese.*

The commas keep each item in the list <u>separate</u>. Notice that there is no comma before the "<u>and</u>".

... or to **Add Information**...

You can use commas to include <u>extra bits</u> of information in your sentences. This can be done at the <u>start</u>, <u>end</u> or even right in the <u>middle</u> of a sentence.

> *After the match, we all went to Kathy's house for tea and toast.*

"After the match" is an <u>adverbial phrase</u>...

... so it's <u>separated</u> from the rest of the sentence by a <u>comma</u>.

In this example, commas are used like <u>brackets</u> to include information in the <u>middle</u> of the sentence.

> *Annie and Ali, who live next door, have built a new shed.*

... or to make the **Meaning** of a sentence **Clear**

Commas also help to make the <u>meaning</u> of a sentence <u>clearer</u>.

> *Before leaving Jo Ben and Sue turned off the TV.*

This sentence is <u>ambiguous</u> — it's not clear who turned off the TV.

> *Before leaving, Jo, Ben and Sue turned off the TV.*

> *Before leaving Jo, Ben and Sue turned off the TV.*

Adding a <u>comma</u> makes this much <u>clearer</u>. In the left-hand sentence Jo, Ben and Sue turned off the TV. In the right-hand sentence, Ben and Sue turned off the TV.

Don't stick them in **All Over** the place

You sometimes need a comma before direct speech. There's more about this on p.7.

There are a few different rules for using commas, so make sure you know them. It's no good putting them in randomly and hoping you've used them correctly. Be sure to <u>only</u> use them when they're <u>necessary</u>.

REVISION TASK

Learn where to put commas

It's no good chucking commas around willy-nilly — you <u>need</u> to know the <u>right</u> way to use them. Try covering this page and writing down three uses of commas.

Colons

A whole page about colons for you to get your head around now. Colons are pretty useful — you can use them to <u>introduce lists</u> and <u>explanations</u>. Read this page to find out how.

Use **Colons** to **Introduce** a **List**

This is a <u>colon</u>:   ⟶   **:**

If you want to <u>introduce</u> a <u>list</u>, you use a colon.

> *This is what you need to go camping: one tent, a gas stove, board games, two saucepans, a kettle and a torch.*

<u>Only</u> use a colon to introduce a list if it follows a <u>main clause</u> (see p.2). If this sentence started with "you need", you <u>wouldn't</u> use a colon because that's <u>not</u> a main clause.

A **Colon** can **Introduce** an **Explanation**

Colons are also <u>handy</u> for showing that you're about to <u>explain</u> a point you've just made.

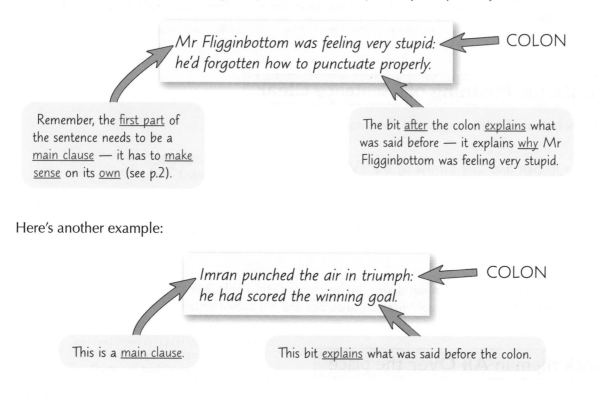

> *Mr Fligginbottom was feeling very stupid: he'd forgotten how to punctuate properly.*   ⟵ COLON

Remember, the <u>first part</u> of the sentence needs to be a <u>main clause</u> — it has to <u>make sense</u> on its <u>own</u> (see p.2).

The bit <u>after</u> the colon <u>explains</u> what was said before — it explains <u>why</u> Mr Fligginbottom was feeling very stupid.

Here's another example:

> *Imran punched the air in triumph: he had scored the winning goal.*   ⟵ COLON

This is a <u>main clause</u>.

This bit <u>explains</u> what was said before the colon.

Use colons to introduce things

Colons are quite easy to get the hang of. Just remember that you use them to <u>introduce</u> things, like <u>lists</u> or <u>explanations</u>. If you can use them properly, you'll <u>really impress everyone</u>. Honest.

Semicolons

Semicolons are a bit harder than colons, but they're still straightforward when you know how to use them. Helpfully, this page will tell you <u>all you need to know</u> to make you a semicolon expert.

Use **Semicolons** to **Break Up Lists**

This is a <u>semicolon</u>:   **;**

<u>Semicolons</u> can help you to organise <u>long lists</u> and make them <u>easier</u> to <u>read</u>.
They're <u>particularly</u> handy when you want to <u>organise</u> a list containing <u>other punctuation</u>.

The <u>first part</u>
of the sentence
is a <u>main clause</u>.

> *Lizi's reasons for not going to school were quite simple:*
> *she really hated being told where to go and when;*
> *the compulsory school dinners always tasted foul;*
> *and the uniform, a bright pink, wasn't her colour.*

The list is <u>introduced</u> by
a <u>colon</u>, then divided into
<u>sections</u> with <u>semicolons</u>.

Unlike with commas,
you <u>do</u> need a semicolon
before "<u>and</u>" in this list.

For more on clauses see p.2.

Semicolons can **Join Clauses** in a **Sentence**

You can use semicolons to <u>join</u> clauses together.
Both clauses need to be <u>about the same thing</u>.

> *Katie married her childhood friend;*   ← SEMICOLON
> *her brother, Jacob, missed the wedding.*

<u>Both clauses</u> could be
sentences <u>on their own</u>...

...and they're <u>equally</u>
<u>important</u> points.

Here's another example:

> *Joel ordered a rhubarb pie;*   ← SEMICOLON
> *Ashley asked for a crumble.*

This is a <u>main clause</u>.

This is a main clause <u>too</u>.

Semicolons separate items in a list and join clauses...

You're likely to need semicolons at some point, be it to <u>separate</u> items in a long list or <u>join</u> two related <u>main clauses</u>. Have a go at writing two example sentences of your own — one using semicolons to break up lists and one to join two clauses.

Apostrophes

Apostrophes can be tricky but you have to learn when you <u>should</u> use them and when you <u>shouldn't</u>.

Use **Apostrophes** to **Show** who **Owns Something**

You need to use an apostrophe when you're writing about things that <u>belong</u> to people.

Kulvinder's goldfish have all died.

The apostrophe shows that the goldfish <u>belonged</u> to Kulvinder.

<u>Plurals</u> that <u>don't</u> end in 's' follow the same rule.

The women's race was cancelled.

Remember — you don't need an apostrophe to show something's plural. "We bought some carrot's." is just plain wrong.

There's an <u>important</u> rule for words <u>ending</u> in '<u>s</u>':

James's garden is bigger than mine.

If a <u>singular noun</u> ends in '<u>s</u>', you <u>still</u> need to add an <u>apostrophe</u> and an '<u>s</u>'...

I washed the players' kits after the match.

...but when it's a <u>group</u> of something ending in '<u>s</u>', add an <u>apostrophe</u>, but <u>no 's</u>'.

You can also use **Apostrophes** to **Shorten** words

When you're <u>shortening</u> a <u>word</u>, you need to use an <u>apostrophe</u> to show there are <u>missing letters</u>. These are called <u>contractions</u>. Here are some common examples...

e.g. does + n<u>o</u>t = doesn<u>'</u>t

This one is <u>irregular</u>. will + not = won't

| I'm | I've | we'll | who's | doesn't |

| I'd | he's | can't | they're | here's | won't |

You should only shorten words using apostrophes when writing <u>informally</u>. If you are writing something like an <u>essay</u> or a <u>formal letter</u>, then <u>don't</u> use contractions.

Turn to p.30-1 for more on formal and informal writing.

Its and **It's** are **Two Different Words**

Getting <u>it's</u> and <u>its</u> mixed up is a mistake that people make all the time — make sure you know the difference.

The dog chewed <u>its</u> bone.

Its = <u>belonging</u> to it.

<u>It's</u> raining outside.

This is short for '<u>It is</u>'.

<u>It's</u> been a lovely day.

This is short for '<u>It has</u>'.

REVISION TIP

Apostrophes are tricky

Use apostrophes to show that something <u>belongs</u> to someone or to show that there are letters <u>missing</u> in a word. <u>Don't</u> use an apostrophe to show that there's more than one of something.

Section One — Writing Properly

Inverted Commas

Inverted commas (or speech marks) are used to show when someone's speaking.
All you've got to do is use them in all the right places. You've guessed it — learn this page...

Inverted Commas show when someone is Speaking

Every time someone speaks in a sentence, you need to use inverted commas. Inverted commas go at the start and end of the speech.

"Don't leave the cage door open," warned Sally.

Inverted commas surround the exact words Sally said. This is called direct speech.

Sally warned him not to leave the cage door open.

This doesn't need inverted commas because no one's actually speaking. This is called indirect speech.

Start with a Capital Letter...

Make sure that the spoken bit always starts with a capital letter, even if it isn't at the beginning of your sentence. If there's a bit before the direct speech, you need to add a comma before the inverted commas.

You need a comma before the direct speech.

Harry said, "Don't worry, I won't."

It starts with a capital letter.

... and End with the Right Punctuation

The spoken bits of your sentences need to end with either a full stop, a comma, a question mark or an exclamation mark. No matter what punctuation you use, it needs to go INSIDE the inverted commas.

Ruby said, "I knew you shouldn't have trusted Harry."

The sentence is finished, so you need a full stop.

"He's useless," she declared.

The speech has finished but the sentence hasn't, so you need a comma here instead of a full stop.

"Did we feed the bear before it escaped?" asked Jill.

This speech is a question, so it ends with a question mark.

Careful — you don't need to use a capital letter after the punctuation within the inverted commas.

Don't forget to use inverted commas
You also have to use inverted commas when quoting. There's more on using quotes on pages 72-3.

Brackets, Dashes and Hyphens

Brackets, dashes and hyphens are up next. Read on to find out how to use them correctly.

Brackets are used to add Extra Information

If you want to add extra information that is less important than the rest of the sentence, you can include it in brackets. The sentence must still make sense if the bit in brackets is removed.

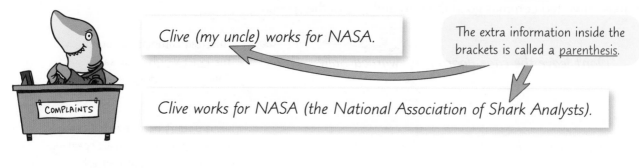

Clive (my uncle) works for NASA.

The extra information inside the brackets is called a parenthesis.

Clive works for NASA (the National Association of Shark Analysts).

Dashes have Multiple Uses

Pairs of dashes are used like brackets to separate extra information from the rest of the sentence...

Clive — my uncle — works for NASA.

Jacob missed his sister's wedding — she had nobody to walk her up the aisle.

... while single dashes can join two related main clauses together, just like a semicolon.

Link Words Together with Hyphens

Hyphens join words together to make the meaning clearer.

a man eating shark

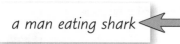

The example on the left describes a man who is eating shark meat, but the one on the right describes a shark that eats men.

a man-eating shark

Hyphens can also be used to attach a prefix to a root word. This is particularly important if the root word...

anti-French

co-owner

re-cover

... starts with a capital letter.

... starts with the same vowel that the prefix ends with.

... becomes a word with a different meaning but the same spelling as another word.

Brackets, dashes and hyphens make your writing clearer

You must write clearly in your essays — if you don't, you'll struggle to get your point across. Brackets, dashes and hyphens help you make your point with as little confusion as possible.

Tenses

Switching between tenses is a common mistake that you should avoid in your writing. You'll need to know how to choose the right tense and then stick to it if you want to keep your work error-free.

The **Tense** of a **Verb** tells you **When** something **Happens**

There are lots of tenses to choose between, but most of them can be divided into the past, the present and the future.

There are several more tenses other than the ones mentioned below.

This is the simple past. It describes an action that was completed in the past.

> *The Prime Minister __delivered__ a speech.*

This is the simple present. It describes an action that is happening right now or something that happens regularly.

> *The Prime Minister __delivers__ a speech.*

This is the simple future. It describes an action that hasn't happened yet.

> *The Prime Minister __will deliver__ a speech.*

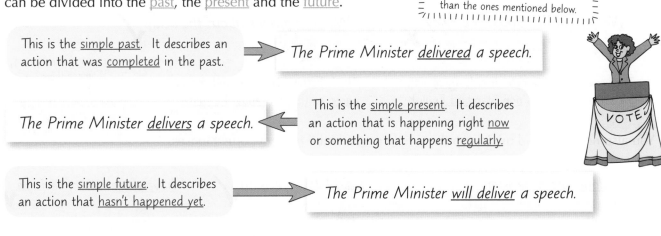

Don't **Switch** between tenses **Accidentally**

Once you've picked the right tense, you'll need to use it consistently. If you don't, it's bound to lead to confusion for the reader.

> *Pearl Harbour __was__ a turning point in World War Two. It __outrages__ the public to the point where the United States __will have__ no choice but to join the war.* ✘

Switching tenses between past, present and future makes this example confusing.

The tenses in this example are all the same, making it much clearer.

> *Pearl Harbour __was__ a turning point in World War Two. It __outraged__ the public to the point where the United States __had__ no choice but to join the war.* ✔

There are some **Exceptions**

In cases where there is a good reason for it, it might be acceptable for you to switch between tenses.

This sentence compares the present to the past, so it uses both tenses.

> *Students today __spend__ countless hours on their homework each week, which is much more than their parents __did__ in the 1980s.*

Words like "today" and "in the 1980s" make sure the sentence is still clear.

Tense consistency is key

Switching tenses is a common mistake that pupils make, especially when writing under pressure in exam conditions. Always check that your tenses are consistent.

Standard English

Standard English just refers to the sort of English that everyone agrees is correct. This means that everything you write should be written in Standard English. Here are a few common mistakes to watch out for.

The **Subject** and **Verb** should **Always Agree**

In Standard English, the verb always has to agree with who or whatever is doing the action.

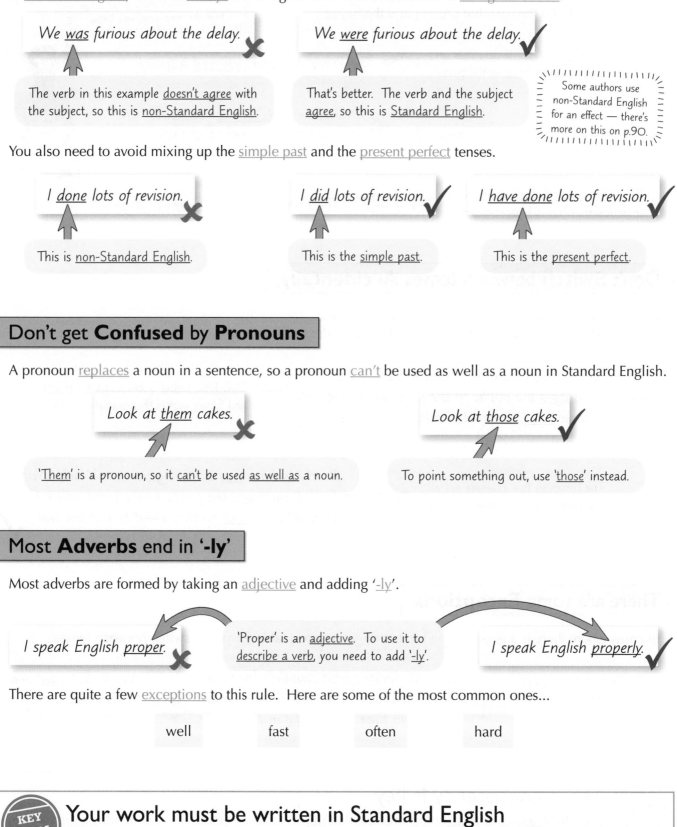

We _was_ furious about the delay. ✗

The verb in this example _doesn't agree_ with the subject, so this is _non-Standard English_.

We _were_ furious about the delay. ✓

That's better. The verb and the subject _agree_, so this is _Standard English_.

Some authors use non-Standard English for an effect — there's more on this on p.90.

You also need to avoid mixing up the simple past and the present perfect tenses.

I _done_ lots of revision. ✗

This is _non-Standard English_.

I _did_ lots of revision. ✓

This is the _simple past_.

I _have done_ lots of revision. ✓

This is the _present perfect_.

Don't get **Confused** by **Pronouns**

A pronoun replaces a noun in a sentence, so a pronoun can't be used as well as a noun in Standard English.

Look at _them_ cakes. ✗

'_Them_' is a pronoun, so it _can't_ be used _as well as_ a noun.

Look at _those_ cakes. ✓

To point something out, use '_those_' instead.

Most **Adverbs** end in '**-ly**'

Most adverbs are formed by taking an adjective and adding '-ly'.

I speak English _proper_. ✗

'Proper' is an adjective. To use it to describe a verb, you need to add '-ly'.

I speak English _properly_. ✓

There are quite a few exceptions to this rule. Here are some of the most common ones...

well   fast   often   hard

KEY TERM **Your work must be written in Standard English**
There's no two ways about it — if it isn't written in Standard English, it isn't strictly correct.

Revision Summary for Section One

You've got to learn all of this punctuation, even the little bitty things like full stops and apostrophes. It's no good being sort of vaguely aware of it. You have to know it back to front and inside out — so that you don't make mistakes, even when you're in a hurry. You don't want to get the easy bits wrong. Answer all of these questions correctly to prove that you really are a punctuation genius.

1) What's wrong with the following sentence?
   I've got tickets to see the raiders play the vikings on saturday.

2) How many exclamation marks should you put at the end of a sentence?

3) Are these proper sentences? If not, write a proper sentence instead:
   a) I enjoyed my holiday.
   b) The sea was warm.
   c) To the beach.

4) What is...
   a) a clause?
   b) a phrase?

5) Put commas in the right places in this sentence to show which bit is the extra information:
   The dancer her hair streaming out behind her finished the routine perfectly.

6) What punctuation could you use in the following situations?
   a) To introduce a list
   b) To separate an adverbial from the start of a sentence
   c) To break up the items in a list

7) What two things do apostrophes do?

8) Circle the mistakes in the sentences below, and write out the correct version.
   This food mixer is brilliant. It's slicing attachment chops vegetables really quickly.
   Its got a separate liquidiser for soups and milkshakes.

9) Put inverted commas and correct punctuation into this sentence:
   There's nothing better than a nice cosy armchair murmured Harry.

10) What's wrong with the following sentence?
    Terry said "next week I can show you how the equation was solved"

11) What name is given to the information inside a pair of brackets?

12) Give two uses of dashes.

13) Rewrite these sentences so that the verbs are all in the correct, consistent tense.
    Yesterday, I leave school early, because I had to go to the dentist. He examines my teeth and cleans them. It only took ten minutes, so I will go to the shops afterwards.

14) Rewrite these sentences in Standard English.
    I were going to do it later, but he asked me to help set up the stage.
    Them people was too lazy to help proper, so we done it ourselves.

15) How are most adverbs formed?

Paragraphs

You <u>must</u> use paragraphs in your writing. They make your writing <u>much clearer</u>, but only if you learn how to <u>use them properly</u>. In fact, they're <u>so important</u> that they get a whole section all to themselves.

Always use Paragraphs

It's not enough to use paragraphs <u>some</u> of the time — you need to use them <u>all</u> the time — in <u>stories</u>, <u>essays</u>, <u>letters</u>... in <u>ANYTHING</u> and <u>EVERYTHING</u> you write.

Paragraphs make things Clear

A paragraph is a <u>group</u> of <u>sentences</u>. These sentences talk about the <u>same thing</u>, or <u>follow on</u> from each other.

Leave a <u>little gap</u> before the first word of the next paragraph.

Every new paragraph must have a space between the margin and the first word. Then leave another space every time you start a new paragraph. This shows you're writing about something different.

When you finish the <u>last line</u> of the paragraph, <u>just stop</u>.

Some people leave a whole line when they start a new paragraph. It doesn't matter which method you choose, as long as you're clear and consistent.

Start a New Paragraph for Each Point in an essay

Paragraphs help make your essays <u>clearer</u>.
A new paragraph shows that you're writing about <u>something new</u>.

This is a <u>new point</u>, so start a new paragraph.

The idea that school uniforms hide differences between rich and poor is false. Everyone can tell whose uniform came from a discount shop and whose cost a lot. Supporters of school uniform say that they don't want to turn school into a "fashion parade". In fact, this is exactly what they are doing when they point out the tiny ways in which a skirt or jumper doesn't quite fit the rules.

EXAM TIP

You absolutely must write in paragraphs

Start a <u>new paragraph</u> each and every time you start a new sentence with a <u>new idea</u>, <u>angle</u> or <u>argument</u>. Make it clear as day to whoever's reading that you have a new point to make.

Using Paragraphs

You need to know when to start a new paragraph — you can't just guess. It may be tough, but you'll have to learn the rules. Here's a nice golden rule to start with...

Here's the **Golden Rule** for **Paragraphs**

Start a new paragraph every time something changes.

Here's a useful tip — use TiPP. That stands for Time, Place, Person. Each time one of these three things changes, it's a pretty safe bet that you'll need to start a new paragraph.

Start a new paragraph for a **Different Time...**

This is talking about later that day, so start a new paragraph.

> At last it was over. The voice called out again, "Are you alright?" I barely had the strength to answer. Relief flooded through me in a warm, drowsy wave. Soon I would be out of the cave and home.
>   An hour later, I was sitting in the coastguard's van, drinking hot tea from a flask. I could hear people talking all around me, but I couldn't really understand what they were saying. It was all a bit too much for me to take in. All I knew was that I was safe and everything was going to be alright.

...or a **Different Place**

> The shopping centre was utterly deserted. The uniformed security guards scratched their heads. What were they supposed to do now there was no one to watch?
>   Outside Bernie's gourmet chip shop on the High Street, it was a rather different story. The crowd was three deep around the shop, all pushing and shoving to get to the door. "Give us battered cod!" they clamoured. "What kind of chip shop runs out of cod?"

The story has moved from the shopping centre to the chip shop, so this needs a new paragraph.

Paragraphs make your work easier to read

If your writing is all in one massive chunk, it makes it really hard to read and will lose you a lot of marks. So remember, always start a new paragraph when your writing changes either time or place.

Using Paragraphs

You need to start a <u>new paragraph</u> when you talk about a <u>new person</u> or someone new <u>speaks</u>.

When you talk about a **New Person**

Tanya looked at the scene in despair. She couldn't believe that eight soldiers could make such a mess. She sighed and started to pick up the biscuits and crisps.

This paragraph is about <u>Tanya</u>.

A friendly face popped round the door. It was Brian. He watched Tanya grovelling around in the mess for a second or two before he spoke up.

This paragraph is about <u>Brian</u>.

When **Someone New** speaks

The <u>same person</u> is speaking here, so you <u>don't</u> need a new paragraph.

Someone <u>new</u> is speaking, so you need a <u>new paragraph</u>.

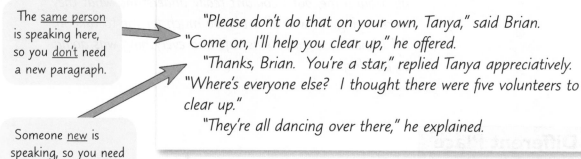

"Please don't do that on your own, Tanya," said Brian. "Come on, I'll help you clear up," he offered.

"Thanks, Brian. You're a star," replied Tanya appreciatively. "Where's everyone else? I thought there were five volunteers to clear up."

"They're all dancing over there," he explained.

Remember — <u>TiPP</u> stands for <u>Time</u>, <u>Place</u>, <u>Person</u>. Start a new paragraph every time one of these things changes.

Paragraphs aren't optional

Every time you talk about a <u>new person</u> or <u>someone new is speaking</u>, you <u>have</u> to use a new paragraph. No ifs, no buts — it's as simple as that. It's got to be second nature to you.

Linking Paragraphs

One final word on paragraphs. To make your writing fabulous, you need to link your paragraphs together. It might seem like a small thing, but it makes a huge difference.

Link your Paragraphs together

Paragraphs need to flow smoothly from one to the other. This keeps your writing organised.
Here are a few words and phrases you can use at the start of your paragraphs to link them together:

Firstly...   Therefore...   Furthermore...   Secondly...

On the other hand...   Another view is...   Moreover...   In addition...

Linking your paragraphs Improves your Writing

Linking paragraphs together massively improves the quality of your writing, especially in essays. Here are a couple of examples of how to use linking words:

...that's one of the main reasons why I'd make a good prefect. Furthermore, I work very hard, especially in a team...

The word "furthermore" shows that this paragraph links to the previous one.

The phrase "on the other hand" shows that you're going to look at both sides of the argument.

...which shows that Caliban is a really evil character. On the other hand, Caliban has every reason to hate Prospero...

...emphasises the poet's sadness and anger about the horrors of warfare. In conclusion, the poet uses a variety of techniques to...

The phrase "in conclusion" shows your essay is coming to an end, and you're about to summarise your key points.

REVISION TASK

Improve your writing by linking your paragraphs

Linking your paragraphs together is essential to writing well, so you need to know a variety of linking phrases. Cover this page and jot down all the linking phrases that you can remember, then use a thesaurus or a dictionary to add another 10 words or phrases to the list.

Revision Summary for Section Two

Well, here we are at the end of another section, and what do you know, it's time for a set of Summary Questions. Remember, the point of these is to make sure that you've learnt something from the last four pages. Go through them, and don't you dare move on to the next section until you've got them all right.

1) What is a paragraph?

2) Using paragraphs makes texts...
   a) more interesting.   b) more complicated.   c) clearer.

3) True or false: "You don't need to use paragraphs if you're writing a letter."

4) What should you do at the start of a paragraph?

5) What is the golden rule for when you should start a new paragraph?

6) What might suggest to the reader that a piece of writing has changed time?

7) A piece of writing describes what Dan, Carol and Adrian look like.
   How many paragraphs is this piece of writing likely to have?

8) Do you need to start a new paragraph when the same person carries on speaking?

9) What's the rule for when a new person starts speaking?

10) Give an example of a linking phrase that...
   a) shows that the new paragraph is going to follow on from the previous paragraph.
   b) shows that the new paragraph is going to talk about a different side of the argument.

11) The following piece of writing is really confusing. Make it nice and clear
    by re-writing it with proper paragraphs:

    "Where's the dog?" Kim asked, looking worried. "Dunno," said Rob, who was so engrossed
    in his comic book that he didn't even look up. "Lucy is going to kill us if we've lost her dog,"
    Kim replied, panic rising in her voice. "You know how much Lucy loves that mutt." Meanwhile,
    Oscar the dog was having a lovely nap upstairs under a bed. It was nice having a bit of
    peace and quiet away from Kim and Rob.

12) Write three paragraphs of a story, using the rules in this section.

Avoid Repetition

You've got the hang of the basics, so now it's time to take your writing to the next level. These handy tips will help you to make your writing the best it can be.

Don't use "And" and "Then" too much

This is something loads of people do, but it makes your writing a bit boring.

I went to the beach and I put on my trunks and I walked to the sea and the water was warm and I swam for an hour. ✗

Instead of using "and" all the time, try to use commas, full stops and semicolons.

I went to the beach, put on my trunks and walked to the sea. The water was warm; I swam for an hour. ✓

We went to the bank then we had a coffee and then we went back to the car. Then we drove to the supermarket and did some shopping, then we drove home. ✗

Changing the word order helps you not to use "then" all the time.

After going to the bank, we had a coffee. Then we went back to the car and drove to the supermarket. We did some shopping and drove home. ✓

Don't start all your sentences the Same Way

This is another thing that makes your writing dull and boring.

Think of different ways to start your sentences — it'll make your writing a lot more interesting to read.

There was a chill in the air as Jo walked towards the house. There was nobody around. There was a big oak door and Jo knocked on it. There was a scream from inside the house. ✗

This is much more interesting — the shorter sentences help to build tension.

There was a chill in the air as Jo walked towards the house. Nobody was around. Jo knocked on the big oak door. A scream came from inside. ✓

Keep an eye out for repeated words
When proofreading your work, look out for any words used repeatedly and replace them.

Avoiding Repetition

Here are some more tips on how to avoid repeating the same things over and over. This page will help you to vary your verbs and cut out the clichés.

Make your Verbs more Interesting

Using the same verb over and over again is another thing that can make a text unexciting. Look at this little piece of writing. It becomes a lot more interesting just by adding two new verbs instead of repeating "ran" three times.

> If you're struggling to come up with a variety of verbs, have a look at the word wheels on p.21 for inspiration.

> I ran to the post box with a letter, then I ran to the shop for some chocolate. After that, I ran home so I wasn't late for tea. ✗

> I ran to the post box with a letter, then I hurried to the shop for some chocolate. After that, I raced home so I wasn't late for tea. ✓

Better still, you can include some adverbs to describe your verbs in even more detail.

> I ran quickly to the post box with a letter, then I hurried anxiously to the shop for some chocolate. After that I raced excitedly home so I wasn't late for tea. ✓✓

> An adverb is a word that describes a verb, an adjective or another adverb.

Don't use too many Clichés — they get Boring

Some figures of speech are used so often that they become boring. These are called clichés. You can get away with using some clichés in your writing, but don't use too many — people will think you haven't got anything original to say. Instead of using...

The atmosphere is electric.   Now that he's finished his homework, he's as free as a bird.

He was as sick as a parrot.   She was as cool as a cucumber.

Try saying something like:

The atmosphere is crackling with anticipation.   He was free from the shackles of homework.

Waves of nausea swept through his body like a tsunami.   She was unflappable.

REVISION TASK

More adverbs, fewer clichés

Have a go at adding some adverbs to this sentence: "Ginny jumped out of bed and scurried downstairs. She hopped over the skateboard, opened the front door and grabbed the parcel."

Using Adjectives and Comparisons

One sure-fire way to improve your writing is by making it more descriptive — here's how you can do it.

Adjectives will make your writing more Interesting

Adjectives are describing words. They're a quick and easy way to spice up your writing.

Just one little adjective can completely change the impression you get from a sentence.

I ate a meal. ✗   I ate a _delicious_ meal. ✓   I ate a _disgusting_ meal. ✓

And with two or three adjectives, you can really start to build up a picture. Try to use adjectives with different meanings so that the reader can imagine what you are describing really clearly.

But DON'T do this every time or it'll get a bit dull.

I ate a _horrible, awful, disgusting_ meal. ✓   This is OK, but the adjectives mean the same thing.

I ate a _disgusting, rancid, undercooked_ meal. ✓✓   This is better — the adjectives are more varied.

Make Comparisons to Create a Picture

1) Comparisons are a great way to build up a picture of something. They sound interesting and they help the reader to imagine what you're describing really clearly.

2) Similes and metaphors are a type of comparison which can improve your descriptions (see p.32).

This is a simile. → The meal was _as hot as a lump of burning coal_.

The meal was _a lump of burning coal_. ← This is a metaphor.

3) You can use comparative adjectives too — adjectives which end with '-er'.

The forest was _green_. → The forest was _greener than a polished emerald_.

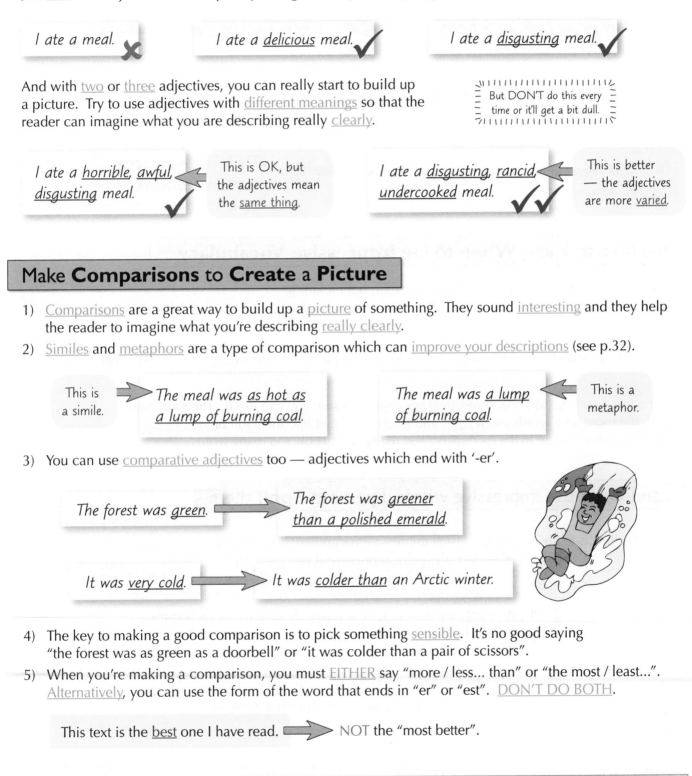

It was _very cold_. → It was _colder than_ an Arctic winter.

4) The key to making a good comparison is to pick something sensible. It's no good saying "the forest was as green as a doorbell" or "it was colder than a pair of scissors".

5) When you're making a comparison, you must EITHER say "more / less... than" or "the most / least...". Alternatively, you can use the form of the word that ends in "er" or "est". DON'T DO BOTH.

This text is the best one I have read. → NOT the "most better".

Use descriptions to make your writing interesting

Adjectives and comparisons are two ways to make your writing stand out. Turn over for some more...

Using Impressive Vocabulary

Using <u>impressive vocabulary</u> will improve the <u>quality</u> of your writing.

Great Vocabulary really Stands Out

Using <u>different</u> words is a good start, but if you can use vocabulary that
is both <u>different</u> and <u>impressive</u> your writing will really stand out.

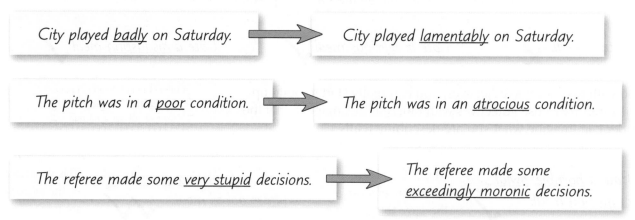

City played <u>badly</u> on Saturday.	*City played <u>lamentably</u> on Saturday.*
The pitch was in a <u>poor</u> condition.	*The pitch was in an <u>atrocious</u> condition.*
The referee made some <u>very stupid</u> decisions.	*The referee made some <u>exceedingly moronic</u> decisions.*

You have to know When to use Impressive Vocabulary...

Not <u>every</u> word you write can amaze your reader, but including
<u>impressive vocabulary</u> now and then will really <u>improve</u> your writing.

Every <u>now and then</u>, try to replace a <u>short</u> and <u>simple</u> word with a <u>longer</u>, more <u>impressive</u> one.

Of course, you have to know some <u>great vocabulary</u> before you can use it. The more you
<u>read</u>, the more new words you'll <u>learn</u> and <u>remember</u>. Get into the habit of <u>looking up</u>
words you don't know in the <u>dictionary</u>. You really can't know too many words.

...and Only use impressive words if you can Spell them

If you're on a computer, don't forget to use the spellchecker. And make sure you learn the correct spelling.

1) Spelling is <u>really important</u>. Using impressive vocabulary is like doing
    a trick on a skateboard — it's only really impressive if you get it right.

2) If you're not sure how to spell a word, check it in the dictionary.
    Then try to <u>learn</u> the spelling for the next time you need it.

3) And one last thing — <u>DON'T</u> use a long
    word if you're <u>not sure</u> what it means.

Use better vocabulary if you can spell it
The more impressive a word, the harder it can often be to spell. You can work around this
by keeping a list of all of the words you struggle to spell and testing yourself regularly.

Using Impressive Vocabulary

Word wheels are a great tool for incorporating an assortment of interesting words into your work.

Vary your Vocabulary as much as Possible

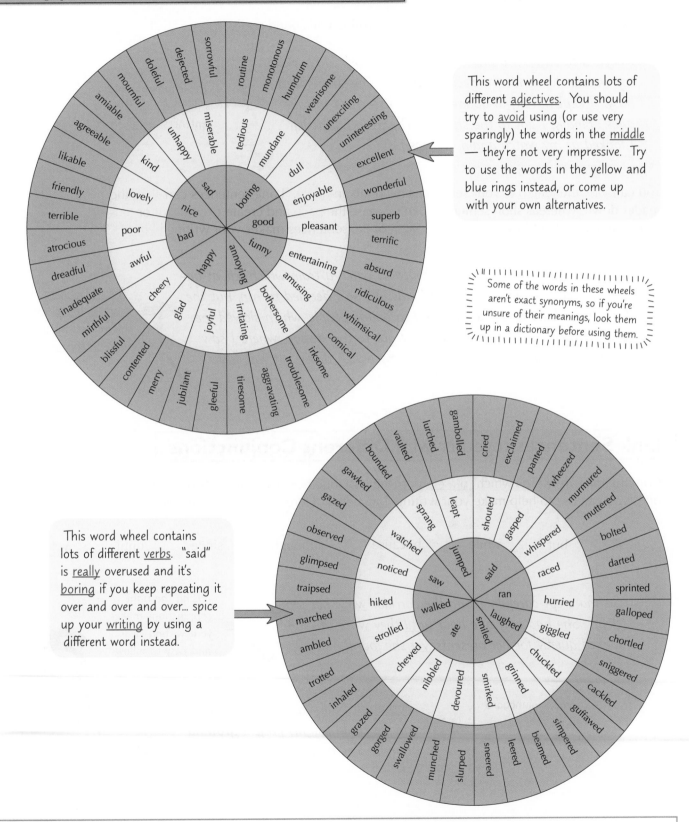

This word wheel contains lots of different adjectives. You should try to avoid using (or use very sparingly) the words in the middle — they're not very impressive. Try to use the words in the yellow and blue rings instead, or come up with your own alternatives.

Some of the words in these wheels aren't exact synonyms, so if you're unsure of their meanings, look them up in a dictionary before using them.

This word wheel contains lots of different verbs. "said" is really overused and it's boring if you keep repeating it over and over and over... spice up your writing by using a different word instead.

 Use these word wheels to improve your writing

Have a go at making your own word wheel. Put some words that you tend to use a lot in the centre, then use a thesaurus to fill in the second and third layers with alternative words.

Varying Sentence Length

And last but not least — mixing up the length of your sentences is a great way to make your writing better.

Use a **Variety** of **Short** and **Long** sentences

If your sentences are all the same length, your writing will sound really boring:

> *I needed to catch a train. It left at one o'clock. I checked my watch. I was late. I decided to run. The streets were busy. I kept having to dodge people. It seemed to take ages. Finally, I got to the station. The train hadn't left. I looked at my watch again. It was fast.*

This chunk of writing is dull because the sentences are all short.

You can vary the length of your sentences to create an effect. Long sentences can slow the reader down, whereas short sentences can increase the pace and create excitement or tension. Here's an example of how varying the length of the sentences makes your writing better:

> *I was walking to the station. I needed to catch a train which left at one o'clock. I checked my watch and I was late so I decided to run, but the streets were busy and I kept having to dodge people, which slowed me down. Finally, I crossed the road and got to the station, where I saw that the train hadn't left. I looked at my watch again. It was fast.*

The mix of long and short sentences makes this version much more interesting.

Link Sentences together with **Different Conjunctions**

Conjunctions are words which join clauses (see p.2) together. There are lots of different ones you can use to help make your writing flow better. Here are a few examples:

| if | but | while | because | although | since | until | yet |

> *Sienna crept carefully along the corridor while her family slept. She had only one hour until they woke up. She looked quietly for her presents, yet she found nothing.*

Using the right conjunctions makes your writing clear and easy to follow.

Some conjunctions can go at the start of a sentence as well as in the middle.

> *Although Nicky had two pairs of gloves on, he could feel his fingers growing numb. The breeze was bitterly cold.*

Don't make all your sentences the same length

Now that you know lots of ways to make your writing interesting, remember to think about them all when you're writing. Practise them and they'll soon become second nature to you.

Warm-Up Questions

The last six pages have some really useful tips on how to make your writing interesting. These questions will help you check you've taken it all in.

Warm-up Questions

1) What can you use instead of using 'and' and 'then' all the time in your writing? *coma*

2) Give two verbs which could sensibly replace the underlined verbs in the passage below.
   "I'm completely exhausted," said Harriet, struggling to catch her breath. — *said → Singhsd*
   "This is so boring," said Milo, low enough so that Carlos wouldn't hear.
   "Come on guys! Not much longer to the top of the mountain," said Carlos.

   comp Cark

3) Match up the verbs on the left with the most suitable adverb on the right.
   a) sang   uncontrollably
   b) sobbed   grumpily
   c) muttered   happily

4) Is this statement true or false?
   "Using clichés all the time shows you're being imaginative." *True*

5) Pick out the three sentences you think your teacher would be most impressed by:
   a) The band stopped playing and we all turned to face the bride and groom.
   b) Omar picked up the battered, grimy book and brushed the dust off the wrinkled spine.
   c) After a bone-shaking three hours, the bus gasped to a halt by a deserted-looking building.
   d) The twins looked at each other, nodded and pressed the button.
   e) I had never seen such a hairy, flea-bitten, pitiful mongrel in all my life.

6) Match these beginnings and endings so that these comparisons make sense.
   a) She smiled like   a biscuit and a cake in one.
   b) It made a sound like   a crocodile with a good dentist.
   c) He was as lazy as   two trumpets and a sick donkey.
   d) It tasted like   a toad at the bottom of a well.

7) Which of these two versions of the same story is better, and why?
   a) *She stopped. She saw nothing. Then, the sounds began. The whispering and rustling and pattering sounds which suddenly surrounded her drove her further into the forest, running for her life.*
   b) *She stopped but there was nothing and then the sounds began which were whispering and rustling and pattering sounds which suddenly surrounded her and drove her further into the forest and made her run for her life.*

8) Fill in the blanks using three different conjunctions.
   a) _While_ the road was blocked, we had to get out of the car and proceed on foot.
   b) Francine was extremely stressed about the exam _but_ it wasn't for another two weeks.
   c) _While_ Jasper cycled with all his might, Kim relaxed on the back of the tandem.

Revision Summary for Section Three

This section's given you loads of tricks to help make your writing more interesting. Now you just need to learn them all and remember to use them. Interesting writing isn't something you can do just like that — you have to practise it. The next time you write a letter, a postcard or even a shopping list, have a go at popping in just a little of the fancy stuff — an inexpensive pumpkin, a lemon as sour as my sister, a bottle of chilli sauce as hot as the sun... And don't forget to keep reading every day — it will also help to improve your writing.

1) Which two words do many people use too much?
   a) "and" and "then"
   b) "if" and "when"
   c) "since" and "because" □

2) Why is it a bad idea to start all your sentences the same way? □

3) How can you add more detail to your verbs? □

4) When is it OK to use clichés?
   a) Now and again
   b) Most of the time
   c) All of the time □

5) Why is it good to use adjectives?
   a) They join sentences together.
   b) They help to describe things and build a picture.
   c) You can use lots of them in every sentence you write. □

6) Which of these are wrong?
   a) You're weirder than me.
   b) She's my bestest friend.
   c) He's more helpful, though.
   d) I'm the most funniest. □

7) When should you aim to use impressive vocabulary?
   a) Never
   b) All the time
   c) Every now and again □

8) When you read a word and you don't know what it means, what should you do? □

9) If you know a piece of vocabulary that'd be really appropriate for something you're writing, but you're not 100% sure how to spell it, what should you do? □

10) "Keeping your sentences all the same length makes your writing interesting for the reader." True or false? □

11) What type of word can you use to link clauses together? □

Fiction and Non-Fiction

Now it's time to dive into the wonderful world of reading. First up is fiction and non-fiction.

Texts can be either Fiction or Non-Fiction

1) Fiction texts are made up. There might be some elements of real life in fiction texts, e.g. the *Harry Potter* books have scenes set in London, but the characters and the events of the story are entirely imaginary.

2) Non-fiction texts are about real life. It's writing that isn't made up.

Fiction Entertains the Reader

The three main types of fiction text are:

Poems ➡ There are lots of different types of poem. Some are short, while others are quite long. Some rhyme, like limericks, but others don't, like free verse. There's loads more about poems in Section 8.

Plays ➡ A play is a piece of writing that's intended to be acted out. It's mostly made up of lines of dialogue, often with some stage directions too. See Section 9 for more information on plays and drama.

Stories ➡ Stories are pieces of prose such as novels — see pages 87-94 for more. There are lots of different genres — this just means the type of story it is. Here are a few examples:

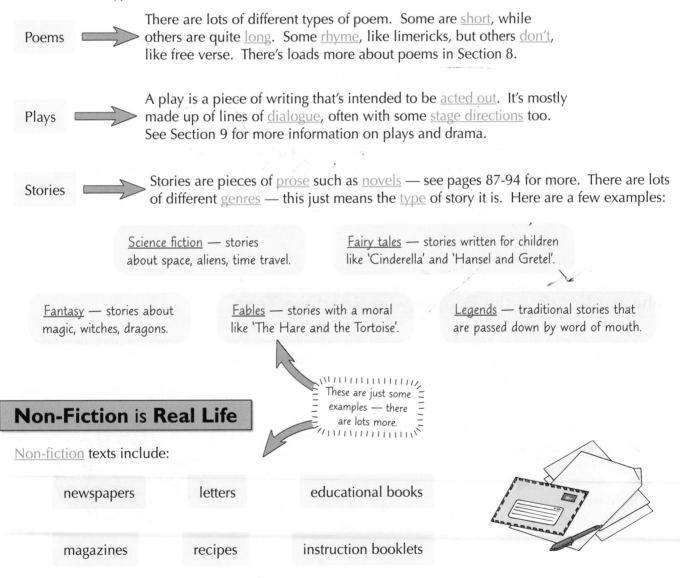

Science fiction — stories about space, aliens, time travel.

Fairy tales — stories written for children like 'Cinderella' and 'Hansel and Gretel'.

Fantasy — stories about magic, witches, dragons.

Fables — stories with a moral like 'The Hare and the Tortoise'.

Legends — traditional stories that are passed down by word of mouth.

These are just some examples — there are lots more.

Non-Fiction is Real Life

Non-fiction texts include:

newspapers	letters	educational books
magazines	recipes	instruction booklets

Don't get fiction and non-fiction confused

REVISION TIP

Get the difference between fiction and non-fiction clear in your mind. Fiction isn't real life, non-fiction is. If it helps you to remember, "fiction" and "fake" both start with "f".

Purpose and Audience

Writers of both fiction and non-fiction think about what the <u>purpose</u> of their text is, who their <u>audience</u> is and what <u>layout</u> and <u>language</u> they want to use. Just remember <u>PALL</u> — purpose, audience, layout, language.

The **Purpose** of a text is the **Reason** it has been **Written**

1) Here are some of the <u>most common purposes</u>:

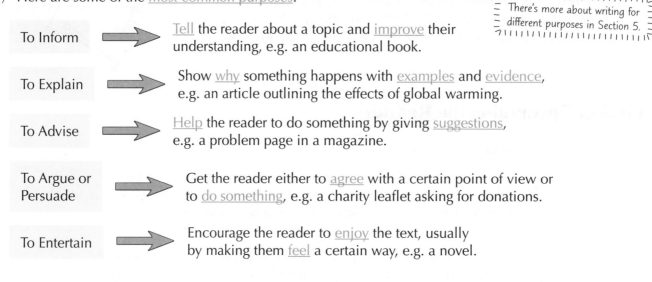

To Inform	<u>Tell</u> the reader about a topic and <u>improve</u> their understanding, e.g. an educational book.
To Explain	Show <u>why</u> something happens with <u>examples</u> and <u>evidence</u>, e.g. an article outlining the effects of global warming.
To Advise	<u>Help</u> the reader to do something by giving <u>suggestions</u>, e.g. a problem page in a magazine.
To Argue or Persuade	Get the reader either to <u>agree</u> with a certain point of view or to <u>do something</u>, e.g. a charity leaflet asking for donations.
To Entertain	Encourage the reader to <u>enjoy</u> the text, usually by making them <u>feel</u> a certain way, e.g. a novel.

> There's more about writing for different purposes in Section 5.

2) Some texts can have <u>more than one purpose</u>. For example, a <u>persuasive</u> text might also try to <u>inform</u> its audience about a topic.

3) You need to think about <u>how</u> the purpose has <u>affected</u> the text that you're reading. Authors tailor the <u>layout</u> and <u>language</u> (see pages 27-31) of their texts to suit the purpose and audience.

The **Audience** is the **People** who **Read** the **Text**

1) Sometimes an audience can be quite <u>general</u>, for example teenagers. Sometimes the audience can be very <u>specific</u>, for example teenagers studying English. Some texts will have <u>more than one audience</u>.

2) <u>Language</u> can often tell you about a text's audience.

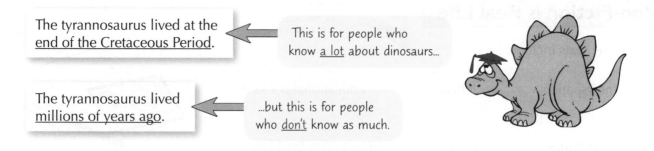

The tyrannosaurus lived at the <u>end of the Cretaceous Period</u>.

This is for people who know <u>a lot</u> about dinosaurs...

The tyrannosaurus lived <u>millions of years ago</u>.

...but this is for people who <u>don't</u> know as much.

PALL — Purpose, Audience, Layout, Language
You must think about these when reading a text — hop over to the next page to learn about layout.

Section Four — Understanding Fiction and Non-Fiction

Layout

How the text <u>looks</u> on the page can have an <u>effect</u> on the reader too. That's why writers use different <u>layout features</u>. The features they choose depend on the purpose of the text and the audience.

Layout is how the text is Presented

1) The layout the writer uses depends on what <u>type</u> of text it is, for example the text in a newspaper article will often be presented in columns.

2) Non-fiction texts often use <u>more</u> layout features than fiction texts.

3) Here are some <u>examples</u> of layout features:

> Layout is different to structure. Structure is how the words, sentences and information in a text have been organised. Layout is about how a text looks. There's more about structure on pages 92 and 97.

titles, headings and subheadings

text presented in columns

text split into boxes

bullet points and numbered lists

photos, images, illustrations

the style, colour and size of the font

graphs and tables

Layout features Affect the Audience

As well as being able to <u>spot</u> layout features, you may also need to say <u>why</u> the writer has <u>chosen</u> to include them. Think about the <u>effect</u> that they have on the <u>reader</u>. For example, <u>graphs</u> present information <u>clearly</u> and <u>subheadings</u> make it <u>easier</u> for the reader to find information.

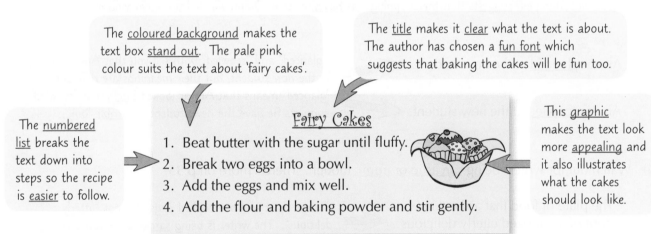

The <u>coloured background</u> makes the text box <u>stand out</u>. The pale pink colour suits the text about 'fairy cakes'.

The <u>title</u> makes it <u>clear</u> what the text is about. The author has chosen a <u>fun font</u> which suggests that baking the cakes will be fun too.

The <u>numbered list</u> breaks the text down into steps so the recipe is <u>easier</u> to follow.

Fairy Cakes

1. Beat butter with the sugar until fluffy.
2. Break two eggs into a bowl.
3. Add the eggs and mix well.
4. Add the flour and baking powder and stir gently.

This <u>graphic</u> makes the text look more <u>appealing</u> and it also illustrates what the cakes should look like.

Some Fiction texts use Layout Features too

1) Fiction texts tend to use <u>fewer</u> layout features than non-fiction texts.

2) Some fiction texts might use <u>illustrations</u>, especially if they're aimed at a <u>younger audience</u>.

3) A fiction book written in the style of a <u>diary</u> might use a font that looks like <u>handwriting</u>.

4) The layout of a poem often depends on its <u>form</u>, for example, limericks always have 5 lines.

5) Some <u>poems</u> might be laid out in an unusual way, e.g. a line in a poem might be <u>shorter</u> than the rest of the lines in a stanza. There's an example of this in the poem on p.112.

Think about the effect the layout has

REVISION TASK

A good layout often makes information easier to read. List all the layout features on this page and think about why the author has included them and the effect they have on the reader.

Language and Inference

Authors think very carefully about the words they use. Sometimes they don't want to make what they mean obvious — you may need to make an inference.

Sometimes you have to make an Inference

> An inference is a conclusion reached on the basis of hints given by the author. For example, if a character shivered, you might infer that they are cold.

1) When you're reading a text, the writer won't always say exactly what they mean.

2) This means that you need to make an inference — look closely at the text and pick out anything that gives you a clue to the writer's thoughts. Often the language used will give you an idea:

> The menu was unexciting — nothing inventive or out of the ordinary. The dining room, with its drab colours and small windows, was gloomy and uninviting.

Words like "unexciting" and "uninviting" are very negative. From this, you can infer that the writer disliked the restaurant.

3) Many words have connotations — an impression you get from the word on top of the actual meaning.

> Quinn put the shopping on the table.

> Quinn dumped the shopping on the table.

Both sentences tell you where Quinn placed the shopping. "Put" doesn't tell you anything else, but "dumped" suggests that the shopping was heavy, or that Quinn was fed up of carrying it.

> Anwar glanced at the new student.

> Anwar scowled at the new student.

"glanced" and "scowled" both tell you that Anwar looked at the new student, but their meanings are different. "glanced" means that Anwar looked briefly, but "scowled" suggests he gave the new student a horrible look.

4) Watch out for writers being sarcastic or ironic though. There's more on p.35.

> The plate of food that arrived in front of me looked utterly delicious — burnt toast and overcooked eggs.

"burnt toast and overcooked eggs" are not "utterly delicious". The writer is being sarcastic — you can infer they're very unhappy about their meal.

Use phrases to show that you've made an Inference

Here are some helpful phrases to use in your essays to show that you've inferred something:

> This suggests that..   This implies that..   The author seems to be...

Think about the connotations of words

It can take a while to get the hang of making inferences, so be sure to get lots of practice. Look closely at the words the author uses and think about the impression you get from them.

Section Four — Understanding Fiction and Non-Fiction

Tone, Register and Style

Tone, register and style might sound quite confusing, but this page should help to make them clearer. Tone is the feeling of the text, register is the language used and style is the way the whole text is put together.

Tone is the **Feeling** of the language

1) A writer's tone is the way they use language to put across their feelings or attitude. This creates a particular mood (see p.94). Think of a writer's tone as being like someone's tone of voice when they're talking.

2) Tone can be identified by the language used. Slang and humour create a personal or light-hearted tone, whereas technical language creates a more serious, informative tone.

3) The tone used by the writer will depend on the purpose and audience of the text. For example, a text that informs the reader how to operate heavy machinery will usually have a serious tone, whereas texts aimed at young children might have a playful, light-hearted tone.

Register is the **Vocabulary** that the author uses

Authors must choose the register that best suits the text's audience. A text's register can be formal, informal or somewhere in between. For example:

A letter written to your town council asking them to improve the local park would need a formal register, e.g. "The current state of the park is appalling and requires urgent attention". A formal register is needed because you don't know the councillors and you want them to take the matter seriously.

An article for your school newsletter might use an informal register, e.g. "If we don't do something soon, the park will get even more run down". You can be more informal because the audience are your classmates, and you don't want them to be put off by complicated language.

Style is how the whole text is **Written**

1) Style includes the language, structure and layout of a text.

2) There are lots of different styles that writers use. For example, a text with a journalistic style will usually inform the reader and present information in a balanced way. Writing with a conversational style will use an informal register and will be written to sound like natural speech.

3) When you're reading, think about how the purpose and audience influence the style of a text.

4) Take a look at this example:

Will you protect the elephants? Or will you let them die?
Every year, elephants are brutally poached for their tusks. These incredible animals are left to die in the dust while men profit from their ivory. We must do something to save these beautiful creatures once and for all.

The author uses a serious tone and a formal register to convey the importance of their message.

The author uses rhetorical questions (p.36) and emotive language (p.54) to create a persuasive style.

Tone, register and style — make sure you know the difference

It's important that you understand what these terms mean — don't get them mixed up. Tone can be a tricky one to figure out sometimes, but the more you practise, the easier it gets.

Informal Style

Now you know what style is, let's look at <u>informal style</u> in more detail.

An **Informal Style** is **Personal**

1) Writers use an <u>informal</u> style when they know their audience <u>well</u> or they want to <u>connect</u> with their audience. For example:

> a letter to a friend   an agony aunt column   a magazine article for children

2) An informal text usually has some of the following <u>features</u>:

> <u>CHATTY LANGUAGE / SLANG</u> — informal texts use <u>chatty</u>, simple language, e.g. "<u>cool</u>" rather than "superb". They might also use <u>slang</u> words like "<u>grub</u>" instead of "food".

> <u>PERSONAL LANGUAGE</u> — informal texts are more likely to use <u>second person</u> (e.g. "you") or <u>first person plural</u> pronouns ("we"). This makes it sound like the writer is talking <u>directly</u> to the audience.

> <u>HUMOUR</u> — informal texts might use <u>jokes</u> to make the text more <u>light-hearted</u>.   <u>CONTRACTIONS</u> — informal texts might use <u>shortened</u> versions of words, like "won't" instead of "will not".

> <u>SHORT SENTENCES</u> — informal texts avoid complex sentences and mostly use <u>short</u>, <u>simple</u> ones.

Writers use an **Informal Style** to **Connect** with the **Reader**

Look at this example of a text written in an <u>informal style</u>:

> The new RunRun trainers are really awesome. They're dead comfy — you'd be mad not to get yourself a pair. They're only £29.99 too — what a bargain! Don't hang about, RunRun out and buy a pair today!

The author uses <u>contractions</u> like "they're" and <u>slang</u> like "dead comfy" to create a <u>chatty tone</u>.

The writer uses <u>second person</u> pronouns (i.e. "you") to speak <u>directly</u> to the reader.

The writer makes a <u>joke</u> with the brand name to add some <u>humour</u> to the text.

The writer uses these techniques to make the text <u>friendly</u> and <u>relatable</u> in order to <u>persuade</u> the reader to get the trainers. If the reader feels like the text is written by <u>someone like them</u>, they'll be <u>more likely</u> to buy the trainers.

Learn the typical features of informal writing

REVISION TASK

The five features above are very common in informal texts. Make sure you know them off by heart, then try writing your own short text that includes them all.

Formal Style

Formal texts <u>don't</u> engage with the reader like informal texts do — they're often more <u>detached</u>.

Formal Texts tend to be more Serious

1) Writers use a <u>formal</u> style when their audience is someone they <u>don't know</u>, or don't know very well. For example:

Broadsheet newspapers tend to report serious topics.

| a job application | a school report | a broadsheet newspaper article | a letter of complaint |

2) Formal language usually has some of the following <u>features</u>:

STANDARD ENGLISH — formal texts are usually written in Standard English with <u>correct</u> grammar, punctuation and spelling. Authors of formal texts often avoid using <u>contractions</u>, e.g. they'd write "do not" rather than "don't".

FORMAL VOCABULARY — formal texts might use more <u>sophisticated</u> vocabulary. For example, "<u>I demand</u>" rather than "I want".

IMPERSONAL LANGUAGE — the writer of formal texts will often <u>distance</u> themselves from the subject. They might say, "Jack's work is considered terrible", rather than, "I think that Jack's work is terrible". They often do this by using the <u>passive</u>. In a passive sentence, something is <u>done to</u> the <u>subject</u>, e.g. "The man was bitten by the dog" rather than, "The dog bit the man".

TECHNICAL LANGUAGE — formal writing sometimes includes <u>technical terms</u>. For example, a recipe might say "<u>Dice</u> the apples" instead of "Cut the apples into small chunks".

LONGER COMPLEX SENTENCES — formal writing usually includes <u>complicated</u> sentence structures, e.g. "Oscar iced the cake skilfully, crafting his masterpiece one layer at a time, pausing to think about each and every detail."

Authors use a Formal Style for different Effects

1) It's <u>not</u> enough to just <u>recognise</u> whether a text is formal or not. You've got to be able to spot the <u>techniques</u> that the author is using and explain <u>why</u> they're using them.

2) The <u>effect</u> of these techniques will depend on the text's <u>audience</u> and <u>purpose</u>, for example:

Average worldwide temperatures have increased by about 1 °C in the last hundred years, mainly due to the increased emission of gases such as carbon dioxide.

This author uses <u>technical</u> language such as "emission" and "carbon dioxide" to appear <u>knowledgeable</u>.

This author uses <u>formal</u> language such as "individual" and "wealth of experience" to impress the reader and to appear <u>professional</u>.

If you were to hire me, you would find me a responsible, hardworking individual with a wealth of experience.

Use features to help you identify the text's style

When you're reading a text, keep an eye out for the features above to help you identify if it's formal or not. For example, if a text includes slang, it's not a formal text.

Figurative Language

Time for some information about <u>figurative language</u>.

Figurative Language makes texts more Interesting

Writers use different types of <u>figurative language</u> to create interesting <u>effects</u>.
Examples of figurative language include:

exaggeration   personification   onomatopoeia

alliteration   metaphors   similes   imagery

A Simile says something is Like something else

A <u>simile</u> is a way of <u>describing</u> something. Similes usually use the words "<u>as</u>" or "<u>like</u>".

I wandered <u>lonely as a cloud</u>.

Daffodils — William Wordsworth

This is a <u>simile</u>. It tells you <u>how alone</u> the author was.

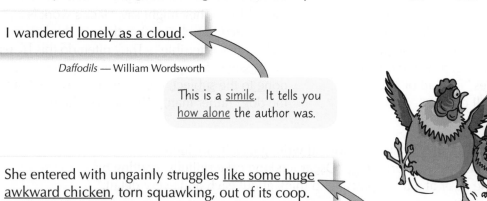

She entered with ungainly struggles <u>like some huge awkward chicken</u>, torn squawking, out of its coop.

The Adventure of the Three Gables — Arthur Conan Doyle

This is also a <u>simile</u>. It tells you <u>how awkwardly</u> the character moved.

A Metaphor says something Is something else

<u>Metaphors</u> describe something by saying that it <u>is</u> something else.
They never use "like" or "as". For example:

All the world's a stage,
And all the men and women merely players,

As You Like It — William Shakespeare

This is a <u>metaphor</u>. The world isn't actually a stage, but it describes how <u>dramatic</u> life can be.

There are many different types of figurative language

Figurative language is a great way for writers to spice up their texts, and there are all sorts of different types. Similes and metaphors are very common ones, so make sure you know them.

Figurative Language

Here are some more examples of figurative language. It's a good idea to get your head around these before you move on to the rest of the section.

Personification is another kind of Comparison

Personification is when an animal or an object is described as having human qualities.

> The ... gruff old bell was always peeping slily down at Scrooge...
>
> *A Christmas Carol* — Charles Dickens

Bells can't see, but personification brings the object to life.

> ...a pale moon, lying on her back as though the wind had tilted her...
>
> *Dr Jekyll and Mr Hyde* — Robert Louis Stevenson

Moons don't lie down, but this use of personification suggests that the wind is so strong, it's blown the moon over.

Imagery uses words to Create a Picture in the Reader's Mind

Imagery is when writers use descriptive or figurative language to create a really clear picture of something in the reader's imagination.

> He began to dance and his laughter became a bloodthirsty snarling.
>
> *Lord of the Flies* — William Golding

The author uses imagery to make the character sound like an animal. This emphasises how he has become less human.

> Imagine the soft hush of the waves and submerging your feet in warm, sapphire water. Your own island paradise is only a short flight away...

The writer appeals to the reader's senses of sound, touch and sight. Painting an inviting picture for the reader makes them want to visit the island.

> I saw that the bride within the bridal dress had withered like the dress, and like the flowers, and had no brightness left but the brightness of her sunken eyes.
>
> *Great Expectations* — Charles Dickens

Describing the bride as "withered" and having "sunken eyes" suggests she looks like a dead body. The description implies she's given up on living.

You need to learn to spot personification and imagery

Here's a handy way to remember what these two are — personification means describing things as a person, and imagery is about painting a picture in the reader's mind.

Figurative Language

I told you there were <u>lots</u> of different types of figurative language — here are <u>three</u> more. These techniques often appear in <u>non-fiction</u> texts as well as fiction writing.

Writers **Exaggerate** for **Effect**

<u>Exaggeration</u> is when something is said to be a <u>lot better</u> or a <u>lot worse</u> than it actually is.

He was going to kill me.

Anita and Me — Meera Syal

The character has stolen some money to buy sweets and her dad is about to find out. He's not really going to kill her, but this <u>exaggeration</u> suggests that the dad is going to react <u>very angrily</u>.

Writers sometimes exaggerate to <u>persuade</u> the reader to see their point of view:

These cashmere socks are incredibly soft and cosy — <u>I'm never taking them off</u>.

The writer exaggerates to make the socks sound <u>really good</u>.

Alliteration is when **Sounds** are **Repeated**

<u>Alliteration</u> is often used in poetry, or for <u>short snappy slogans</u> in adverts and leaflets. It grabs the reader's <u>attention</u> and often makes the text more <u>memorable</u>.

While I <u>n</u>odded, <u>n</u>early <u>n</u>apping, suddenly there came a tapping

The Raven — Edgar Allan Poe

Onomatopoeia — **Sounds Like** what it's talking about

Writers use onomatopoeia to make their <u>descriptions</u> come to life.

We hiss'd along the polish'd ice

The Prelude — William Wordsworth

The verb "hiss'd" <u>imitates</u> the sound of ice skates and makes the movement seem <u>smooth</u> and <u>effortless</u>.

<u>Swoop</u> through trees then enjoy the view as you <u>whizz</u> along the fastest zip wire around.

"Swoop" and "whizz" sound like someone moving <u>quickly</u> along a zip wire, so these verbs give the reader an idea of how <u>thrilling</u> the zip wire will be.

Exaggeration is also called hyperbole

Hyperbole just means exaggeration. Onomatopoeia is a tricky one to spell — try putting the letters to the tune of 'Old MacDonald had a farm, ee ei ee ei oh'. It works. Honest.

Oxymorons, Irony and Sarcasm

Writers have lots of <u>tricks</u> up their sleeves. Up next are oxymorons, irony and sarcasm.

Oxymorons put Contrasting ideas together

Writers often use oxymorons to <u>emphasise</u> something:

> JULIET: Good night, good night! Parting is such sweet sorrow...

Romeo and Juliet — William Shakespeare

Shakespeare uses lots of oxymorons. Have a look at p.136 for more examples.

"Sweet" and "sorrow" don't typically go together. Juliet means that she's sad that Romeo has to <u>leave</u>, but happy since he's organising for them to get <u>married</u>.

Sometimes oxymorons make a piece of writing more <u>humorous</u>:

The opening of the new community gardens was organised chaos — most people turned up half way through the ceremony because they'd been told the wrong time.

Putting "organised" and "chaos" together <u>emphasises</u> that the opening <u>wasn't</u> organised well. The contradiction also makes the text <u>funnier</u>. You can use the word '<u>oxymoronic</u>' to describe contradictory language like this.

Irony is when you Mean the Opposite of what you say

<u>Irony</u> is often used by writers to get across their <u>point of view</u>, but in a <u>funny</u> way.

> "...nobody can ever be introduced in a ball-room."

Pride and Prejudice — Jane Austen

Elizabeth uses irony to <u>make fun</u> of Mr Darcy — people <u>can</u> be introduced in a ballroom. She's suggesting that Mr Darcy isn't being very <u>sociable</u>.

Sarcasm is Angrier than Irony

Sarcasm is used to express the writer's <u>anger</u>, usually through <u>irony</u>. It can also be used to <u>mock</u> someone, usually by <u>praising</u> or <u>complimenting</u> them when the <u>opposite</u> is true.

I stood at the till for several minutes while the shop assistants chatted amongst themselves. I had never experienced such attentive service until that moment.

The writer uses sarcasm to express his <u>anger</u> at the shop assistants <u>not</u> doing their job. Saying the service is "attentive" sounds like a <u>compliment</u>, but the writer is actually <u>mocking</u> them.

Make sure you know which technique is which

Three language techniques here — make sure you know the effects of each one.
When you're ready, have a go at writing your own examples of the techniques above.

Fact, Opinion, Lists of Three and Rhetorical Questions

Some features are much more <u>common</u> in non-fiction texts than fiction texts. Have a read through them...

Fact is not the same as Opinion

Not all non-fiction is <u>fact</u>. If you can <u>prove it</u>, it's fact. <u>Opinion</u> is what someone <u>thinks</u>.

"The capital of Spain is Madrid."

Fact: You can look it up in an encyclopedia.

"Football is better than television."

Opinion: Not everyone would agree.

<u>Facts</u> and <u>statistics</u> often make non-fiction writing feel more <u>reliable</u>.

80% of people surveyed thought that a vegan diet was healthier than a non-vegan diet.

Statistics make the writer sound more <u>knowledgeable</u>. They can also be used to make a text more <u>persuasive</u>.

Lists of Three are used to Emphasise

Writers sometimes use a <u>list of three</u> words or phrases to make their point <u>stand out</u>.

The mayor's decision was <u>reckless</u>, <u>rushed</u> and <u>wrong</u>.

The three <u>adjectives</u> and <u>alliteration</u> emphasise that the writer <u>disagrees</u> with the mayor's decision.

To really make their point <u>clear</u>, writers will repeat the <u>same</u> word or phrase three times.

The <u>mayor's decision</u> was reckless.
The <u>mayor's decision</u> was rushed.
The <u>mayor's decision</u> was wrong.

The writer could have just written one sentence. By writing three similar sentences, it <u>emphasises</u> to the reader that there are <u>multiple</u> things that the writer <u>dislikes</u> about the mayor's decision.

Rhetorical Questions involve the reader

Writers sometimes ask questions that <u>don't</u> need an <u>answer</u> — these are <u>rhetorical questions</u>. It seems like the writer is making the reader <u>think</u> about their answer, when actually the writer is <u>persuading</u> the reader to <u>agree</u> with them.

Do we really want the next generation to suffer the consequences of global warming?

The reader will most likely answer <u>no</u> to this question — this is exactly what the writer <u>wants</u> them to say.

Make sure you can spell "rhetorical"

These techniques can often be found in persuasive texts — especially speeches. If you're writing a speech for your Spoken Language task, you'll impress your teacher if you use them.

Narrative

Now you know your onomatopoeia from your oxymorons, it's time to move on to narrative.

The **Narrator** is the voice that **Tells** the story

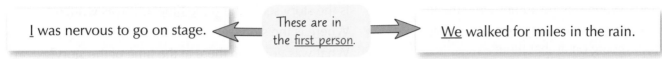

There's more on narrators on p.93.

1) Most fiction texts have first-person or third-person narrators.

2) A text that uses "I" or "we" has a first-person narrator. The reader follows the character through the story and sees the same things, whilst also knowing the character's thoughts and feelings.

I was nervous to go on stage. ← These are in the first person. → We walked for miles in the rain.

3) A story that uses "he", "she" or "they" has a third-person narrator. They tend to give a wider view of the story than first-person narrators and often tell the reader about lots of different characters.

She was nervous to go on stage.

They walked for miles in the rain.

These are in the third person.

Non-fiction texts often use the **Second Person**

The second person uses the pronoun "you". Some fiction writing uses the second person, but it's much more common in non-fiction writing.

In fiction writing, using "you" helps the reader to put themselves in the character's shoes. In this text, the reader can picture the action as they can imagine themselves climbing a tree, just like the character does.

→

You steady your foot on the branch and reach your fingertips higher and higher. You grasp the branch tightly and pull yourself up.

You should make yourself a revision timetable. That way you know what to study and when, and you can break your revision up to make it more manageable.

←

Using "you" in texts that advise makes the reader feel like the advice is directed at them. In this text, students can relate to the advice as it feels personal.

Newspaper Articles often use the **Third Person**

Some newspaper articles (especially those in broadsheets) use the third person to report events in an unbiased way. Using the third person helps to remove the writer from the story.

The city's residents have been affected by the war. They have attempted to flee to the countryside to escape the violence.

←

The use of the passive voice (see p.31) and the third person makes the writer sound detached.

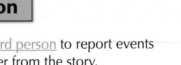

Every story has a narrator

If you write 'first person' as numbers (1st person) it looks a bit like the word 'I'. Do the same for 2nd person and remember that 'two' rhymes with 'you'. That should help you remember.

Context

When you're reading a text, think about its context — it will help you to understand it better.

The Context is When and Where a text is written

The context will affect the events, language and style of a text.
Here are some questions to ask about a text to help understand its context.

There's more about the context of Shakespeare on pages 131 and 141.

History
- When did the author write the text?
- Were there any important events going on at that time?

The setting of the story
- Is the story set in the same time as it was written?
- Where is the story set?
- What was going on there at the time of the story?

The author
- Where is the author from?
- Has their background influenced the text?

Society and culture
- What was society and culture like at the time?
- How is it different from today?
- Is the author positive or negative about it?

It's likely you'll study a text from the Victorian era, so it's worthwhile learning more about life at this time.

Setting Affects the Language in a text

1) The time the story is set in or written in will affect the language used by characters and the narrator.

I am sorry, with all my heart, to find you so resolute. We have never had any quarrel, to which I have been a party.

A Christmas Carol — Charles Dickens

A Christmas Carol is set in Victorian London. The language used by the characters reflects how people spoke at that time...

It was cold, bleak, biting weather: foggy withal...

A Christmas Carol — Charles Dickens

... some words, such as "withal", were used back then, but aren't really used today.

2) The setting can also influence the way the characters speak. Writers might include the local dialect in their text — words and phrases specific to a certain region.

I s'pose you're glad. Ever'body knowed you'd mess things up. You wasn't no good.

Of Mice and Men — John Steinbeck

Of Mice and Men is set in America so the characters speak with an American accent and use American dialect words.

Texts Reflect what Society was like

1) Texts often represent society at the time they were written. Some things that happen in texts written long ago might seem strange now, but it was quite normal at the time.

2) Jane Austen's *Pride and Prejudice* was published in 1813. Back then, upper class women couldn't go to work, so it was important they married someone rich. In *Pride and Prejudice*, Mrs Bennett gets very excited whenever a wealthy single man appears because she has five daughters to marry off.

Context

The **Author's Background** can influence texts

The writer's own life and experiences sometimes influence plots, settings and characters.

Anita and Me by Meera Syal
- The plot of Meera Syal's novel is fictional, but the setting and some characters are loosely based on the author's childhood.
- Meena is the main character and her life is inspired by Syal's childhood. Meena's parents emigrated to England from India, like Syal's parents did in real life. Syal went to a grammar school and at the end of the novel, Meena sits an exam to get into grammar school.

Use **Spider Diagrams** to make notes about **Context**

Take a look at this spider diagram which summarises the context of Mary Shelley's novel, *Frankenstein*, which was published in 1818.

Language of the novel reflects the language of the 19th century

Shelley was a woman. Female authors less likely at this time, especially writing science fiction / gothic horror stories.

Novel has an unhappy ending. Suggests that Shelley felt negatively about these experiments.

SOCIETY & CULTURE

In 1800s, scientists were carrying out experiments to find out if electricity could bring things to life. Main character tries to bring a monster to life with electricity.

Part of the story set in Geneva, Switzerland, but written by an English author

SETTING

'Frankenstein' by Mary Shelley published 1818

HISTORY

Lots of interest in polar expeditions at this time. One of the characters tries to find "passage" through the Arctic.

Shelley spent time in Geneva — provided inspiration for setting

AUTHOR

Think about the context of the text you're studying...

REVISION TASK

Make a spider diagram like the one above for the text you're studying. Think about the text's author, and how history, society and culture have affected the language, setting and events.

Grammar and Punctuation

Grammar and punctuation — everyone uses them, but sometimes writers use them for a particular effect.

Don't overlook **Tenses**

1) Most fiction texts are written in the past tense.
2) Some non-fiction texts, such as newspaper articles, are written in the past tense too...
3) ... whereas some might use the present tense.

> The situation is desperate.

⬅ Persuasive texts often use the present tense. The writer wants their text to sound more urgent.

4) Some non-fiction texts, especially recipes and instructions, might use the imperative.

> Sieve the flour and add the sugar.

⬅ This is the imperative — it's a command. The writer is telling the reader exactly what to do.

5) These are just a few examples of the different tenses that you might come across. When you're answering questions about texts, make sure you think about what tense has been used and its effect on the reader.

Punctuation can be used to create an **Effect**

1) Ellipsis (...) indicates a pause in a text. These pauses are often used to build suspense.

> "If it was my master, why did he cry out like a rat, and run from me? I have served him long enough. And then..." The man paused and passed his hand over his face.

⬅ The ellipsis shows that the character stops talking midway through a sentence. It creates suspense as it suggests that he can't bring himself to admit what has happened.

Dr Jekyll and Mr Hyde — Robert Louis Stevenson

2) Exclamation marks can indicate different emotions, like anger or surprise. They can also make the tone of a text more emotional or light-hearted.

> "I never meant you, Meena! It was all the others, not yow!"

⬅ This character is pleading with Meena. The exclamation marks show how strongly he feels.

Anita and Me — Meera Syal

3) Bullet points are more commonly found in non-fiction texts than fiction. They are used to lay out information in a way that's easy to read.
4) The use of punctuation marks in poetry is important — have a look at p.111 for more about the effects.

Don't ignore grammar and punctuation
Every sentence will have some grammar and punctuation — it's up to you to work out its effect.

Warm-Up and Worked Practice Questions

Time for some questions — have a go at the warm-up ones first to get your brain in gear.

Warm-up Questions

1) Picture this scene: "Charlie opened the present with a sneer."
   What does the word "sneer" tell us about Charlie's reaction to the present?
2) Give three features of an informal text.
3) Name five types of figurative language.

Worked Practice Questions

This paragraph is from a brochure about biking holidays abroad.

> One of Europe's most exciting, yet least known, mountain biking areas lies deep in southern France. Full of technical trails and rocky single-tracks, the limestone region of Roquefort, just west of the Cevennes National Park, is a mountain-biker's playground. Cutting through the plateaux are the steep gorges of the Tarn, with their challenging climbs and descents, and in the eastern part of the region fast trails sweep through the cool chestnut and oak woodlands of the Cevennes. It's the perfect area for fit and experienced bikers looking for a workout.

1. What is the purpose of this text?
   To persuade readers to go on a cycling holiday in France.

2. How does the brochure try to make the holiday sound appealing to mountain bikers?

   This first point looks at the connotations of the language.

   The brochure calls the destination "a mountain-biker's playground". The word "playground" has connotations of being fun and exciting, so this would make the holiday sound appealing to cyclists.

   The second point talks about the use of technical language.

   The brochure also uses technical language, such as "technical trails and rocky single-tracks", which shows that the writer knows a lot about mountain biking. This makes the holiday seem appealing because the readers would feel as though their holiday is being organised by mountain bike experts.

   Make sure you think about what the effect on the reader is.

Worked Practice Questions

Here are some more worked practice questions. They show you how you can use all the advice you've read so far to write a good answer.

Worked Practice Questions

This is the beginning of a story by Paul Jennings called *Spaghetti Pig-Out*.

> Guts Garvey was a real mean kid. He made my life miserable. I don't know why he didn't like me. I hadn't done anything to him. Not a thing.
>
> He wouldn't let any of the other kids hang around with me. I was on my own. Anyone in the school who spoke to me was in his bad books. I wandered around the yard at lunch time like a dead leaf blown in the wind.
>
> I tried everything. I even gave him my pocket money one week. He just bought a block of chocolate from the canteen and ate it in front of me. Without even giving me a bit. What a rat.
>
> After school I had only one friend. My cat — Bad Smell. She was called that because now and then she would make a bad smell. Well, she couldn't help it. Everyone has their faults. She was a terrific cat. But still. A cat is not enough. You need other kids for friends too.

1. What type of narrator does the story have?

   first person

2. What register does the author use? Give an example to support your answer.

   Informal — "a real mean kid"

3. a) Which simile in the second paragraph describes how lonely the narrator was?

   "I wandered around the yard at lunch time like a dead leaf blown in the wind."

   b) Explain why this phrase is effective.

   A leaf being blown by the wind is drifting around with no real place to go, just like the narrator.

4. Explain how the tone changes slightly in the last paragraph.

   In the first three paragraphs the tone is quite sad because the narrator is telling us how miserable and lonely he is. In the fourth paragraph he introduces a touch of comedy by talking about his cat who makes bad smells.

   This question is about spotting a change, so the answer talks about the sadness of the first bit and the comedy of the second bit.

Practice Questions

Now have a go at these practice questions.

Practice Questions

This abridged extract is from *Persuasion*, a novel by Jane Austen. It was first published in 1817.

> Lady Dalrymple's carriage, for which Miss Elliot was growing very impatient, now drew up; the servant came in to announce it. It was beginning to rain again, and altogether there was a delay, and a bustle, and a talking, which must make all the little crowd in the shop understand that Lady Dalrymple was calling to convey* Miss Elliot. At last Miss Elliot and her friend, unattended but by the servant, were walking off; and Captain Wentworth, watching them, turned again to Anne, and by manner, rather than words, was offering his services to her.
>
> "I am much obliged to you," was her answer, "but I am not going with them. The carriage would not accommodate so many. I walk: I prefer walking."
>
> "But it rains."
>
> "Oh! very little, Nothing that I regard."
>
> After a moment's pause he said: "Though I came only yesterday, I have equipped myself properly for Bath already, you see," (pointing to a new umbrella); "I wish you would make use of it, if you are determined to walk."
>
> She was very much obliged to him, but declined it all, repeating her conviction, that the rain would come to nothing at present, and adding, "I am only waiting for Mr Elliot. He will be here in a moment, I am sure."
>
> *convey — collect

1. Give an example of how the language of the extract reflects the time it was written in.

   ....

   ....

2. What do you think Lady Dalrymple's social status is? Explain your answer.

   ....

   ....

   ....

3. How does the extract reflect what society was like in the 1800s?

   ....

   ....

   ....

Practice Questions

Read the non-fiction text below and answer the following question.

Practice Questions

HOW TO EAT 10 PORTIONS OF FRUIT AND VEG PER DAY

With nutritionists now recommending that we should eat even more fruit and veg each day, it can be hard to find ways to include more portions in your diet. We've planned out two days of delicious meals below that will help you reach that 10-a-day goal.

Day One	Day Two
Breakfast	Breakfast
• Fruit salad (2 portions)	• Omelette with ham and tomatoes (1 portion)
Lunch	Lunch
• Winter veg soup (3 portions)	• Baked sweet potato with veg (3 portions)
Dinner	Dinner
• Chicken stir fry with greens, peppers and onions (2 portions)	• Ratatouille (3 portions)
Snacks	Snacks
• An apple (1 portion)	• An orange (1 portion)
• A banana (1 portion)	• Carrot batons and dip (1 portion)
• Berries and yoghurt (1 portion)	• A handful of grapes (1 portion)

Choose three layout features from the text above and explain what effect they have.

Layout feature 1: ....

Effect: ....

....

Layout feature 2: ....

Effect: ....

....

Layout feature 3: ....

Effect: ....

....

Practice Questions

Here's another extract and some practice questions for you to get your teeth into.

Practice Questions

In this extract, the writer begins to describe what it might be like to be attacked by piranhas.

Swim with the fishes *by Greg Emmanuel*

These are no ordinary fish. Although piranhas aren't much larger than a good-sized goldfish, they have the dentition* to clear the flesh off any animal's bones — including yours. A piranha can go from open mouth to clenched teeth in less than five milliseconds — that's less time than it takes you to blink. Their jaws have an interlocking design: the top triangular teeth fit snugly into the gaps between the bottom teeth, snapping shut like a steel trap. And each individual tooth is as sharp as a razor blade.

Piranhas also have excellent senses: good vision, a well developed sense of smell, and a system of pores along their body that allows them to detect distant disturbances in the water. When your splashing feet enter their territory, the nearest piranha is thirty yards away — but can cover that distance in a few seconds. As you wrestle with your canoe, pushing and pulling it over the sandbank, you suddenly feel an unspeakable pain and yank your left foot out of the water.

* dentition — teeth

---

1. a)   Find two examples of technical language from the text.

    ....

    ....

   b)   What effect does this technical language have?

    ....

    ....

2. How does the writer use similes to emphasise how dangerous piranhas are?

    ....

    ....

    ....

3. How else does the writer suggest that piranhas are a serious threat?

    ....

    ....

    ....

Revision Summary for Section Four

Phew, that was a lot of techniques. When you're feeling confident about what you've read in this section, go ahead and run through these questions. If any of them stump you, go back through the section until you find the answer.

1) Name three examples of fiction texts and three examples of non-fiction texts.

   Tudort stories, autobiogrphy, Cindecella

2) Name four purposes of texts.

3) Give three layout features that could be used in a recipe.

   It gives you info

   method, recipe

4) Make an inference from the following sentence:

   "Haroon groaned when the teacher said that sports day was cancelled."

   hes upseat that sports day is cancel

5) What is register?

   Its one to see whose here

6) Give three features of a formal text.

   no slang - no score, address numb

7) Decide whether the following sentences are similes or metaphors:

   a) The palms of her hands were sandpaper.

   b) He was a beast with the ball.

   c) The car was like an oven.

   d) The snow lay over the fields like a white blanket.

8) Which words in these sentences are examples of onomatopoeia?

   a) The snake hissed unhappily as they looked at it through the glass.

   b) They uncorked the bottle of champagne with a loud pop.

   c) The collection of tins clanged and clattered in the boot of the car.

9) Which sentence below contains an oxymoron?

   a) Paul's sofa is really comfortable — you can feel all the springs when you sit down.

   b) Daisy's new haircut went down like a lead balloon with her mum.

   c) After Milo the dog dug holes all over the garden, it looked really tidy.

10) What is a rhetorical question?

    Its a yes or no question

11) "Third-person narrators tend to focus on one character." True or false?

12) What is context?

    it has a meaning behind it

13) Give three things about context that you should think about when reading a text.

14) "Dice the onion, add it to the frying pan and cook over a low heat for 5 minutes." This sentence uses imperative verbs. What effect does this create?

15) What effect does using ellipsis often create?

    It creats suspene

Writing Fiction

This section is all about using different styles of writing for different purposes. You might be asked to write a piece of fiction or non-fiction, and so you need to know how to tackle both of them.

Plan your story Before you start Writing

1) It's tempting to start your story by writing "Once upon a time..." and hope that you'll be able to make up what happens in your story as you go along. But that's a really bad idea.

2) Before you start writing, you should already have a good idea of how your story is going to end and what will happen in the middle. If you don't, you'll have all sorts of problems.

3) Making a quick plan will help with this — the plan doesn't need to decide every detail of your story, but a good plan will help to keep the whole thing on track.

> Q. Write about an exciting journey you have made. It can be real or imaginary.

PLAN: Going on holiday on a plane (100 words).

Lots of people got very ill from the food (150 words).

Went to the cockpit — pilot was unconscious (100 words).

I talked to air traffic control over the pilot's radio and they told me what to do (150 words).

I landed the plane safely (50 words).

Everyone went to hospital — they were all fine (100 words).

The plan is a summary of the story you're going to write.

When you write the story, you could have two or three paragraphs about each of these points.

It's useful to have an idea of roughly how long each part of the story will be.

You've planned how it's going to end, so you always know what you're aiming towards.

Start with something Exciting

1) Nobody wants to read a story with a boring start — the beginning of a story should grab the reader's attention and make them want to read on.

2) There are lots of ways you can do this, but here are a few examples:

START IN THE MIDDLE OF THE ACTION — e.g. "Naomi moved away. The edge of the cliff crumbled and she plunged backwards".

All of these examples engage the reader by creating a sense of mystery or tension.

DESCRIBE AN UNUSUAL CHARACTER — e.g. "Everyone in the town had heard of Barnabas Billington, although very few of them had actually seen him in person."

DIRECTLY ADDRESS THE READER — e.g. "Have you ever had the feeling that something's not quite right? Well, I'm going to tell you about one of the strangest days of my life."

3) You don't need to explain everything at once, you just need to make the reader want to read on.

Starting a story is often the hardest bit...

REVISION TASK

Pick one of the ways you could start a story from the blue boxes above, and try to write an exciting opening. Flick to Section 3 for a reminder about making your writing interesting.

Writing Fiction

There's a lot <u>more</u> to writing fiction than having a good plan and an engaging opening...

Use a **Variety** of **Literary Techniques**

1) You'll want to make sure that your story is as <u>interesting</u> to read as possible. Using different <u>techniques</u> is a really good way to keep your reader <u>engaged</u>, and also shows that you not only know about literary techniques, but that you can <u>use them</u> in your <u>own work</u>.

2) Here are a few of the things you should consider when writing your story:

<u>NARRATIVE VIEWPOINT</u> — most stories feature a <u>first</u> or <u>third-person</u> <u>narrator</u> (page 93), although some stories do use the <u>second-person</u>.

<u>MOOD</u> — the <u>language</u> you use will depend on the <u>mood</u> of your story (page 94). E.g. a <u>funny</u> story would need very <u>different language</u> from a <u>sad</u> or <u>scary</u> story.

<u>FIGURATIVE LANGUAGE</u> — include some techniques like <u>metaphors</u>, <u>similes</u>, <u>imagery</u>, <u>personification</u>, <u>alliteration</u>, <u>exaggeration</u> and <u>onomatopoeia</u> (pages 32-34). Using a mixture of these techniques will make your story more <u>engaging</u>, but <u>don't</u> use them too often or they'll lose their effect.

Make sure your story has a **Clear Focus**

1) While it's important to make your story interesting, you should also keep it as <u>focused</u> as possible.

2) A common <u>mistake</u> people make when writing fiction is <u>filling the story</u> with <u>too many</u> different <u>things</u> — too many characters, lots of different settings, a confusing amount of events, etc.

3) A story that follows <u>one character</u> through a <u>single situation</u> can often be <u>more interesting</u> than a story that follows too many <u>indistinct characters</u> through a series of <u>unclear events</u>.

Finish with a **Good Ending**

1) The ending is <u>really important</u>. Try to make it <u>memorable</u> so it sticks in your reader's mind. If it's really good, it will give your reader a <u>positive impression</u> of everything you've already said.

Even if you're only asked to write part of a story, make sure you finish it with a strong ending.

2) Just like starting a story, there are <u>lots of ways</u> you can end one. Here are a few examples:

<u>WRAP EVERYTHING UP NICELY</u> — e.g. "As he set sail for the open sea, Tamar gazed back at the town, happy in the knowledge that he had performed his job brilliantly."

<u>INTRODUCE A PLOT TWIST</u> — e.g. "The brothers stepped towards the villain's door with anticipation. As they slowly turned the handle, they were shocked to discover their grandfather."

<u>CREATE A CLIFFHANGER</u> — e.g. "The prison guard slammed the door of the cell. Kerry looked around at the bare space in front of her — how on earth was she going to get out of this one?"

3) However you choose to finish your story, just make sure you <u>don't</u> end with a <u>cliché</u> (see p.18).

A clichéd ending can ruin the entire story

Nobody wants to spend time reading a story only for it to end with something like "and they all lived happily ever after" or "it was all a dream" — show the reader that you can be <u>original</u> instead.

Writing Letters

Now you've got the hang of writing fiction, it's time to look at writing non-fiction. Let's start with letters.

Always **Plan** a letter

1) Letters can be written in a formal or an informal style.
2) Planning a letter is just as important as planning a story or an essay.
3) If you don't plan it out first, you won't do the best job that you possibly can.
4) To make your plan, just jot down the main points that you want to make in the letter.

> PLAN: *letter to Space Age Washing Machines*
>
> *Intro — writing to complain*
>
> *Problem with the machine*
>
> *Phoning the helpdesk (mention 30 minute wait)*
>
> *Would like a refund and the machine removed*
>
> *Hope the problem is resolved quickly*

The full letter has been included on the next page.

In the introduction, you want to establish why you are writing to the recipient, e.g. to complain, to enquire, to inform, to ask for something.

In most cases, you should end your letter with a summary of your main idea or argument.

Use **Formal Language** in a **Formal Letter**

1) When you write a formal letter, you have to use a more formal style (see page 31).
2) This style is used in important documents, e.g. a letter from school, a job application.
3) Here are some key features of letters written in a formal style:

- They might have a detached tone.
- They often use more complex vocabulary, and avoid slang terms.
- They avoid using contractions.
- They don't use exclamation marks.

Informal Letters use casual **Chatty Language**

1) When you write an informal letter, you can use a more informal style (see page 30).
2) This style is more appropriate when you're writing to someone that you know.
3) Here are some key features of letters written in an informal style:

- They often sound like they're talking to the person you're writing to — the letter sounds more natural.
- They still use proper sentences even though they are written in a more friendly way.
- They use contractions, chatty language and exclamation marks.

Informal writing doesn't mean it's poorly written

Make sure that any letter that you write completes the task in the question and is written in the most appropriate style. Even if the letter is to a friend, you need to make sure the letter is written well.

Writing a Formal Letter

Formal letters follow a strict set of rules — these are shown in blue in the letter below.
Look at the letter and learn the rules for writing them.

Formal Letters have certain Features

Name and address of the
person you are writing to.

Your address.

1 Tippins Lane
Waterford
WA3 6PP
5th May 2017

Write the date out in full.

Mrs V Sutton
Space Age Washing Machines PLC
Huyton
HU5 7EZ

If you don't know their name, just put "Dear Sir/Madam".

Dear Mrs Sutton,

Put what the letter is about here.

Re: Performance of your washing machines

The first bit gives your reason for writing.

I am writing to complain about the standard and performance of my week-old
Space Age washing machine.

When I turned it on, the machine made a high-pitched whining noise. After five
minutes, the whole machine began to vibrate violently, sending tremors through my kitchen.
The washing machine then began to froth around the door until foam was escaping across
the kitchen floor.

Space between paragraphs makes the letter easier to read.

At this point, I attempted to phone your company's help desk. I was left on hold
for thirty minutes listening to a terrible selection of music whilst waiting for an operator to
speak to me.

Clear paragraphs for each point.

This is clearly an unacceptable product. At the very least I would like a full refund
and the removal of this machine as soon as possible.

Formal language is used.

I hope that you resolve this matter immediately.

Yours sincerely,

To end your letter, use "Yours sincerely" when you know the person's name.
If you've put "Dear Sir/Madam" at the top, then put "Yours faithfully" here.

A.S. Coleridge
Ms Alia S. Coleridge

Your signature, with your full name below it.
Put "Mr", "Ms" or "Miss" before your name.

Learn the layout rules for formal letters

It might seem like there's a lot to learn here, but <u>don't worry</u>. Try covering up this page
and writing a list of all of the features of a formal letter in the order they would appear.

Writing an Informal Letter

If you're writing to someone you <u>know well</u>, then you can write an <u>informal letter</u>. Informal letters are more <u>friendly</u> and you <u>don't</u> have to bother so much with formal language. Take a look at this letter...

Informal Letters also have certain Features

Give your address (it makes it easier for the other person to reply).

7 The Square
Benwich
Yorkshire
BE4 6RT
5th July 2017

First name, because you're writing to a friend.

Dear Zina,

You don't need to say what your letter is about — you can just get straight into writing it.

Cheers for the letter — it made me smile and even chuckle a little. I just can't believe what you got up to — you're a terror!

Chatty, friendly style.

I don't get many chances to get up to much stuck here in the country, but it has its moments when it's <u>not</u> as dull as dishwater.

You can use contractions.

Last week, we had the annual marrow competition. You should have seen them — some so large you could barely pick them up! Nadja, Will and H painted a courgette, stuck it on a plastic leaf and entered it into the 'Most Unusual Marrow' category. It was cool, but they didn't win. Never mind, it was great fun. Better luck next year...

You still need spaces between paragraphs.

We had a bit of excitement just this morning when the cows from the local farm went on the rampage. They invaded the village centre and stole Mr Lambert's vest from the washing line. It was so funny! It also meant that I was a whole hour late for school — so I missed science. Fantastic!

You can use exclamation marks.

Dad says to say 'hi' from him. He's got a new job as a gardener at one of those big houses on the edge of the village. The best part is that the owner has no kids, so she's said I can go and use the swimming pool any time Dad's working. I can't wait.

Paragraphs for each point or different part of the story (it makes the letter easier to read).

Must dash, stay good and write soon.

Take it easy,   Informal ending.

Nasreen   Just sign your first name.

Informal letters have a less strict layout

An informal letter <u>doesn't</u> have as many <u>strict rules</u> as a formal letter, but that doesn't mean you can just write all over the place. Your writing still needs to be <u>organised</u>, so it's important to make a <u>plan</u>.

Writing to Persuade and Argue

Now you've got formal and informal letters clear in your head, it's time to think about writing to persuade and argue. There's loads to learn here, so best get cracking...

Persuading and Arguing are quite Similar

1) Writing to persuade is about encouraging the reader to do something, e.g. to recycle more, to eat a healthy breakfast, to support a charity.

2) Writing to argue is more about getting people to agree with your opinions and showing why other people's opinions are wrong (or at least not as good as yours). For example, you might argue that a longer school day is unfair or that a local bus route shouldn't stop running.

3) Persuading is usually more subtle than arguing — it focuses more on emotion, while arguing focuses more on facts and uses more forceful language to get the point across.

4) When you're writing to argue or persuade, you need to give clear and convincing reasons to support what you say.

5) Texts that persuade or argue could be written in lots of different forms — letters, speeches, newspaper articles etc. As well as using the language techniques on these pages, you may need to include the features of the form too. There's more about form on p.97.

Use 'A Forest' in your writing

1) 'A Forest' is a really useful mnemonic to help you remember some of the techniques you can use in your arguments or persuasive writing.

2) It stands for anecdotes and alliteration, facts, opinions, rhetorical questions, emotive language, statistics and the magic three.

3) These techniques are covered in more detail over the next few pages and are a great way to make your writing even stronger.

4) As with any technique, don't overuse them in the same piece of writing — they won't be as effective.

A — Anecdotes and alliteration
F — Facts
O — Opinions
R — Rhetorical questions
E — Emotive language
S — Statistics
T — The magic three

Anecdotes and Alliteration can engage the reader

1) An anecdote is a short story about a real event. Anecdotes are often personal to you, but they can be about other people or things you've heard too. For example:

> *When I was a child, my parents would always tell me about the importance of eating a healthy breakfast.*

Starting your writing with an anecdote is a really good way to engage your reader and make them want to read on.

2) As you'll remember from page 34, alliteration is when sounds are repeated. For example:

Alliteration is a really useful way of getting the reader's attention — it also emphasises the point you're making.

> *Some people believe that the best way to start your day is with a big bowl of berries for your breakfast.*

Writing to Persuade and Argue

Use **Facts** to support what you say

1) Facts are true — they can be proven. This means they are a really good way to convince or persuade your reader.

2) To make your argument more believable, you should include lots of facts. Using facts makes you seem more knowledgeable.

Statistics are a type of fact — there's more about these on the next page.

Porridge is often made from oats.

This is a fact — you could look it up in an encyclopedia to prove that it is true.

Make your **Opinion** clear throughout your writing

1) Opinions are just what someone thinks — unlike facts, they can't be proven. This means that different people often have different opinions.

This is an opinion — there's no way to prove that it's true.

Eating a bowl of porridge is the best way to start the day.

2) You can disagree with someone else's opinion. A really good way to strengthen your argument is to give the opinion of the other side, then explain why you think they're wrong (see p.56).

3) It's important to make your opinion as clear as possible — you can mention the other side of the argument, but just make sure that you don't sit on the fence.

Use **Rhetorical Questions** to make your points

1) Asking people a question is a great way to make them sit up and take notice — even though you don't want them to reply (this type of question is called a rhetorical question).

2) The trick is to phrase the question so that there can only be one possible answer.

Do you really think that cereal full of sugar and additives is a healthy breakfast option?

This question has been phrased so that the reader would say "no".

3) Alternatively, you can ask a question, then go on to answer it yourself.

So why do companies make unhealthy breakfast cereal? I'll tell you why. It's because they don't care about people's health — they just want to make a profit.

Writing to Persuade and Argue

Use **Emotive Language** to create **Sympathy**

1) <u>Emotive language</u> is any language that makes the reader <u>feel</u> something.

2) In persuasive writing, it's mainly used to make the reader <u>sympathise</u> with the writer's cause, although it can be used to create <u>other feelings</u> as well.

> The <u>emotive language</u> here creates a feeling of <u>sympathy</u>, but also a feeling of <u>guilt</u>.

> *Ignoring young people's thoughts about environmentalism is not only <u>insensitive</u>, it's downright <u>irresponsible</u>.*

3) <u>Emotive language</u> can make your argument <u>more persuasive</u>, but be careful it doesn't become too <u>aggressive</u> — this might <u>offend</u> people and make them stop reading.

> *People who refuse to recycle are stupid and selfish.* ✗

> *Recycling is a simple way to help protect our beautiful planet from irreversible damage.* ✓

Statistics are really strong pieces of **Evidence**

1) Statistics are pieces of <u>information</u> that come from studies which are presented using <u>numbers</u> — e.g. measurements, percentages, tables, charts.

2) Using <u>statistics</u> is an effective way of showing the reader that <u>you know your stuff</u>.

3) It tells them that you've <u>researched</u> the area you're talking about and that you can <u>support</u> your <u>points</u> with solid <u>evidence</u>.

> *Studies show that up to 95% of 18-24 year-olds feel that their stance on environmentalism is being ignored.*

> Using <u>statistics</u> like this can make your argument sound much more <u>convincing</u>.

4) It's best to use only <u>key statistics</u> — you don't want to bombard the reader with lots of <u>numbers</u> or they might <u>lose interest</u>.

The Magic Three makes your points **Stand Out**

POWER OF THREE

<u>Three</u> is a <u>magic number</u> when you're <u>arguing</u> or <u>persuading</u>. Using three <u>adjectives</u> to describe something sounds much <u>more effective</u> than only using one or two.

> The three adjectives should all <u>add</u> something to the description. Using three words with the <u>same</u> meaning (e.g. "dirty, grubby and filthy") <u>isn't</u> as effective.

> *Fossil fuels are <u>dirty</u>, <u>dangerous</u> and <u>outdated</u>.*
>
> *Renewable energy is <u>clean</u>, <u>safe</u> and <u>efficient</u>.*

> You may have heard this technique called 'tricolons', 'triplets' or 'the power of three'.

REVISION TIP

'A Forest' isn't the only way to remember these techniques
You might have heard of similar <u>mnemonics</u> like 'FORESTRY' or a completely different one like 'PERSUADE', but you could even <u>make up</u> your own if you find it <u>easier</u> to remember.

Writing to Persuade and Argue

Now that A FOREST has been covered, it's time to look at some more great techniques you can use when writing to persuade and argue. First up, it's exaggeration.

Exaggeration is also known as Hyperbole

"hyperbole" is pronounced "hy-per-bo-lee".

1) It might sound a bit unfair to exaggerate how good your own arguments are. But don't worry — everyone does it. If you don't exaggerate, people might think your points are weaker than they are.

2) This works really well in articles and speeches, and also in texts that are trying to sell a product.

3) Take a look at the examples below. The first one isn't very convincing...

Global warming could be quite a problem. Some people think the earth is getting warmer quite quickly. That might mean that a fair bit of farmland turns into desert, so people might not have enough food.

The vague language in this example makes it sound as though the writer isn't really sure of what they're saying.

4) This one is much more persuasive:

"Many" instead of "some" is more persuasive — it sounds like loads of people agree with your argument. The term "scientists" (rather than "people") is more convincing too, because they're experts who know their stuff.

Global warming is a massive threat to the very future of humanity. Many scientists believe the earth is getting warmer at a frightening rate. If this continues, huge areas of farmland will turn into desert, causing billions of people to starve.

Words like "massive", "frightening" and "huge" are stronger than words like "quite" or "a fair bit".

It says "will" instead of "might".

It talks about "billions of people" instead of just saying "people".

Using "starve" is scarier than "not have enough food".

...but Don't Lie

Be careful — you're allowed to exaggerate, but you're not allowed to lie. You can't say things that aren't true, such as "global warming will cause aliens to take over the Earth".

If you say things that obviously aren't true, people won't trust the rest of your argument.

Exaggeration can be very effective

Exaggeration is an important trick for persuasive writing. It can make your argument sound more convincing. Just make sure you don't lie, or it's less likely that your reader will agree with you.

Writing to Persuade and Argue

As well as exaggerating the good points in your own argument, you
can also point out the flaws in the opposition's argument.

Make your **Opponents** sound **Weaker**

1) You can also exaggerate what the people who disagree with you say in order to
weaken their points — it's a great tactic when you're writing an argument.

2) Putting your opponents' point of view in your own words is a good way to make them sound bad.

> Some business owners believe we have no responsibility
> to the environment. They think it doesn't matter if we
> keep on churning out deadly greenhouse gases. All
> they care about is making profits.

Phrases like "no responsibility",
"it doesn't matter" and "all they
care about" exaggerate the negative
parts of the other side's argument.

3) You can be harsh, but as always, it's important that you don't tell any actual lies.

4) Don't spend too much time criticising your opponents though — make sure you
concentrate on presenting your own argument clearly and persuasively.

Work out the **Opposite** view — then say why it's **Wrong**

1) Write down a list of all the reasons why you think people might not agree with your argument.

2) Then go through your list and work out how to prove them wrong.

Here's how you
might plan a speech
trying to persuade
people to support a
ban on fox hunting.

> _Notes: Reasons why people disagree with banning fox hunting_
>
> 1. _Countryside jobs — but there aren't that many_
>
> 2. _Need to cull foxes — but there are more humane ways_
>
> 3. _Tradition — but so was bear-baiting_

These are reasons it
should NOT be banned.

Here's how you can say
these reasons are wrong.

> _Why fox hunting should be banned_
>
> _Supporters of fox hunting say that it's a tradition, but in
> the past it has also been traditional to bait bears. Times
> change and societies move on. Just because something is
> traditional, it does not mean that we have to keep doing it._

And here's
how you could
write out one of
those points.

3) Show that while you've thought about what your opponents have to say, you still disagree with them.
That way you'll have more chance of convincing other people that your view is right.

Writing to Persuade and Argue

Keep your **Criticisms General** and **Impersonal**

Don't make direct attacks on your opponents. It'll make you sound angry and aggressive, and anyone who's neutral might be turned off by your attitude.

If you think animal testing is acceptable, I think you're wrong. ✗

Using the pronoun "you" sounds as though you're criticising the reader directly. Some people might find this offensive and stop reading.

Some people think that animal testing is acceptable, but I think they're wrong. ✓

Using "Some people" instead of "you" makes this criticism more general. However, you're still targeting a group of people, which can come across as a bit aggressive.

It is sometimes said that animal testing is acceptable, but I think that's wrong. ✓✓

This version criticises the practice of animal testing — it's more impersonal.

Make your **Positive** points **Personal**

1) For positive points, you can be as personal as you like because you're less likely to offend someone.
2) Using "you" is an easy way to involve the reader — it makes them sit up and listen to what you have to say.
3) You can also involve the reader by using "we" — this makes it seem like the reader is on your side, and so they might be more likely to agree with you.

You can make a difference by not buying this company's products. If we work together, we can bring this awful practice to an end.

This sort of personal language is especially effective when you use it as an ending.

It's fine to be personal when the point is positive

Part of writing politely is making your negative points impersonal. Being aggressive just turns people away. When points are positive, though, it's a good idea to talk directly to your audience.

Writing to Inform, Advise and Explain

Now you know how to persuade and argue, it's time to learn how to <u>inform</u>, <u>advise</u> and <u>explain</u>.

There are some Key Things to Consider for each style

1) Writing to <u>inform</u>, <u>advise</u> and <u>explain</u> are quite <u>similar</u>. They are all about passing <u>information</u> on to the reader.

2) But there are some <u>subtle differences</u> between them — so make sure you know how to <u>suit</u> your writing to match each purpose.

3) They can either be written in a <u>formal</u> or an <u>informal</u> style — you need to work out which would be the most <u>appropriate</u> style for your audience.

4) Remember to think about the <u>form</u> of the text too — you may be asked to write a <u>letter</u>, a <u>speech</u>, a set of <u>instructions</u> etc. — so you may want to include some <u>layout features</u> like headings, numbered lists or diagrams.

Turn to p.27 if you'd like a reminder about layout features.

5) You can make notes about <u>language</u>, <u>form</u> and <u>structure</u> in your <u>plan</u>.

> Q. Your teacher has asked you to write a text about your favourite animal. Write about half a page of A4 informing people about your favourite animal.

This text will need a <u>formal</u> style because it is being written for a <u>general reader</u>.

You can use an <u>informal</u> style for this letter because it's being written to a <u>friend</u>. You'd need to include the features of an <u>informal letter</u> too (see p.51).

> Q. Imagine you are going on holiday. Write a letter to a friend informing them that you'll be away for a few weeks.

Informing is about Providing Information

1) Writing to <u>inform</u> is all about <u>telling</u> the reader what you know about a certain topic.

2) This means that you need to include <u>plenty of facts</u> — you don't need to use these facts to persuade or argue though, you just have to present them to the reader in an <u>engaging</u> way.

3) Informative writing can be <u>personal</u> — e.g. a letter to a friend about a film you saw recently. Or it can be more <u>practical</u> — e.g. a section from a textbook or a leaflet about snakes.

STRUCTURE — INFORMATIVE TEXTS

- Often, you'll have <u>lots</u> of facts that you could include in your answer, but it's important <u>not</u> to <u>overwhelm</u> the reader. It's a good idea to write down all the <u>facts</u> you would like to cover, and then pick the <u>most important</u> ones to get your point across.

- Informative texts are usually quite <u>balanced</u> and may contain both the <u>positive</u> and <u>negative</u> aspects of a topic. For example, a text informing people about caring for horses may say that horse ownership is <u>fun</u> and <u>good exercise</u>, but that it's also <u>expensive</u> and <u>time-consuming</u>.

- There are different ways you can <u>structure</u> your text. If you're writing about an <u>event</u>, you could write in <u>chronological order</u> (this just means the order in which things happened). If you're writing about a general topic, like boa constrictors, you may want to structure your text <u>thematically</u> by <u>grouping similar information</u> into separate chunks, for example, a boa constrictor's diet, habitat, behaviour etc.

- Making a <u>plan</u> before you start writing will make sure that you're using the best <u>structure</u>, and remember to <u>link</u> your paragraphs together with <u>conjunctions</u> (see pages 15 and 22).

Writing to Inform, Advise and Explain

LANGUAGE — INFORMATIVE TEXTS

- Technical language, or jargon, are words that an average reader might not know. For example, a car mechanic would know what "clutch", "torque" and "drive belt" mean, but someone who didn't know anything about cars wouldn't have a clue.

- Using technical language in an informative text can make you sound knowledgeable, but make sure you're aware of your audience — you may need to explain some technical terms to help readers understand.

LAYOUT — INFORMATIVE TEXTS

- Sometimes a diagram or a chart might be the clearest way to present information. For example, a labelled picture showing the locations of the organs inside the human body might be easier to follow than a block of text.

- Headings and subheadings can also help the reader navigate a text, especially if a text has been structured thematically. Headings help the reader to pick out the information that they need easily.

Advising is about Giving Suggestions

1) Writing to advise means trying to help someone, usually by giving them suggestions or instructions, e.g. safety advice for driving in snow or an advice column in a magazine.

2) However, don't fall into the trap of telling the reader what to do — no one likes a bossyboots...

STRUCTURE — WRITING TO ADVISE

- 'Writing to advise' texts are usually structured logically — you want to make it as easy as possible for the reader to follow your advice.

- You may want to tell your reader why they should listen to your advice and to reassure them that you know your stuff. For example, "I've been a snake owner all my life, so I know a thing or two about how best to look after boa constrictors."

- Texts that advise may give the reader consequences of not following the advice, (e.g. "Make sure you apologise to your friend soon. The longer you leave it, the harder it will be for her to forgive you.") or reasons why the reader should follow the advice ("Eating breakfast will keep your energy levels topped up until lunchtime.").

- Texts that advise might end by summarising the advice so that the reader can clearly see how to follow the suggestions. They might use bullet points or numbered lists to summarise the key points.

LANGUAGE — WRITING TO ADVISE

- Most 'writing to advise' texts are written using second-person pronouns (e.g. "you"). This makes the text feel more personal — it's as though you're talking directly to the reader.

- Think about the tone of your writing. If you're writing an agony aunt column, you may want to sound sympathetic. If you're giving advice about driving in the snow, you may want to sound knowledgeable.

LAYOUT — WRITING TO ADVISE

- The layout of your text will depend on its form, e.g. whether it's an agony aunt column for a magazine or a leaflet giving advice about saving money, so make sure you use the right text type.

Writing to Inform, Advise and Explain

You've learnt about <u>informing</u> and <u>advising</u>, so now it's on to <u>explaining</u>...

Explaining is about Helping the reader to Understand

1) When you <u>explain</u> something, you're answering the question "<u>why?</u>" or "<u>how?</u>".

2) Explanations often give <u>examples</u> and <u>evidence</u> to help someone <u>understand</u> something.

3) One of the best ways to explain something is to state the <u>fact</u> (just like when you're writing to inform) and then go on to <u>explain why</u> this is the case. This tells the reader everything they need to know in one chunk, which helps them to piece everything together nicely.

4) It's best to assume that your audience <u>knows nothing</u> about your topic and go right back to basics — even if something seems obvious to you, there's no way of knowing if it will be obvious to the reader.

STRUCTURE — EXPLANATORY TEXTS

- Explanatory texts can be structured in different ways, so you need to decide which structure is the most <u>suitable</u>.

- If you're explaining '<u>how</u>', (e.g. how to ride a bike) you may need to explain the process <u>step by step</u>. You might want to use a <u>numbered list</u> or <u>bullet points</u> to separate the steps out.

- If you're explaining '<u>why</u>', (e.g. why football is your favourite sport) you may want to structure your text <u>chronologically</u> or <u>thematically</u> instead.

- Regardless of which structure you use, make sure your explanation is <u>clear</u> and <u>easy to follow</u>. You can do this by using <u>short</u>, <u>simple sentences</u> and by linking your paragraphs <u>clearly</u> with <u>conjunctions</u>.

LANGUAGE — EXPLANATORY TEXTS

- Explanatory texts use <u>clear</u>, <u>unambiguous</u> language. If you use technical language, you need to make sure it's been <u>properly explained</u>.

- If you're explaining '<u>how</u>', you may want to use <u>imperatives</u> (command words) for example, "<u>Press</u> the button to start the device".

- If you're explaining '<u>why</u>', you might use <u>statistics</u> to help <u>reinforce</u> your point, e.g. "Our survey found that 15% of children don't eat breakfast in the morning because they don't have enough time."

- Use a <u>confident</u> tone — if you sound <u>unsure</u> or explain things in a <u>vague</u> way, then the reader is likely to become <u>confused</u>. Just make sure you don't sound <u>bossy</u>, as this could <u>annoy</u> the reader.

LAYOUT — EXPLANATORY TEXTS

- Like informative texts, think about whether a <u>labelled diagram</u>, <u>chart</u> or <u>picture</u> would help your reader to understand the text <u>more clearly</u>.

- <u>Headings</u> and <u>subheadings</u> may also help to <u>split</u> the information into separate chunks.

You might have to write in more than one of these styles

Sometimes these styles <u>overlap</u> — e.g. you might have to inform and explain in one text, or advise and explain in another. This book is a perfect example of all three: it <u>informs</u>, <u>explains</u> and <u>advises</u>.

Warm-Up and Worked Practice Questions

These warm-up and worked practice questions should get you firing on all cylinders.

Warm-up Questions

1) Is this statement true or false?
   "When you are writing to inform, you should include plenty of facts."

2) Write out these options in the order they should appear in a formal letter:
   a) what the letter is about
   b) Yours sincerely/Yours faithfully
   c) addresses
   d) your name and signature

3) Is this statement true or false?
   "Informal language still has to be written in proper sentences."

Have a look at this worked example answer to a question about writing to persuade.

Worked Practice Question

This is an extract from a national newspaper report.

> **EATING OURSELVES TO DEATH?**
>
> Britain is facing a medical time bomb as young people opt for more and more unhealthy eating choices. They prefer to snack on junk food rather than eat balanced meals and this, doctors say, is leading to an increase in obesity, diabetes and asthma amongst our nation's schoolchildren.
>
> What can be done to change youngsters' eating patterns?

1. Write an article for your school magazine about unhealthy eating in school. You should try to persuade other pupils to take the issue seriously, and suggest what action should be taken.

<u>Notes</u>

Planning is really important. Remind yourself who your audience is and what your purpose is.

Audience — other schoolchildren

Purpose — persuade them healthy eating is important

Intro — set scene — national problem — focus on school dinners

1. Say what's wrong — fizzy drinks, vending machines etc. — litter —

   poor choice of school dinners — horrible dining hall

2. Say what changes to make — change food — nicer room — more info.

3. Deal with objections — finish with need for action

This plan has been turned into a full answer on the next page.

62

Worked Practice Question

Here's how you could turn the plan on the previous page into a good answer.

Worked Practice Question

Starting with a question engages the reader straight away.

Do you want to be unhealthy? No, neither do I, but from the way the newspapers carry on you'd think all young people want to do is eat themselves into an early grave. It's time to realise that the problem starts with the disgraceful standard of school dinners.

We all know what the problem is. The school dinners on offer are tasteless, unwholesome and usually cold. Vending machines offer unlimited supplies of crisps, chocolate and fizzy drinks and cause mountains of litter. Our dining hall is more like a railway station than somewhere to enjoy a meal. It's crowded, noisy and uncomfortable and they herd us through like cattle. It's no wonder we try not to think about what we're actually eating.

Use 'magic threes'.

Exaggeration makes your points more forceful.

Use comparisons.

Get the readers on your side by saying 'we' and 'our'.

So what can we do to change the situation and save ourselves from an unhealthy future? There needs to be some major changes to the quality of both the food and the eating conditions in our school. We must demand a wider range of healthy foods such as salads, fresh fruit and vegetables and vegetarian options rather than chips, burgers and more chips. We need to put pressure on our school, through the school council, to provide us with a more comfortable dining room with better seating and more information about the food on offer. Most importantly, we need to make healthier choices ourselves. If it's all there for us, we'll have no excuse.

300 words is about the right length.

Finish by knocking down the main objection.

Some people will say that these changes will be too expensive, but surely picking up the bill for the unhealthy adults we could become will be even more expensive in the end. If we can show our school that we want to take our health seriously then perhaps our school will take us seriously and give us the school dinners that we need.

Remember to end on a positive note.

Section Five — Writing Fiction and Non-Fiction

Practice Questions

Time to have a go yourself. Make sure you think about the text's audience, form and purpose.

Practice Questions

Imagine this notice went up in your school.

> ### NOTICE TO ALL STUDENTS
>
> Following damage to classrooms during the lunch break, it has been decided that all students will be asked to leave the building during breaks and lunchtimes. Students may leave their belongings in classrooms, which will be locked until five minutes before the start of afternoon lessons.
>
> This arrangement will apply to all year groups.

1. Write a letter to your head teacher on behalf of your year group, persuading him or her to change this decision.

This is an extract from a newsletter published by a local community group.

> ### TIME FOR CHANGE
>
> Our surveys last month showed up some worrying facts:
>
> *   Local traffic is up by 30% on its normal daytime levels during the hours when children are going to and coming home from school.
>
> *   There was an increase in new cases of asthma this January. Doctors say that an increase in car exhaust fumes during the winter months is partly to blame.
>
> *   The number of children involved in road accidents around school gates and school crossings doubled last year. Our research suggests this was due to congestion caused by parents picking up and dropping off their children in cars, which cuts down how far people can see when crossing the road.

2. You are asked to write a speech to be given at your school's open evening. You should argue that it is better to walk and cycle to school as much as possible.

Revision Summary for Section Five

You wouldn't think there were so many tricks to doing something as simple as writing, but trust me — knowing all the stuff in this section will make a huge difference. Don't think you can wing it. Go over this section until you can answer every one of these questions.

1) What should you always do before you start writing a fiction text?

2) Give two ways that you could start a fiction text.

3) Why should you avoid filling your story with too many characters?

4) What sort of ending should you avoid writing in a story?

5) How should you start and end a formal letter if you don't know the name of the person you're writing to?

6) How should you end a formal letter if you do know the name of the person you're writing to?

7) You can use contractions (e.g. 'didn't', 'he'd') in an informal letter. True or false?

8) Give one difference between writing to persuade and writing to argue.

9) The 'e' in the mnemonic 'A Forest' stands for:
    a) entertaining
    b) ellipsis
    c) emotive language

10) What is an anecdote?

11) Why should rhetorical questions only have one possible answer?

12) Which of these is a good example of exaggeration?
    a) "Companies that make guns cause some suffering in the world."
    b) "Companies that make guns are responsible for causing untold misery to millions."
    c) "Companies that make guns are to blame for global warming."
    What is wrong with the other two sentences?

13) Which of these is a good example of criticising without being personal?
    a) "I think it's wrong of people to wear real fur."
    b) "You should be ashamed of yourself for wearing real fur."
    c) "Wearing real fur still occurs today, and many disagree with the practice."

14) You should always include your opinion in an informative text. True or false?

15) Why are many advice columns written in the second person?

Essays: The Basics

Have no fear — essays are no problem if you can keep your head and remember the basics.

Essays **Aren't** as **Scary** as they seem

1) People tend to think that there's one great secret to writing essays — but it's just not true.

An essay is a piece of writing that answers a question.

2) A simple 'yes' or 'no' might answer most essay questions, but it won't impress the reader — you need to explain your answer.

3) This may sound like a tricky thing to do, but it's best just to think of an essay as an opportunity to share your own thoughts and opinions on a certain topic or text.

You might write about your **Own Views** or about a **Text**

Here are two different types of essay you might come across:

1) You might get asked to write a narrative essay about your own views on a certain topic, e.g. your favourite sport, a journey you've made or an issue that's important to you.

2) You might get asked to write an essay about a text that somebody else has written. You'll need to provide quotes and analyse the text to answer the question.

Read the **Question**

1) It's always tempting to start writing straight away, but it's not a good idea.

2) Take the time to read the question and think about what it's asking you to do — this will usually take a few minutes to do properly.

3) Identify and highlight the key words in the question so you don't forget about them.

4) Make sure you know exactly what you're supposed to write about before you get going.

5) If you're given an essay that isn't a direct question, turn it into a question:

> Q. Write an essay about your favourite sport.

Turn the essay into this question:

> Q. Why is your favourite sport good to play and fun to watch?

Now all you have to do is:
1) Think of reasons why it's a good sport for people to play, and write about them.
2) Think of reasons why it's fun to watch, and write about them too.

Read the question very carefully

It sounds an obvious thing to say, but reading the question carefully is incredibly important. No matter how good your answer is, if it doesn't do what the question asks you, it's no good.

Essays: The Basics

Depending on what the question is asking you to do, you'll need to write your answer in a certain style.

Short Essays and Long Essays need a Different Approach

1) Always look at how many marks a question is worth before you answer it.

2) The number of marks indicates how much you need to write. For example, you'd need to write a lot more for a question worth 20 marks than you would for a question worth 8 marks.

3) Even if you have lots of really good points for a short essay question, it's better to just include your very best ones rather than trying to write about them all. It's even more important with shorter questions that you write a few really clear points instead of lots of confusing ones.

4) If you're in an exam, you should also use the number of marks to see how much time you should spend writing your answers. Make sure you spend more time answering the question that's worth more marks.

Good writing is Focused writing

1) Here's the golden rule for answering writing questions:

> Good writing makes a point. It doesn't just ramble on about nothing.

2) Plan before you start writing — if you dive straight in without planning first, it'll all go horribly wrong.

3) One page of well planned, well thought out writing is always better than five pages written off the top of your head.

4) Have a good think about what you're going to write about before you start. You don't need to know exactly what you're going to write, but you need to have a rough idea.

Jot Down your Points into a Rough Plan

1) It's a good idea to jot down a plan of the points you want to make before you start writing. That way you won't waffle, and you won't get to the end and realise you've forgotten something.

2) A plan doesn't have to be in proper sentences. It's just a reminder for you to use. Try to keep your plan brief — you should use the majority of your time to write your answer.

3) If you're writing an essay about a text, jot down the quotes you want to include too.

4) You may not need a full plan for a short essay, but you won't lose marks for scribbling down a few ideas.

Your essays should have both style and substance

A plan should help you take care of the 'substance' part, and there's more info about 'style' on p.68. Before you move on, have a look at the plan on the next page to make sure you know your stuff.

Planning Essays

A <u>plan</u> is <u>crucial</u> for any good answer. You need to know <u>what you're going to include</u> before you begin.

Include your Best Points on your Plan

Have a look at this example plan.

> Q. How does the character of Sheila Birling change in *An Inspector Calls*?

There's more about structuring your essay on page 69.

This question is about how a character <u>develops</u>, so it makes sense to start with some examples of what she's like at the <u>beginning</u> of the play.

Try to include some <u>quotes</u> or examples to support your points.

You need to mention what the character is like by the end of the play so you can explain how she's <u>changed</u>.

Work out how you're going to <u>end</u> your essay. It's good to end with something <u>impressive</u> — it's your last chance to wow your reader.

<u>PLAN</u>: Sheila Birling

<u>Intro</u> — Sheila changes a lot. Starts by being immature, but ends up being the most mature.

<u>At the start</u>
Childish — behaves in a "rather excited" manner; uses slang ("squiffy").

Privileged & selfish — uses her influence at the shop to get Daisy/Eva sacked.

<u>During the play</u>
Sharp — she knows what the Inspector is doing "he's giving us the rope — so that we'll hang ourselves".

<u>At the end</u>
Regretful — feels guilty about her part in Eva's death ("probably between us we killed her").

Changed — hands back the engagement ring to Gerald.

<u>Conclusion</u> — Sheila changes the most during the play. Writer suggests that people can change for the better.

There's <u>more than one way</u> to write a plan — the one shown above is just an example. Some people prefer other methods, like <u>spider diagrams</u>. Use whichever method you prefer.

A plan doesn't have to be a masterpiece
Your plan can be a bit <u>rough</u>, as long as it <u>focuses</u> on the <u>question</u> and includes your <u>main points</u>. Write your own plan for this essay: Explain why littering is harmful.

Writing Essays

When you're writing your essay, you'll need to use interesting and appropriate language.

Vary the Verbs in your Essay

It's just as important to keep the reader interested when writing a formal essay as it is in creative writing. This means you should avoid using the same verbs all of the time.

> The use of the word 'livid' <u>shows</u> how angry the writer is. She uses an exclamation mark at the end of the sentence to <u>show</u> her frustration. There is a lot of imagery involving the colour red, which also <u>shows</u> how furious she is. ✗

> Repeating the word 'show' soon becomes boring.

> Changing some of the verbs makes this example far more interesting.

> The use of the word 'livid' <u>highlights</u> how angry the writer is. She uses an exclamation mark at the end of the sentence to <u>express</u> her frustration. There is a lot of imagery involving the colour red, which also <u>emphasises</u> how furious she is. ✓

Here are some more great verbs you could use in an essay:

| states | implies | indicates | develops |
| supports | presents | hints | considers |

Essays need Adjectives too

Just because essays don't usually include long descriptions it doesn't mean they shouldn't contain any adjectives. In fact, you'll need to use a variety of adjectives to make your point clearly.

> The author uses a lot of <u>nice</u> imagery to describe how <u>nice</u> the scenery is. The comparison between the sea and a "flawless sapphire" is particularly <u>nice</u>. ✗

> The adjectives on the right make this example much more convincing.

> The author uses a lot of <u>striking</u> imagery to describe how <u>picturesque</u> the scenery is. The comparison between the sea and a "flawless sapphire" is particularly <u>effective</u>. ✓

Here are just a few interesting adjectives you can use to make your point in an essay:

| positive | powerful | subtle | gloomy |
| negative | dramatic | vivid | surprising |

Variety makes your essay more interesting

It's really easy to improve your writing and make it more interesting. Sprinkle in a bit of variety in the vocabulary you use and you'll be halfway there. It really is that simple.

Structuring Essays

All essays follow a similar structure — they should have a <u>beginning</u>, a <u>middle</u> and an <u>end</u>.

An **Introduction** outlines what you're going to say

1) Writing an <u>introduction</u> is really important — it tells the reader what you're going to <u>discuss</u> in your essay.

2) A <u>good introduction</u> should be <u>one paragraph</u> long and should <u>outline the points</u> you're going to make in the main part of your essay — good introductions make the reader want to <u>read on</u>.

> *Do you want to live a healthier life? Luckily, living healthily doesn't have to be complicated. There are three simple things you can do to improve your health: eat more fruit and vegetables, exercise regularly and eat less junk food.*

This introduction <u>clearly</u> sets out <u>what</u> the essay is going to cover and in <u>what order</u>. This way the reader knows exactly what they're going to find in the essay.

The **Main Body** should contain all your points

1) The <u>main part</u> of your essay should cover all of the key <u>points</u> you want to make.

2) Write a <u>new paragraph</u> for <u>each point</u> — this helps to keep your writing <u>clear</u> and <u>focused</u>.

3) Try to use the <u>P.E.E.D.</u> structure for each of your paragraphs if you can:

<u>P.E.E.D.</u> stands for <u>Point</u>, <u>Example</u>, <u>Explain</u>, <u>Develop</u>

There's an example of a P.E.E.D. paragraph on the next page.

- Make a <u>point</u> to answer the question you've been given.
- Give an <u>example</u> that supports your point (see pages 71-5 for more on this).
- <u>Explain</u> how your example backs up your point.
- <u>Develop</u> your point. You can do this in lots of ways — e.g. you could say <u>how</u> it <u>affects</u> the reader, what the <u>writer wanted to achieve</u> or even give your <u>own opinion</u>.

Your **Conclusion** should tie up all your points

1) You need a <u>conclusion</u> at the end of your essay to <u>sum up</u> your answer to the question.

2) A <u>good conclusion</u> should be <u>one paragraph</u> long and <u>bring together</u> all your <u>main points</u> — you don't want to introduce any new points at this stage, as it will only <u>confuse</u> the reader.

3) It's often good to include a short sentence in your conclusion that <u>links back</u> to what you said in your <u>introduction</u> — this helps bring the whole essay together nicely.

> *In conclusion, eating more fruit and vegetables, exercising regularly and eating less junk food are great ways to improve your health. So, if you want to live a healthier lifestyle, doing these three things is a great way to start.*

This conclusion <u>brings together</u> the <u>main points</u> of the essay and <u>links back</u> to the question from the introduction — this <u>engages the reader</u> and <u>makes them think</u>.

End your writing on a high

Your conclusion is the <u>last impression</u> your reader will take away with them, so make sure it's good. In a persuasive text, the ending is a <u>great opportunity</u> to make a <u>bold statement</u>.

Drafting and Editing Essays

Once you have your plan and know how you're going to structure your essay, it's time to start writing.

Keep Referring to your Plan

1) Before you start writing, look over your plan to make sure you're happy with everything — it's better to make any changes now rather than when you're writing.

2) Start by writing your introduction — make sure it's engaging and grabs the reader's attention.

3) Then you can start building up the main body of your essay. Look back at the plan before you start each paragraph so you know what point you need to make.

4) Use P.E.E.D. to help structure each paragraph — it will help keep your ideas focused and make sure everything is clear for the reader. Here is an example:

> Q. How does the writer use language to show how she feels about going to the dentist?

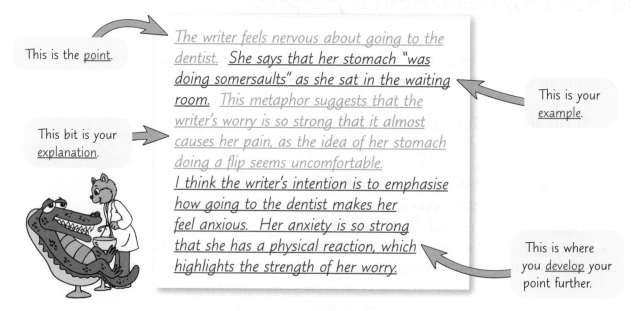

This is the point.

The writer feels nervous about going to the dentist. She says that her stomach "was doing somersaults" as she sat in the waiting room. This metaphor suggests that the writer's worry is so strong that it almost causes her pain, as the idea of her stomach doing a flip seems uncomfortable.
I think the writer's intention is to emphasise how going to the dentist makes her feel anxious. Her anxiety is so strong that she has a physical reaction, which highlights the strength of her worry.

This is your example.

This bit is your explanation.

This is where you develop your point further.

5) Finally, finish your essay with a conclusion — make sure you bring everything together and leave a good impression on the reader.

Editing your essay allows you to Make Changes

There's more about checking your work on pages 78-9.

1) Once you've written your essay, you can go back and make any changes.

2) If you're writing under exam conditions, you may not have much time, but always save five minutes at the end for checking your work.

3) Read through the whole essay and check it against the plan to make sure you haven't missed anything.

4) If you've missed something, simply add an asterisk (*) where the missing bit should go, then add another asterisk underneath your essay and write what you want to include next to the second asterisk. Make sure any corrections are made neatly. It's no good correcting something if the reader can't understand it.

P.E.E.D. stands for Point, Example, Explain, Develop

Whether you're writing your essay by hand or on the computer, using P.E.E.D. should help you to include examples and explanations for all your points — this will make your essay much clearer.

Using Examples

You have to give <u>reasons</u> for the points you make — use <u>examples</u> to show you've <u>understood</u> the text.

Every Time you make a Point — give an Example

1) It's sometimes easy to <u>forget</u> to give examples from the bit of writing you've read. But your answer will make <u>more sense</u> and have a <u>clearer structure</u> if you give <u>proof for every point</u> you make.

2) It's best to <u>imagine</u> that the person reading your answer has <u>never seen the text</u> you're talking about.

3) Another way of making sure you always give an example is using the <u>P.E.E.D.</u> structure (see page 69).

4) If you <u>don't</u> give examples, your answer won't show <u>you actually know</u> what you're talking about. <u>Examples</u> show that you know your stuff. Here's a handy example...

> *The women at the book club aren't very friendly. In fact, they're very rude.* ✗

This answer <u>doesn't</u> give any reasons...

> *The women at the book club aren't very friendly — they ignore Mrs Armstrong when she tries to say hello. In fact, they're very rude — they look at her, but then they start talking among themselves.* ✓

...but this answer gives a <u>reason</u> from the writing to justify every point it makes. That's loads better.

Put examples in Your Own Words

1) <u>Don't</u> just <u>copy out</u> what the text says word for word. Anyone can do that — it <u>doesn't prove</u> that you've <u>understood</u> it.

2) Read this extract from a story:

> Mrs Armstrong started to introduce herself, but the sour-faced woman turned away and muttered something to her companions.

3) In order to prove you've understood what you've read, you should use your <u>own words</u>. This is called <u>paraphrasing</u>. Look at the two examples below.

> *When Mrs Armstrong started to introduce herself, the sour-faced woman turned away and muttered something to her companions.* ✗

This <u>isn't</u> a good way to talk about the story. It uses all the <u>same words</u> as the story — it <u>doesn't</u> show that you actually <u>understand</u> it.

> *The unpleasant-looking woman paid no attention to Mrs Armstrong when she tried to introduce herself. Instead, she turned to the other women and said something to them under her breath.* ✓

The <u>meaning</u> here is the <u>same</u>, but the <u>words</u> are <u>different</u> — it proves you know what's going on.

Never forget to back up your points

A <u>sure-fire</u> way of writing really good essays is to make sure you put loads of <u>examples</u> in your answer. <u>Reasons</u> and <u>examples</u> — <u>nothing else</u> is going to do.

Using Quotes

Remember <u>inverted commas</u> from Section One? Well, they're also used when <u>quoting</u>. If you need a quick refresher, have a flick back before starting these pages — they'll still be here when you return...

Quote, Quote, Quote — and **Quote** some **More**

1) As you'll remember from the last page, it's <u>not</u> a good idea to copy out what a text says <u>word for word</u> — that said, <u>quoting</u> is a great way to <u>improve</u> your answer.

2) Quotes are useful because they show <u>exactly</u> which bit of the text you've got your answer from.

3) Quoting <u>isn't</u> the same as stealing words from the text you've read. There's a <u>difference</u>...

Quotes have **Inverted Commas**

1) <u>Inverted commas</u> make all the difference. They show that you're <u>quoting</u>, not stealing words.

2) Here's an extract from a story:

> Mrs Armstrong started to introduce herself, but the sour-faced woman turned away and muttered something to her companions. <u>All of the other women glanced briefly at Mrs Armstrong</u>.

3) Here is an <u>example</u> of how to quote from the text above. Everything <u>inside</u> the inverted commas is a <u>quote</u>. It has to be what the text says <u>word for word</u>.

Notice how the quote is <u>separated</u> from the rest of the answer by a dash. This isn't wrong, but <u>embedding</u> the quote (see below) would make it even <u>better</u>.

The women at the book club are rude. They talk among themselves even though they all know Mrs Armstrong is there — "<u>All of the other women glanced briefly at Mrs Armstrong</u>". ✓

Embedded quotes are **Even More Impressive**

The women at the book club are rude. This is shown by the way they "<u>glanced briefly at Mrs Armstrong</u>", but continue talking among themselves even though they know she is there. ✓✓

By <u>embedding</u> the quote into the rest of your sentence, you avoid <u>interrupting the flow</u> of your writing.

Just because you're embedding a quote <u>doesn't</u> mean it has to go in the <u>middle</u> of the sentence. The quote in this example is <u>still embedded</u>.

The women at the book club are rude because they continue talking among themselves even though they know Mrs Armstrong is there. We know this because they all "<u>glanced briefly at Mrs Armstrong</u>". ✓✓

Quote early and quote often

Remember — <u>copying</u> = <u>bad</u>, but <u>quoting</u> = <u>good</u>. Remember these two important rules: quotes always have to be copied out <u>word for word</u> from the text and they have to go inside <u>inverted commas</u>.

Using Quotes

Ever wanted more information on how to use quotes? If the answer is 'yes', then this page is just for you...

Some quotes are a Bit Trickier

1) If you're quoting more than one line of poetry, put a '/' to show where a new line starts:

> William Wordsworth, in his poem 'Daffodils', describes his happiness when he thinks about daffodils: "my heart with pleasure fills, / And dances with the daffodils".

2) If you're quoting from a play, you must make it clear who's speaking:

> In Act 2, Scene 2, Romeo claims that "Juliet is the sun".

Never quote more than a Few Words

Remember — you need to explain your quotes too. There's more about this on the next page.

1) Some people think that you'll write a better answer just by using longer quotes, but it's not true — in fact, it'll probably be worse.

2) As quotes show that you've read and understood the bit of text you're talking about, you usually only need to quote a few words to make your point.

> In Act 2, Scene 2, Romeo compares Juliet to the beauty of nature:
> "But soft, what light through yonder window breaks?
> It is the east, and Juliet is the sun.
> Arise, fair sun, and kill the envious moon,
> Who is already sick and pale with grief,
> That thou, her maid, art far more fair than she."

This quote is far too long. If your quotes are muddled, you'll sound unsure. Extra long quotes could also confuse your reader.

This quote is loads better. It's short and has everything you need to make your point.

> In Act 2, Scene 2, Romeo compares Juliet to the beauty of nature: "It is the east, and Juliet is the sun."

3) Quote often, but using the fewest number of words you can — don't be afraid to quote a single word if it's enough to make your point.

4) You can cut words out of the middle of the quote if you need to. Just use ellipsis (...) to show that there are words missing. Here's an example of how you can modify a quote.

The middle of the quote is unnecessary, so it's been cut and replaced with "...".

> In the gloom the courtyard looked of considerable size, and as several dark ways led from it under great round arches, it perhaps seemed bigger than it really is.

> The character says that "the courtyard looked of considerable size... it perhaps seemed bigger than it really is" which suggests that he initially feels overwhelmed by his surroundings.

Dracula — Bram Stoker

Quotes should be as short as possible

Don't quote vast chunks of text — just the bit that makes the point. It's quicker, too.

Explaining Quotes

Once you've picked out your quote, you need to explain it.

You need to **Explain Every Quote** you use

Just giving an example doesn't really tell the reader anything — to make it clear why you've chosen a quote, you need to explain what the quote shows.

> The writer describes one of the women as "sour-faced".

This answer isn't complete — it doesn't really make a point. You also need to explain why you think the quote is important or what effect it has on the text.

You can put the **Quote Before** the explanation...

In the example below, the quote is used first and the explanation comes after.

> The writer describes one of the women as "sour-faced". That makes us think she's not a very pleasant person.

The quote gets in there first.

Then the answer explains why it's relevant to the point — that she isn't a nice person.

... or you can put the **Explanation Before** the quote

1) In this example, a quote is used to back up a reason that's been given.

> The women at the book club are rude. They talk among themselves even though they all know Mrs Armstrong is there. We know this because the writer states that "All the other women glanced briefly at Mrs Armstrong".

The answer makes a point — it says the women are rude.

Then there's a reason to back it up — the women talk among themselves and ignore Mrs Armstrong.

Now there's a quote from the text — the quote proves the point that the women know Mrs Armstrong is there.

2) This is a slightly different order from P.E.E.D. on page 69, but it gives you another way you could structure your point — it still gives a clear example and explains it well.

3) If you really wanted to impress your reader, you could then develop the point further.

> This encourages the reader to feel sorry for Mrs Armstrong and to dislike the other women.

When you develop a point, you could discuss the effect on the reader.

Always explain why the quote is relevant

One of the key things to remember with quotes is that while you know why you've chosen your quote, the examiner doesn't — therefore you need to tell them why it's been used.

Explaining Quotes

Every answer you write should contain lots of <u>short quotes</u> and <u>explanations</u>, so it's helpful to know how to link the two together.

Use **Linking Phrases** to make your point **Clear**

Once you've found the right quote to <u>back up</u> what you're trying to say, you need to <u>explain</u> your point in a way that makes it <u>clear</u>. For example:

> This phrase <u>links</u> the point you're making to the quote so it's <u>clear</u> to the reader.

Wordsworth describes how "my heart with pleasure fills" when he thinks about daffodils. <u>This shows that</u> the memory of daffodils is almost as good as the real thing.

Don't **Always** use the **Same Words** and **Phrases**

1) Learning only one linking phrase and using it <u>all the time</u> is no good — you need to <u>mix it up</u> to impress the reader and hold their attention.

> Using the <u>same</u> linking phrase over and over makes your answer sound <u>repetitive</u>.

Wordsworth describes how "my heart with pleasure fills" when he thinks about daffodils. <u>This shows that</u> the memory of daffodils is almost as good as the real thing. He goes on to say that his heart "dances with the daffodils". <u>This shows that</u> few things make him happier than being in close contact with nature. ✗

Wordsworth describes how "my heart with pleasure fills" when he thinks about daffodils. <u>This shows that</u> the memory of daffodils is almost as good as the real thing. He goes on to say that his heart "dances with the daffodils", <u>which suggests that</u> few things make him happier than being in close contact with nature. ✓

> To really <u>impress</u> the reader you need to use a <u>mix</u> of interesting phrases.

2) Here are some other useful <u>verbs</u> you can use to link your quote to your explanation.

underlines	emphasises	reiterates	illustrates
highlights	implies	signifies	reinforces

Link your quotes and explanations with lots of interesting words
Using lots of short quotes is a good start, but they need <u>explaining</u> too. Cover up this page and scribble down lots of verbs that you might use to link quotes and explanations.

Comparing Texts

Sometimes you might have to compare two texts — don't worry though, it's not as confusing as it sounds.

Look for **Similarities** and **Differences**

1) Comparing means reading more than one text and looking to see how they're similar or different.

2) Some questions might ask you to compare texts that seem very different,
e.g. you might be asked to compare a poem and an extract from a story.

3) You can use linking words to highlight similarities and differences, for example:

similarly	equally	in contrast	instead of
likewise	however	whereas	

Don't write about each text **Separately**

1) When you're comparing texts, don't write about one text at a time — if you write about both texts at the same time, you'll be able to make links between them.

2) For example, you could say how the language in both texts is similar, or different, and give some examples.

3) Here are some things you could look at when you compare texts:

audience	purpose	layout	setting
language	perspective	mood	structure

4) A plan for a comparison question could look a bit like this:

Structure	text 1 is a poem — 4 verses, one rhyming couplet in each text 2 is a story — 12 chapters, one about each character
Language	text 1 has lots of adjectives for description e.g. "ghoulish" text 2 uses metaphors — "the town was a bare wasteland"
Mood	text 1 uses ellipses to create suspense text 2 uses short sentences to create suspense

5) Always try to give an opinion, and don't forget to give evidence to back up your points:

> Both authors create suspense really well, but they do it in different ways. In text 1, the author uses ellipses, whereas the author of text 2 uses short sentences, such as in the lines "It was pitch black. Sam could see nothing. He waited."

You don't need to compare every word

There are loads of things you could mention when you're comparing texts, and you probably won't have to write about all of them. Pick the things that stand out most, and focus on those.

Evaluating Texts

You might be asked to <u>evaluate</u> a text. Don't get caught out — read this page for more info.

Evaluate = Say how Effective something is

1) If you're asked to <u>evaluate</u> a text, you need to judge how <u>effective</u> it is.

2) Sometimes it <u>won't be obvious</u> from the question that you need to evaluate, for example:

> Q. "The writer has succeeded in making this passage truly terrifying". To what extent do you agree with this opinion?

The question is asking how <u>effective</u> the writer has been in making the reader feel <u>scared</u>.

3) You could just write "I agree" or "I disagree" but that <u>won't</u> get you any marks. You need to <u>back up</u> your opinion with examples, and say <u>why</u> the text is effective or not.

4) It's <u>OK</u> to disagree, but you need to be able to <u>justify</u> your response. Often, the extracts you will be asked to evaluate will have been written by <u>successful</u> authors, so if you disagree, you need to make sure you have <u>plenty</u> of <u>well-thought-out criticisms</u>. Writing "I found it boring" just <u>isn't</u> going to cut it.

5) If you're asked to evaluate a text, try to use some of these <u>sentence starters</u>...

> Significantly...

> I believe this is effective because...

> I don't feel the writer is successful at...

> Less important, but still significant is...

> This is vital to...

> Less effective is the writer's...

Always think about the Effect on the Reader

1) Every point you make needs to discuss <u>how</u> the writer has used a <u>technique</u> to <u>impact</u> the reader and <u>create</u> an effect. Then, you need to comment on how <u>successful</u> this is.

2) Here are some things you might analyse in a text:

> descriptions   characters   events   setting   themes

> language   dialogue   mood   structure

> *The writer uses horrible language to describe the character; her lips are "swelled and dark" and her eyes are "bloodshot". This creates a terrifying atmosphere.* ✗

This answer describes a <u>technique</u> and mentions its <u>effect</u>, but it doesn't evaluate how <u>successful</u> the writer has been.

> *The writer uses horrible language to describe the character; her lips are "swelled and dark" and her eyes are "bloodshot". This horrifying and unnatural language would create a gruesome image in the reader's mind. Vivid descriptions are perhaps the most significant technique the writer employs to create a truly terrifying atmosphere.* ✓

When it comes to evaluation questions, practice makes perfect

Try making a plan and writing a response to this essay question: "All teenagers should be expected to get a part-time job." To what extent do you agree with this statement?

Proofreading Essays

When you <u>finish</u> a piece of writing, it's vital that you <u>check your work</u>. These pages will tell you what sort of <u>errors</u> to look out for, as well as how to <u>correct</u> them.

Always check your work

1) If you <u>don't</u> check your work, you won't know if it's full of <u>silly mistakes</u>. Mistakes can be <u>avoided</u> by taking the time to <u>read through</u> your answer.

2) It <u>isn't</u> always possible to read your work <u>out loud</u> (e.g. in an exam), but it gives you the <u>best chance</u> of spotting your own mistakes if you <u>can</u>.

3) Try to read your work <u>sentence by sentence</u>. It's easy to miss mistakes if you skim over your essay.

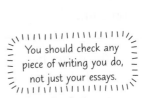
You should check any piece of writing you do, not just your essays.

Correct the **Obvious** mistakes **First...**

Some mistakes <u>stand out</u> like a sore thumb, so it's <u>important</u> to get rid of these <u>first</u>. The <u>most obvious</u> mistakes to check for include:

A homophone is a word that sounds like another word, but is spelled differently, e.g. 'there', 'their' and 'they're'.

1) <u>SPELLING</u> — is everything spelled <u>correctly</u> (especially <u>key words</u> and <u>homophones</u>)?

2) <u>PUNCTUATION</u> and <u>GRAMMAR</u> — do all of your sentences start with a <u>capital letter</u> and contain <u>appropriate punctuation</u> throughout? Is your grammar <u>spot on</u>?

3) <u>CLARITY</u> — do all of your sentences <u>make sense</u> and say <u>exactly</u> what you want them to say?

Go back to Section 1 if you need a reminder about spelling, punctuation and grammar.

... before moving on to **Other Issues**

If you've still got time after correcting the <u>obvious</u> mistakes, there are <u>plenty</u> of other issues to keep an eye out for when checking your work:

1) Make sure you have used a <u>variety</u> of vocabulary. Change any <u>dull</u> or <u>repeated</u> words for something different that is more likely to <u>impress</u> the reader. There's more about this on page 68.

2) If you're writing an <u>essay</u>, check that each point is backed up with at least one <u>example</u> or <u>quote</u>. See p.71.

3) Check that your work contains both an <u>introduction</u> and a <u>concluding paragraph</u>. See p.69

Everyone makes mistakes

Don't let the thought of making a mistake put you off using a range of <u>sentence structures</u> and <u>interesting vocabulary</u>. Just leave yourself enough time to check everything <u>thoroughly</u>.

Proofreading Essays

It's all well and good spotting mistakes in your work, but it's not much use if you don't know how to make the corrections in a neat and tidy way — that's where this page comes in...

Make your **Corrections** with **Care**

1) It's tempting to scribble out any mistakes and write the correction wherever you can find space.

2) However, this often leaves your work looking messy — it may even lose you marks if the reader struggles to understand your correction.

3) You should try to be consistent in the way you make corrections instead.

No Mistake is Impossible to Fix

There are simple ways to correct mistakes that won't leave your work looking messy. Below are some examples of the most common fixes:

> *There   alliteration*
> *(Their) are two examples of (aliteration) in the opening paragraph.*

If you make a spelling mistake, place brackets around the misspelled word, cross it out with two lines and write the correction above.

> *This tells us that the writer wants to create a sense of urgency in the text. // Another method used by the writer is ...*

If you forget to start a new paragraph when moving on to a different point, insert one by writing (//) where you want it to start.

> *   second*
> *... onomatopoeia, which features three times in the ^ paragraph.*

If you miss out a word or two entirely, use a (^) symbol where the missing words should be and then write them above the line.

Finally, if you've missed out more than just a couple of words, you can use an asterisk (*) to add the missing bits. There's more about this on p.70.

A correction isn't correct unless you do it properly

There is definitely a right way and a wrong way to make corrections. If it's extra practice you want, go back to your last piece of English homework and proofread it using your new skills.

Warm-Up Questions

Right, you should be a pro at writing essays now. Have a look over these question pages.

Warm-up Questions

1) Rewrite the following piece of text using your own words.

> Tanya felt like something wasn't quite right as she crept up the stairs to her room. The darkness unsettled her even more.

2) Which of these quotes could be used to back up the following point?

Tanya was afraid of the ghost.

a)
> Tanya woke up when she heard a noise outside.

b)
> Tanya saw a ghost come in through her bedroom window.

c)
> Tanya's teeth started to chatter as the ghost approached her.

d)
> The ghost wailed before disappearing into thin air.

3) Rewrite the following answer so that the quote is embedded into the rest of the sentence. You can shorten the quote if you need to.

> Although the ghost disappears, the author implies that it will come back later in the story — "Tanya had a feeling she hadn't seen the last of the ghost."

Worked Practice Questions

Worked Practice Questions

This extract is the introduction from a non-fiction book aimed at teenagers.
It is a handbook for people who want to be vegetarians.

> It all starts here — with the ultimate guide to going, being and staying veggie.
>
> This book will take you through the change from being a meatie to being a vegetarian — every step of the way. Every question answered, every doubt knocked on the head and every concern sorted.
>
> If you're already a veggie, this book will give you the confidence and knowledge to argue for your beliefs. If your parents are worried, it will put their minds at rest. If you're short of facts, you'll find them here.

1. Pick out a quote that shows that the book contains everything the reader needs.

    "the ultimate guide"

2. Pick out a quote that suggests the writer is talking directly to the reader.

    "this book will give you the confidence"

3. Find an example of repetition from the text. What effect does this have on the reader?

    "Every question... every doubt... every concern". The repetition of "every"

    makes it sound as though the handbook has got everything covered.

4. Using the quotes from the questions above, as well as any other details from the text, make a plan for the following question.

    > Q   How does the author create a reassuring tone?

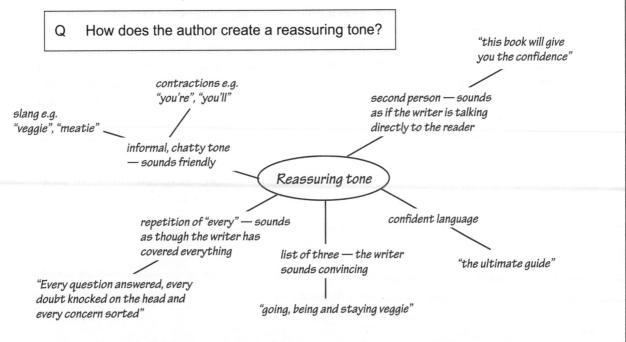

Practice Questions

Read this extract, and then turn to p.83 to answer some questions about it.

Practice Questions

The following extract is adapted from the end of the first chapter of Charles Dickens's novel, *Great Expectations*. Pip, a young boy, is threatened in a churchyard by a convict, who is desperate for food and a tool to cut the chains from his leg.

I said that I would get him the file, and I would get him what broken bits of food I could, and I would come to him at the Battery*, early in the morning.

"Say Lord strike you dead if you don't!" said the man.

At the same time, he hugged his shuddering body in both his arms — clasping himself, as if to hold himself together — and limped towards the low church wall. As I saw him go, picking his way among the nettles, and among the brambles that bound the green mounds, he looked in my young eyes as if he were eluding the hands of the dead people, stretching up cautiously out of their graves, to get a twist upon his ankle and pull him in.

When he came to the low church wall, he got over it, like a man whose legs were numbed and stiff, and then turned round to look for me. When I saw him turning, I set my face towards home, and made the best use of my legs. But presently I looked over my shoulder, and saw him going on again towards the river, still hugging himself in both arms, and picking his way with his sore feet among the great stones dropped into the marshes here and there, for stepping-places when the rains were heavy, or the tide was in.

The marshes were just a long black horizontal line then, as I stopped to look after him; and the river was just another horizontal line, not nearly so broad nor yet so black; and the sky was just a row of long angry red lines and dense black lines intermixed. On the edge of the river I could faintly make out the only two black things in all the prospect that seemed to be standing upright; one of these was the beacon by which the sailors steered — like an unhooped cask upon a pole — an ugly thing when you were near it; the other, a gibbet*, with some chains hanging to it which had once held a pirate. The man was limping on towards this latter, as if he were the pirate come to life, and come down, and going back to hook himself up again. It gave me a terrible turn when I thought so; and as I saw the cattle lifting their heads to gaze after him, I wondered whether they thought so too. I looked all round, and could see no one else. But now I was frightened again, and ran home without stopping.

* *Battery* — a fort where cannons were kept
* *gibbet* — a scaffold used for hanging criminals

Practice Questions

These questions are about the text on p.82.

Practice Questions

1. Find and copy a quote you could use to back up the following points:

   a) The convict is an unpleasant character.

   ....

   b) The author uses eerie imagery.

   ....

   c) Pip is afraid.

   ....

   d) The setting is bleak.

   ....

2. Make a plan for the following question in the box below. You can use the quotes from the question above if you want to, as well as any other details from the text.

   How does the author of the text create a menacing atmosphere?

Practice Question

Practice Question

1. Read the text below, then answer the question.

    "The author has succeeded in making this extract really tense."
    To what extent do you agree with this statement?

    Plan and write your answer on a separate sheet of paper.

The following extract is adapted from Kenneth Grahame's novel, *The Wind in the Willows*. The novel follows the story of several animals, including Mole, Rat and Toad. In this extract, Mole walks through the Wild Wood trying to find Badger.

Everything was very still now. The dusk advanced on him steadily, rapidly, gathering in behind and before; and the light seemed to be draining away like flood-water.

Then the faces began.

It was over his shoulder, and indistinctly, that he first thought he saw a face; a little evil wedge-shaped face, looking out at him from a hole. When he turned and confronted it, the thing had vanished.

He quickened his pace, telling himself cheerfully not to begin imagining things or there would be simply no end to it. He passed another hole, and another, and another; and then — yes! — no! —yes! certainly a little narrow face, with hard eyes, had flashed up for an instant from a hole, and was gone. He hesitated — braced himself up for an effort and strode on. Then suddenly, and as if it had been so all the time, every hole, far and near, and there were hundreds of them, seemed to possess its face, coming and going rapidly, all fixing on him glances of malice and hatred: all hard-eyed and evil and sharp.

If he could only get away from the holes in the banks, he thought, there would be no more faces. He swung off the path and plunged into the untrodden places of the wood.

Then the whistling began.

Very faint and shrill it was, and far behind him, when first he heard it; but somehow it made him hurry forward. Then, still very faint and shrill, it sounded far ahead of him, and made him hesitate and want to go back. As he halted in indecision it broke out on either side, and seemed to be caught up and passed on throughout the whole length of the wood to its farthest limit. They were up and alert and ready, evidently, whoever they were! And he — he was alone, and unarmed, and far from any help; and the night was closing in.

Then the pattering began.

Practice Question

Practice Question

The following answer contains spelling, punctuation and grammar mistakes.
Read the answer carefully and correct all of the mistakes you can find.

Dickens makes us dislike scrooge by portraying him as cruel

and obsesed with money. The first way in which he does this is by

using of a series of adjectives such as "squeezing" "scraping"

"clutching" and "covetous" to describe Scrooge. All of these word

have similar meanings, but Dickens uses multipel words instead of

just one to emphasise his point further. Another way in which

Dickens emphasises Scrooges cruelty is the description of how he

treets the staff in her counting house. We are told that one clerk

works in a "dismal little cell" with no coal for the fire. This shows

how bad he is treated, especially as it is the Winter. Finally, Scrooge

is made to seem cruel in the way he speaks to his nephew, Fred.

When comes to Scrooge's counting house to wish him a merry

Christmas, Scrooge replies only "bah!" followed by Humbug!

Revision Summary for Section Six

By now you should know everything there is to know about writing essays. Remember, there's no way of creating the perfect answer without a clear and thorough understanding of the whole of this section. And there's an easy way to work out if you've got to grips with it — test yourself on these questions, and, if you're unsure of any, go over the section until you can do them all.

1) Why should you check how many marks an essay is worth?

2) "You need to plan out exactly what you'll write in your essay." True or false?

3) What should a good essay introduction include?

4) What does P.E.E.D. stand for?

5) Read the following points about conclusions and correct any points which are wrong.
   a) Conclusions should be two paragraphs long.
   b) They should summarise the points you've made in the main body of your essay.
   c) You should never link your conclusion back to your introduction.

6) What do you have to do to back up every point you make?

7) What is paraphrasing?

8) Which of these is a good example of the best way to include quotes?
   a) Daisy is jealous of Katya's success — "her eyes were vibrant pools of green".
   b) Imagery such as "her eyes were vibrant pools of green" shows that Daisy is jealous.
   c) Daisy's "eyes were vibrant pools of green", showing she is jealous of Katya's success.

9) If you're quoting more than one line of poetry, when should you use this '/' symbol?

10) "Using a few long quotes in your essay is the best way to quote." Is this correct? Why / why not?

11) Why should you always explain the quotes you use?

12) "When comparing texts, you should write about both texts at the same time." True or false?

13) What should you do when you're asked to evaluate a text?

14) Give four obvious mistakes you should check your essays for.

15) If you forget to start a new paragraph, what symbol can you use to show where it should start?

Characters

It's time to look at <u>fiction</u> and <u>non-fiction</u> texts in a little more detail now. If you need a <u>reminder</u> about the difference between fiction and non-fiction, turn to page 25. Let's start with some info about fiction texts...

Characterisation is the way an author presents a **Character**

1) Characters are a really <u>important</u> part of <u>fiction</u> texts — they <u>drive the action</u> and make the reader <u>feel</u> a certain way.

2) Characters have <u>unique personalities</u> — some are <u>good</u>, some are <u>bad</u> but most are <u>somewhere in between</u>.

3) The <u>main character</u> is known as the <u>protagonist</u>.

4) Readers can learn about characters in lots of <u>different ways</u>:

> For more info on characters in plays, turn to pages 122-123.

From the <u>narrator's descriptions</u>...

> Dickens describes Scrooge's <u>appearance</u> in lots of detail. This allows the reader to <u>picture</u> what he looks like really easily.

> The "cold" in Scrooge suggests to the reader that he is a <u>mean</u> character.

The cold within him froze his old features, nipped his pointed nose, shrivelled his cheek, stiffened his gait; made his eyes red, his thin lips blue; and spoke out shrewdly in his grating voice.

A Christmas Carol — Charles Dickens

... what the <u>character says</u>...

"I am no bird; and no net ensnares me; I am a free human being with an independent will"

> This dialogue shows that the character is <u>independent</u>.

Jane Eyre — Charlotte Brontë

... what the <u>other characters</u> say about them...

> Here, Lady Catherine is talking about <u>Elizabeth</u>. From her words, the reader learns that Elizabeth is <u>opinionated</u>.

"Upon my word," said her ladyship, "you give your opinion very decidedly for so young a person."

Pride and Prejudice — Jane Austen

... and what the <u>character</u> does.

I must embrace her before she died, — I must give her one last kiss, exchange with her one last word.

> Jane's actions show the reader that she is a <u>compassionate</u> person.

Jane Eyre — Charlotte Brontë

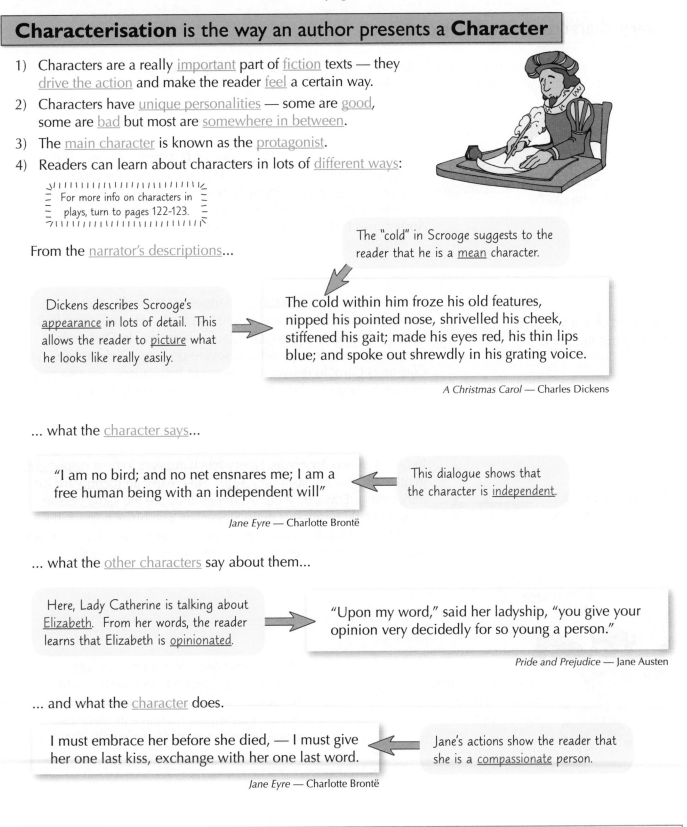

REVISION TASK

There are different ways to find out about characters

Of course, not all characters are straightforward good or evil types. They can be a bit more complicated than that. Learn what's on this page by applying it to your favourite book character — how does the writer shape your feelings towards the character?

Characters

You need to know the characters in the stories you're studying <u>really well</u>. Once you know what the characters are like, you can start to think about <u>why</u> the author has <u>created</u> them.

Every character has a **Purpose**

When reading a story, you need to think about <u>why</u> the author has <u>made</u> the characters the way they are and what their <u>purpose</u> is. Here are a few ideas to get you started:

Does the character have an effect on the <u>plot</u>?

> In *Pride and Prejudice*, <u>Lydia</u> is one of Elizabeth's sisters. She <u>elopes</u> with an unsuitable man which <u>impacts</u> on the <u>plot</u>. Mr Darcy <u>proposes</u> to Elizabeth, but the <u>scandal</u> of Lydia's elopement interferes and it seems like they <u>can't</u> be together. Austen uses Lydia's character to create <u>tension</u> in the story.

Does the character <u>change</u> throughout the story?

> In *A Christmas Carol*, <u>Scrooge</u> changes dramatically after being shown his past, present and future by ghosts. He goes from being <u>bitter</u> and <u>mean</u> to a more <u>charitable</u> character. In Dickens's time, many people experienced severe <u>poverty</u>. Dickens uses *A Christmas Carol* to deliver a message to his readers. For example, he uses Scrooge to show that the <u>rich</u> need to <u>help</u> the <u>poor</u>.

Does the character <u>stand for</u> something?

> In *Dr Jekyll and Mr Hyde*, Henry Jekyll appears to be a <u>respectable</u> gentleman, but he has a <u>dark side</u>. He creates an <u>identity</u> for his dark side — Edward Hyde. Although they are the <u>same person</u>, Edward Hyde represents <u>evil</u>. Stevenson combines respectable and immoral qualities <u>together</u> in one character to make the reader think about whether <u>everyone</u> has the potential to be <u>evil</u>.

This can be linked to the text's theme or message — see the next page.

Does the character make the reader <u>feel</u> something?

> In *Anita and Me*, the reader feels <u>sorry</u> for the <u>main character</u>, Meena, because her loyalty and trust are <u>betrayed</u> by Anita. Having the narrative in Meena's voice helps the reader to <u>side with her</u>.

Characters have a purpose in the story

Authors always have a reason for including their characters. To figure out these reasons, look at what happens to the character, how they relate to the plot and how they interact with other characters.

Setting and Theme

This page is all about two important elements of fiction — setting and theme. Settings help to create a certain effect, whereas a theme is an idea which is repeated in a text.

The Setting is Where the story Happens

1) Writers choose their settings carefully — where the story takes place is important for creating an atmosphere.

2) Look at the language the writer uses and their descriptions, then think about the effect that they're trying to create. Here are a couple of examples:

> The dismal quarter of Soho seen under these changing glimpses, with its muddy ways, and slatternly passengers, and its lamps, which had never been extinguished or had been kindled afresh to combat this mournful re-invasion of darkness, seemed, in the lawyer's eyes, like a district of some city in a nightmare.

The underlined words describe Soho as dirty and depressing. Stevenson uses the word "nightmare" to make Soho and the streets sound frightening.

Dr Jekyll and Mr Hyde — Robert Louis Stevenson

The character of Jane has been wandering the moors looking for food and shelter. The underlined words describe how dismal the setting is and how desperate her situation has become.

> But my night was wretched, my rest broken: the ground was damp, the air cold: besides, intruders passed near me more than once, and I had again and again to change my quarters; no sense of safety or tranquillity befriended me.

Jane Eyre — Charlotte Brontë

The Theme is what the Text is About

1) Texts usually have a theme — an issue or idea that's repeated throughout the story. Texts often have more than one theme.

For more info about themes in Shakespeare plays, turn to pages 145-148.

2) Some common themes are love, gender, social class and power.

The theme of most fairy tales is good against evil. For example, the character of Cinderella represents good and her stepmother and ugly stepsisters represent evil.

3) Once you've identified the theme, think about what the writer is saying about it. This is the story's message or moral.

Not every story has a message or a moral.

Although Cinderella is mistreated by her stepmother and stepsisters, they end up with nothing while she goes to the ball and marries the prince. The message of this story is that good always wins in the end.

4) Sometimes the theme and message are related to the text's context (see pages 38-39). For example, the plot of the novel *Animal Farm* by George Orwell was based on real-life events that happened in Russia.

The theme is the key idea of the story

You can probably think of the themes of your favourite stories quite easily — love, justice, revenge. When you're reading a text, always ask yourself what its themes are.

Language in Fiction Texts

This page looks at some of the language techniques that writers use and why they might use them.

Writers want their words to have an **Effect** on the **Reader**

1) Every word a writer uses is deliberate. Their choice of language will tell you something about the plot, the setting, the characters, the mood of the text or it will make you feel a certain way.

2) When you're reading a text, look out for the language techniques discussed in Section 4, and think about why the author has included them.

What characters **Say** tells the reader a lot about them

1) Dialogue is when two or more characters speak to each other. Dialogue is always in inverted commas. The language characters use when they speak helps the reader to understand what they're like.

"Then why doesn't tha' read somethin', or learn a bit o' spellin'? Tha'st old enough to be learnin' thy book a good bit now."

Several characters in *The Secret Garden* speak with a Yorkshire accent. This is shown using non-standard spelling to mimic the accent.

The Secret Garden — Frances Hodgson Burnett

2) Sometimes you might need to read between the lines and make an inference.

"Four legs good, two legs bad"

The sheep in *Animal Farm* say this over and over again. This suggests they're a bit dim — they can't think for themselves, so they just repeat what they've heard elsewhere.

Animal Farm — George Orwell

Turn to page 121 to learn more about dialogue in plays.

Figurative Language appears in Descriptive Writing

Figurative language is important in poetry too — have a read of page 110.

Writers use figurative language (see pages 32-34) to paint a vivid picture for the reader.

...horses regarded the occasional passers-by with mournful malteser eyes.

Anita and Me — Meera Syal

The metaphor "malteser eyes" tells the reader the colour of the horses' eyes. This childish image also highlights to the reader that the narrator, Meena, writes from a child's point of view.

...like a mountain river... it became the torrent which... swept away all my hopes and joys.

Frankenstein — Mary Shelley

Victor Frankenstein describes his passion for science with a simile. A "mountain river" is powerful and fast, but "torrent" suggests he couldn't control it.

Language tells you a lot about the characters

The language used by characters is especially important if the story has a first-person narrator — their descriptions can tell you a lot about them. There's more info about narrators on p.93.

Language in Fiction Texts

Here are a few more language techniques to look out for...

Objects can **Symbolise Ideas**

1) Authors often <u>repeat</u> key <u>words</u> or <u>imagery</u> to emphasise their <u>importance</u> to the reader — this is known as <u>symbolism</u>.

In *Jane Eyre*, <u>fires</u> are used to show where Jane feels <u>at home</u> and where she <u>doesn't</u> — fires are described <u>positively</u> where Jane feels at home, but she <u>can't</u> get near the fire at the school she dislikes.

In *Lord of the Flies*, the characters blow into a <u>conch</u> (a type of shell) to signify the start of a meeting. During the meetings, whoever is holding the conch has the right to speak, so the conch is associated with <u>order</u> and <u>democracy</u>. However, as the novel progresses, some of the characters become <u>wild</u> and <u>savage</u>, and they <u>destroy</u> the conch. Its destruction <u>symbolises</u> the end of <u>democracy</u> and <u>civilization</u> on the island.

2) If a writer keeps mentioning something <u>over and over again</u>, it's likely that it's <u>important</u> or <u>represents something</u>.

Texts written in the **Past** might sound **Unusual**

There's more on context on pages 38-9.

1) Stories that aren't set in the present day might use words that look <u>unfamiliar</u>, or have a <u>different meaning</u> to those used today.

phaeton ← A 'phaeton' is a type of horse-drawn carriage.

wireless ← In a modern text, 'wireless' means 'without wires'. If the word appears in a text from the mid-1900s, it's referring to a type of radio.

2) Novels that were written a long time ago can sound quite <u>formal</u>. The <u>language</u> is often more <u>sophisticated</u>, the <u>sentences</u> tend to be quite <u>long</u> and the words can be in an <u>unusual order</u>. Take a look at this example.

Although I am not disposed to maintain that the being born in a workhouse, is in itself the most fortunate and enviable circumstance that can possibly befall a human being, I do mean to say that in this particular instance, it was the best thing for Oliver Twist that could by possibility have occurred.

Oliver Twist — Charles Dickens

This sentence is <u>very long</u>. It basically means "Being born in a workhouse isn't a particularly lucky or desirable thing to happen to someone, but in this case, it was the best thing for Oliver Twist."

REVISION TASK

Don't let tricky language put you off...

Texts written in the 19th century can be a bit tricky to read at first, but the more you read, the easier it'll become. Find a copy of *Oliver Twist* by Charles Dickens online, and try to write the first two paragraphs of the first chapter in modern English (you may need a dictionary).

Structure

Fiction texts can have lots of different plot structures. Read on to find out more...

A **Plot** can be **Linear** or **Non-Linear**

1) The <u>plot</u> of a story is all the things that happen — most plots have a <u>beginning</u>, a <u>middle</u> and an <u>end</u>.

2) If the plot happens <u>in time order</u>, it has a <u>linear</u> structure. A linear plot is the most <u>common</u> way to tell a story — it's the <u>easiest structure</u> for readers to follow and it allows the author to build up to <u>an exciting ending</u>.

3) If the events are told <u>out of order</u> then the structure is <u>non-linear</u>. A non-linear structure can be used to <u>grab</u> the reader's <u>interest</u> — starting the book with the ending is <u>unusual</u> and makes the reader want to <u>read on</u>.

Foreshadowing, Flashbacks & Flashforwards keep the reader **Interested**

<u>Foreshadowing</u> is when the author gives the reader <u>clues</u> about what's going to happen <u>later</u> in the story.

<u>Flashbacks</u> are when the action jumps to the <u>past</u>, normally to mention something that's important in the <u>present</u>.

<u>Flashforwards</u> are when the action <u>temporarily</u> moves <u>forward</u> in time. Unlike foreshadowing, the <u>time</u> in the story actually <u>changes</u>.

In *Of Mice and Men*, Lennie did a "bad thing" which is the reason that he and George had to leave town. This <u>foreshadows</u> the end of the novel, when Lennie accidentally kills Curley's wife.

In *A Christmas Carol*, Dickens uses <u>flashbacks</u> and <u>flashforwards</u> to let the reader see Scrooge in the past and the future. This gives the reader a better understanding of his character as they see the action instead of hearing about it from others.

Turning Points change the direction of the **Plot**

Turning points are important <u>events</u> that change the course of the story. Most fiction texts have <u>several</u> turning points.

In *Lord of the Flies*, a major turning point is when the boys <u>split into two groups</u> — one led by Ralph, the other led by Jack. Once the boys are split, the <u>tension</u> between the two groups <u>grows</u>. This eventually leads to Simon's <u>murder</u>.

Cliffhangers create **Tension**

1) Longer stories are split into <u>chapters</u>. Often, writers will have something exciting happen at the end of the chapter — this is called a <u>cliffhanger</u>. Cliffhangers are used to <u>keep the reader interested</u>.

2) Writers try to <u>finish</u> their stories in <u>interesting</u> ways. Some authors tie up all the loose ends in a <u>neat ending</u> which will make the reader <u>happy</u>. Some authors might also use a <u>cliffhanger</u> at the end of the story to leave the reader <u>wanting more</u>.

Structure is very important in fiction writing

There are a lot of technical terms on this page, like foreshadowing and linear structure. Write out the terms and definitions on individual pieces of paper and try to match them correctly.

Narrator

Not all narrators are the same — some know more than others.

Fiction texts usually have **First-Person** or **Third-Person** narrators

> Reader, though I look comfortably accommodated, I am not very tranquil in my mind.
>
> *Jane Eyre* — Charlotte Brontë

Jane Eyre is written in the first person. Jane addresses the reader directly, which establishes a close connection between the narrator and the reader.

> Lennie covered his face with huge paws and bleated with terror.
>
> *Of Mice and Men* — John Steinbeck

Of Mice and Men has a third-person narrator. They tell the reader what happens in a detached way.

Third-person narrators can be anonymous, like in *Of Mice and Men*, or a character in the story, like Harry Potter in the *Harry Potter* series of books.

The reader **Relies On** the **Narrator**

1) The writer uses the narrator to control what the reader finds out in the story.

2) Third-person narrators don't always know everything. A limited narrator might know how one character thinks and feels or they might not know how any of the characters think or feel. An omniscient narrator knows everything.

> The narrator of *Animal Farm* is limited. They only report what the animals see and hear. This means that the reader has to reach their own conclusions about the characters and events in the story.

> The narrator of *Pride and Prejudice* is omniscient and tells the reader everything. The story focuses on Elizabeth, so the reader knows a lot about her thoughts and feelings.

3) The writer might create a narrator who's not entirely trustworthy — they might not reveal everything they know or they might keep things from the reader. This builds suspense in the story.

4) First-person narrators are sometimes unreliable because they tell the story from their point of view.

> In *Anita and Me*, an adult Meena writes about what happened in her childhood. This makes her potentially unreliable as a narrator since she may not remember events accurately. Although she is often honest with the reader, she likes telling stories — these may not be entirely true.

5) Think about why the author chose a particular narrator. Here are some possible reasons:

   - First-person narrators have a more direct relationship with the reader.
   - Third-person narrators tend to be less involved in the story.
   - Third-person narrators can be used to show more than one viewpoint.

Make sure you can identify different types of narrator

It's important to think about the narrator and what they tell you — everything you know about the text is provided by them. Don't always trust the narrator — they might hide information or be inaccurate.

Mood

The mood is all about how a <u>text</u> makes you <u>feel</u>.

Writers use lots of **Techniques** to create **Mood**

1) A text can make a reader feel <u>happy</u>, <u>sad</u>, <u>scared</u> etc.

2) When you read a text, look for <u>words</u> that make you feel a certain <u>emotion</u>. That will help you to work out the <u>mood</u> of the text.

> Don't get confused between mood and tone. Mood describes how a text makes the reader feel. Tone describes how the author feels about the topic they're writing about.

The <u>similes</u> emphasise Scrooge's <u>happiness</u> at getting the chance to change his future.

"<u>I am as light as a feather</u>, <u>I am as happy as an angel</u>, <u>I am as merry as a school-boy</u>. <u>I am as giddy as a drunken man</u>. A merry Christmas to everybody! A happy New Year to all the world! Hallo here! Whoop! Hallo!"

A Christmas Carol — Charles Dickens

3) Writers also use some <u>clever techniques</u> to build the mood. For example, <u>short words</u> and <u>short</u>, <u>sharp sentences</u> can create an atmosphere of <u>tension</u>.

This is a long sentence, but the <u>punctuation</u> breaks it into smaller chunks. This increases the pace and makes the text feel <u>tense</u>.

A cry followed; he reeled, staggered, clutched at the table and held on, staring with injected eyes, gasping with open mouth; [...] he seemed to swell — his face became suddenly black and the features seemed to melt and alter [...]

Verbs like "reeled", "staring" and "gasping" vividly <u>describe</u> what happens to Hyde, but create <u>tension</u> as the reader <u>waits</u> to find out that Hyde is turning into Jekyll.

Dr Jekyll and Mr Hyde— Robert Louis Stevenson

4) Another technique is using <u>ellipses</u> (...) to create <u>suspense</u>:

I feel the dread of this horrible place overpowering me; I am in fear — in awful fear — and there is no escape for me; I am encompassed about with terrors that I dare not think of...

Dracula — Bram Stoker

The ellipsis creates a <u>pause</u> and allows the reader to <u>imagine</u> what these "terrors" are.

5) <u>Nothing</u> in a text is <u>accidental</u>. A writer <u>chooses</u> their words <u>deliberately</u> to make the reader feel a certain way. This creates the mood of a text, which can be:

> These are just a few examples. There are loads more.

playful   mysterious   gloomy   serious   joyful

There's a reason for everything

First learn these techniques that writers use to create a mood. Then try spotting them in the texts you read. It gets easier with practice, so get reading and you'll be great in no time.

Answering Questions About Fiction

Time to bring everything together. Here's how you might answer a question about a fiction text.

Read the question Carefully

When it comes to writing an essay, there are several different areas of the text you could be asked about.

The question might focus on one character...	...or ask you to look at a certain theme (see p.89)...	... or the language the author uses.

Discuss how the author presents Dickon in the following extract.

This question is all about the character of Dickon.

You'd need to write about the techniques that the author uses.

Here are some of the techniques that you should look for when analysing the text below:

- Look out for imagery and figurative language (see pages 32-4) and think about how they're used.
- What does the dialogue reveal about the characters?
- What does the character do?

A boy was sitting under a tree, with his back against it, playing on a rough wooden pipe. He was a funny looking boy about twelve. He looked very clean and his nose turned up and his cheeks were as red as poppies and never had Mistress Mary seen such round and such blue eyes in any boy's face. And on the trunk of the tree he leaned against, a brown squirrel was clinging and watching him, and from behind a bush nearby a cock pheasant was delicately stretching his neck to peep out, and quite near him were two rabbits sitting up and sniffing with tremulous noses — and actually it appeared as if they were all drawing near to watch him and listen to the strange low little call his pipe seemed to make.

When he saw Mary he held up his hand and spoke to her in a voice almost as low as and rather like his piping.
[...]

"I'm Dickon," the boy said. "I know tha'rt Miss Mary."

Then Mary realized that somehow she had known at first that he was Dickon. Who else could have been charming rabbits and pheasants as the natives charm snakes in India? He had a wide, red, curving mouth and his smile spread all over his face.

"I got up slow," he explained, "because if tha' makes a quick move it startles 'em. A body 'as to move gentle an' speak low when wild things is about."

He did not speak to her as if they had never seen each other before but as if he knew her quite well.

The Secret Garden — Frances Hodgson Burnett

The simile compares Dickon's cheeks to poppies. Poppies are beautiful flowers, so the comparison sounds positive and makes the reader think of nature.

The description of Dickon's smile makes him sound warm and friendly.

Dickon speech is in non-standard English which suggests he is of a lower social class.

Dickon speaks to Mary as if he knows her. This suggests that he is warm and welcoming.

Answering Questions About Fiction

Here's some advice on turning those examples into <u>great points</u> in an essay...

Include lots of **Relevant Analysis**

You've spotted a technique, now you need to analyse the <u>effect</u> it has. The more <u>detailed</u> your analysis is, the better — but it must be <u>relevant</u> to the question. Have a read of the examples below:

Dickon's cheeks are compared to "poppies". ✗

This answer <u>isn't</u> very good — it doesn't go into any detail about what this tells us about Dickon.

Dickon's cheeks are compared to flowers using the simile "as red as poppies". Poppies are pretty flowers so this description gives the reader a positive impression of Dickon. ✓

This answer is <u>good</u> — it uses a <u>technical term</u> and it explains what the <u>language</u> tells us about Dickon.

Dickon's cheeks are compared to flowers using the simile "as red as poppies". Poppies are pretty flowers so this description gives the reader a positive impression of Dickon. Comparing Dickon to a flower also suggests that he is close to nature, and this is reinforced by his connection with the animals that gather round him. ✓✓

This answer is even <u>better</u> — it explains the <u>effect</u> of the language, and <u>develops</u> the point to show how this impression about Dickon is supported by other details from the text.

Here's another example of how you might turn a <u>quote</u> from the text into a <u>point in an essay</u>.

Dickon talks with an accent. ✗

This answer <u>isn't</u> very good — there isn't a quote from the text to back up the point, and it doesn't explain what this suggests about Dickon.

Dickon talks with an accent. He says "I know th'art" rather than "I know you are" which suggests that he talks with an accent. This could suggest that he is of a lower social class than Mary. ✓

This answer is <u>good</u> — it uses a <u>quote</u> to develop the point and explains what this tells us about Dickon.

Dickon's dialogue is written in non-standard English, which suggests he talks with an accent — he says "I know th'art" rather than "I know you are". Although this suggests that he is of a lower social class than "Miss Mary", Dickon speaks to Mary as if she is a friend, even though this is the first time that the characters have met. This suggests that he is a warm and friendly character. ✓✓

This answer is even <u>better</u> — it uses <u>technical terms</u>, includes a <u>quote</u> and explains what this tells us about Dickon, as well as developing the point even further.

EXAM TIP

Read the question very carefully...

...so you know exactly what it is asking you to do. You can spend a few minutes doing this.

Section Seven — Analysing Fiction and Non-Fiction

Layout, Form and Structure

Now you're a pro at analysing fiction texts, it's time to look at <u>non-fiction</u>. This page is all about the <u>layout</u>, <u>form</u> and <u>structure</u> of non-fiction texts — they're different from fiction texts.

Don't **Confuse Layout, Form** and **Structure**

1) <u>Form</u> describes the <u>text type</u> that the writer uses, e.g. a newspaper article, a letter, a recipe.
2) <u>Structure</u> is how the <u>ideas</u> and <u>information</u> are <u>ordered</u> and <u>organised</u> within a text.
3) <u>Layout</u> is how the content is <u>presented</u> on the page, e.g. titles, columns, photos.
4) Here are some examples...

There's more about layout on p.27.

FORM
This is a <u>newspaper article</u>.

STRUCTURE
The first paragraph <u>explains</u> what's happened. The second paragraph gives more <u>details</u>.

ARREST AFTER TIGERS ESCAPE

A man is being held by police today after he reportedly let all of the tigers out of the local zoo.

The man, said to be in his early twenties and from the local area, is a trained locksmith, which police believe to be the secret to his success in opening the enclosure on Tuesday morning.

Anyone with information should contact the police.

LAYOUT
Newspaper articles have short, catchy <u>titles</u> which explain what the article is about. The <u>columns</u> make the article easier to read.

FORM
This is a set of <u>instructions</u>.

SNAP!

1) Deal all 52 cards face down.
2) Decide which player will play first. The first player should turn over the top card of their pile and place it in the centre.
3) The second player turns over their top card and places it on the first card. Carry on taking turns to do this.
4) When the top two cards on the pile match, put your hand on the pile and shout "Snap!". Any player can do this.
5) The person who shouts "Snap!" first collects all the cards in the pile and adds them to the bottom of their pile.
6) If a player runs out of cards, they are out of the game. The winner is the player with all the cards at the end of the game.

LAYOUT
The text has a <u>title</u> and uses a <u>numbered list</u>.

STRUCTURE
The first two points explain how to <u>start</u> the game. The middle three points cover how to <u>play</u> it and the final point explains how the game <u>ends</u>. By breaking the game down into <u>simple steps</u>, it becomes <u>easier to follow</u>.

STRUCTURE
<u>Dictionaries</u> are laid out in <u>alphabetical</u> order. This makes it <u>easy</u> for the reader to <u>find</u> the word they're looking for.

mushroom — a type of fungi which is edible
mustard — a spicy condiment often served with meat

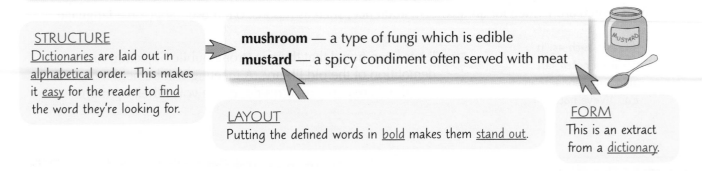

LAYOUT
Putting the defined words in <u>bold</u> makes them <u>stand out</u>.

FORM
This is an extract from a <u>dictionary</u>.

REVISION TASK

A text's layout and structure can be decided by its form

Grab some non-fiction texts and comment on their layout, form and structure.

Language in Non-Fiction Texts

Non-fiction writers use language in different ways from fiction writers.

Non-fiction texts can be **Informal** or **Formal**

1) Non-fiction texts have various purposes, e.g. to advise, to persuade or to inform (see p.26).

2) These texts could use an informal or formal register, depending on the intended audience (see p.26).

3) Some pieces of writing are usually formal, such as informative texts.
This is to make the reader feel that the information is reliable and accurate.

4) Some types of non-fiction text can be formal or informal, for example texts which advise.

> Advice columns in magazines often use informal language and have a friendly tone, e.g "You need to decide what's best for you and just go for it."

> Formal advice, e.g. about finances, might still use "you" but will have a more serious tone, e.g. "You should adjust your monthly budget."

Non-fiction writing uses **Different Perspectives**

1) Non-fiction texts don't have a narrator, but they can be written in the first, second or third person (see p.37).

2) Writers often use the first person ("I" or "we") when they talk about a personal experience or opinion. It might be used in informal texts, e.g. a magazine article about a writer's trip to Hawaii, or in more formal writing, e.g. a letter of complaint to the manager of a restaurant.

3) The second person perspective ("you") is used when the writer wants to address the reader directly, e.g. in advice columns or reviews.

4) The third person ("he", "she" or "they") is used most often. Writers use this perspective, e.g. in newspaper articles, to report information in a detached and factual way.

Texts can use **Emotive** or **Impersonal Language**

1) Non-fiction texts often use emotive language when they want to persuade the reader.

> The performance was thrilling, moving and utterly charming.

> Watch out — writing that uses lots of emotive language might be biased (see p.99).

> The author has used a list of three and emotive adjectives (see p.54) to make the performance sound like it's not to be missed. The writer aims to persuade the reader to see the play.

2) Texts which are written for an unknown audience, such as reports, often use impersonal language.

> Phrases such as "It has been noted" are more impersonal than e.g. "We've noted".

> It has been noted that there is strong public objection to the demolition of the old library. A meeting will be held next month where concerned residents can voice their opinions.

Pay close attention to the writer's language

Think about the purpose and audience of texts — these influence the writer's language.
If you can link these with the effect the language creates, you'll be on track for top marks.

Language in Non-Fiction Texts

Sometimes non-fiction writers include their opinions in texts. Often these opinions are included alongside all the facts, but other times writers miss out things if they want the reader to think a certain way.

The Writer's **Viewpoint** is what they **Think**

1) Sometimes it's clear what writers think, for example in newspaper opinion pieces. Other times you have to look more closely to find out the writer's viewpoint.

2) Look at the writer's language, tone and style to get an idea of their viewpoint.

> The phrasebook's unusual layout was poorly thought out as it makes it difficult to work out the meaning of each word. It's baffling why the author has mixed the words up and has put the Italian word for "bread" next to the English word "orange". There seems to be no logical reason to arrange the contents this way.

> The text's purpose is to inform the reader about what the phrasebook is like. The phrase "poorly thought out" tells the reader that the writer isn't impressed with the phrasebook, whilst "baffling" suggests that the writer finds it confusing and unhelpful.

> The writer informs the reader about the phrasebook using a negative tone. The reader is discouraged from buying it.

> Not all texts have a viewpoint. Some texts, for example recipes or instructions, are deliberately written to be neutral and impersonal.

Texts are **Biased** if they're influenced by the **Writer's Opinion**

1) Most writers give the reader all the information, as well as adding their own viewpoint. Biased writers only put forward one half of the story. They often miss out anything that goes against their viewpoint and exaggerate the points they agree with.

> This cookbook is undoubtedly the best of its kind. Every recipe is a dream to make and couldn't be simpler. The images of the finished results make your mouth water. The writer is a true genius — unrivalled in the art of cakemaking. She has the skills and experience that others can only dream of. Every single amateur baker in the country looks up to her.

> Biased writing makes opinions sound like they're facts. Look out for exaggerated, emotive language like this to help you decide if a text might be biased.

> Generalisations often appear in biased texts. These are statements which supposedly apply to everyone when they actually don't. Not every baker will admire the author of the cookbook.

2) Biased writing and persuasive writing can be quite similar — they share a lot of the same features. Bias tends to be a bit more subtle though, so it isn't always easy to spot — sometimes writers are accidentally biased. Look out for bias in newspaper articles and reviews.

Watch out for viewpoints and bias

Find three newspaper articles about different topics and have a read of them. Work out if the writer includes their viewpoint, and then decide whether the text is biased or not.

Answering Questions About Non-Fiction

Time to bring everything together and look at a question about a non-fiction text.

Think about **Layout** as well as **Language**

> Discuss how the author of the advert tries to persuade the reader.

This question is all about how the advert persuades the reader.

You'd need to write about the techniques that the author uses.

Here are some of the things that you should look for when analysing the text below:

- What sort of language does the author use? Have they used any special techniques?
- How is the text structured?
- What layout features does the advert use?

The text is written in the first person, which makes it sound more personal.

Emotive language helps to persuade the reader.

The cute picture makes the reader feel sorry for the abandoned cats.

ABANDONED. FREEZING. UNLOVED.

Every December, hundreds of families buy kittens as Christmas gifts. By January, some of these tiny, defenceless animals are rejected and left on the streets to fend for themselves.

Here at the Cats and Kittens Trust, we believe every cat deserves love. So we feed, house and love these abandoned cats until we can find them a forever home. If you think cats deserve love, please donate today.

Cats and Kittens Trust
Because *every cat* deserves love

**TEXT 'CAT' TO 85236542
TO DONATE JUST £1**

PROTECTED. WARM. LOVED.

The charity's slogan is an opinion presented as a fact.

A list of three makes the text punchy and memorable.

The donation number is presented in a text box with a bold, coloured font which grabs the reader's attention.

'loved' is in a different colour. This makes the key word stand out.

EXAM TIP

Remember — everything in a text is <u>deliberate</u>

Even if you think you're making a really obvious point, scribble it down anyway to show that you've thought about it. Just don't forget to think about the effect on the reader too.

Answering Questions About Non-Fiction

You've spotted the <u>techniques</u>, now you need to make some <u>great points</u>.

Always think about the **Effect** on the **Reader**

It doesn't matter if you're talking about language, structure or layout, you need to mention the <u>effect on the reader</u>.

The advert uses sad words like "abandoned" and "unloved".

This point could be improved — it doesn't <u>explain</u> or <u>develop</u> the example.

The advert uses emotive language like "abandoned" and "unloved". This makes the reader feel sorry for the cats and more likely to donate to the charity.

This answer is <u>good</u> — it uses a <u>technical term</u> and it explains the <u>effect</u> that the language has on the reader.

The advert is written in the first person, which sounds more personal, as if someone from the charity is talking directly to the reader. In addition to this, the advert uses emotive language like "abandoned" and "unloved". This makes the reader feel sorry for the "tiny, defenceless" kittens which would persuade them to donate to the charity.

This answer is even <u>better</u> — it adds in some extra details about how the first person voice helps to connect with the reader. It also uses the key word '<u>persuade</u>' from the question.

Here's another example of how you might discuss a <u>layout feature</u> in an essay.

The advert uses a picture of a cute kitten.

This point doesn't explain how this <u>persuades</u> the reader.

The advert uses a photograph of a cute kitten to attract the reader's attention. The image would make the reader feel sorry for the "abandoned" kittens and more likely to make a donation to the charity.

This answer is <u>good</u> — it gives <u>two</u> ways that the image would affect the reader.

The advert uses a photograph of a kitten to attract the reader's attention. Kittens tend to be small, which reinforces the description in the text of the abandoned animals being "tiny" and "defenceless". The image makes the issue of neglected cats seem more real, and makes the advert more persuasive, especially to cat lovers and cat owners.

This answer is even <u>better</u> — it <u>links</u> the image to the text and describes the <u>effect</u> that it would have on the reader.

Have a go at writing some points of your own

Look at some of the unused examples from the previous page (e.g. lists of three, coloured fonts) and have a go at turning them into fully explained points like the ones above.

Warm-Up and Worked Practice Questions

Hurrah! You've made it to the end of the section. Time to see whether you've understood it all.

Warm-up Questions

1) What's symbolism?
2) Match up the techniques on the left with the definitions on the right.
   a) flashbacks   when clues are given about later events
   b) foreshadowing   when the story moves to events in the past
   c) flashforwards   when the story temporarily moves to events in the future
3) Is this statement true or false?
   "Cliffhangers can only come at the end of a text."
4) Choose a word from the box below to fill in each of the blanks in the following sentences.

   | figurative | impersonal | emotive |

   a) An author might use _____ language to make the reader feel something.
   b) An author might use _____ language if they're writing for an unknown audience.
   c) An author might use _____ language to create a picture in the reader's mind.

Worked Practice Question

Read the description of Mr Bounderby below.

He was a rich man: banker, merchant, manufacturer, and what not. A big, loud man, with a stare, and a metallic laugh. A man made out of a coarse material, which seemed to have been stretched to make so much of him. A man with a great puffed head and forehead, swelled veins in his temples, and such a strained skin to his face that it seemed to hold his eyes open, and lift his eyebrows up. A man with a pervading appearance on him of being inflated like a balloon, and ready to start. A man who could never sufficiently vaunt* himself a self-made man. A man who was always proclaiming, through that brassy speaking-trumpet of a voice of his, his old ignorance and his old poverty. A man who was the Bully of humility*.

A year or two younger than his eminently* practical friend, Mr. Bounderby looked older; his seven or eight and forty might have had the seven or eight added to it again, without surprising anybody. He had not much hair. One might have fancied he had talked it off; and that what was left, all standing up in disorder, was in that condition from being constantly blown about by his windy boastfulness.

* *vaunt* — boast, brag   * *humility* — modesty   * *eminently* — exceptionally

Extract from *Hard Times* by Charles Dickens

1. How does Dickens present the character of Mr Bounderby?

   Dickens presents the character of Mr Bounderby as an unpleasant and

   unlikable man. Dickens does this using various language techniques to affect the

   reader's perception of the character.

Worked Practice Question

Dickens describes how Mr Bounderby sounds, looks and feels to make the character come to life for the reader. Mr Bounderby is described as being "loud" and he has a "brassy, speaking-trumpet" voice. Comparing Mr Bounderby's voice to a trumpet is effective because it is a recognisable sound to the reader, and it emphasises the loudness and brashness of his voice. Additionally, since trumpets are used for fanfares, this reinforces the idea that Mr Bounderby is a boastful character who is a "Bully of humility".

Embedding your quotes will impress the examiner.

The author also uses imagery to describe Mr Bounderby to the reader. He uses the simile "inflated like a balloon" to make his appearance seem ridiculous. This image of Mr Bounderby being inflated is echoed earlier in the passage when he is described as having a "puffed head" and "swelled veins". Together, these descriptions present a grotesque image of Mr Bounderby, and create the sense that he is swollen with his own self-importance.

Remember to use technical terms, like "metaphor".

The writer uses the metaphor "A man made out of a coarse material" to describe the appearance of Mr Bounderby's skin. Skin is usually smooth, so this metaphor creates an unpleasant image for the reader. The word "coarse" can also be used to describe someone who is rude and vulgar, just like Mr Bounderby, so this word is doubly effective.

As well as spotting language techniques, you can analyse the effectiveness of individual words.

Although Dickens uses language to make Mr Bounderby seem unpleasant, he is a character to be mocked rather than feared. The author uses humour to encourage the reader to ridicule Mr Bounderby. He suggests that Mr Bounderby is balding because he "talked" his hair off. This ridiculous image would cause the reader to laugh at Mr Bounderby's expense.

Keep referring back to the effect on the reader.

In conclusion, Dickens skilfully uses language to present Mr Bounderby as an unpleasant character, but his use of humour means that the audience would find him comical rather than malicious.

Try to finish your essays with a strong conclusion.

Worked Practice Question

You've seen a worked practice question for a fiction text — now it's time to look at non-fiction.

Worked Practice Question

Read the review of a theme park below.

> Why on earth would anyone want to visit a theme park? That's the question I asked myself after taking my kids to one last weekend.
>
> I started to have niggling doubts from the moment we arrived. First of all, we got there an hour after the park had opened, but we still had to sit in a queue of traffic before we could even park the car. Believe it or not, this was a sign of things to come.
>
> Once we were wedged into a parking space the size of a postage stamp, we followed the herd to the entrance gates, a mere 25-minute walk away — not ideal when your kids are already squirming with impatience.
>
> Then, we joined another queue to hand over my hard-earned money to the spotty youth in the ticket kiosk. For a family of four, it cost over 100 quid. My eyes watered as I relinquished the cash.
>
> After what had already seemed like a lifetime, we made it into the park. A luminous information board told us that one of the rides was shut due to strong winds, another was closed due to compulsory maintenance and the rest had queue times of about 80 minutes. By this point, I didn't think the day could get any better.

1. How does the writer convey their attitude to theme parks in this extract?

The author of the text clearly has a very negative opinion of theme parks, and they convey this attitude using several techniques. ← *The introduction is simple but clear.*

Remember to use linking words. → *Firstly, the author grabs the reader's attention with a rhetorical question: "Why on earth would anyone want to visit a theme park?" Usually theme parks are associated with fun, so this overly-negative question takes the reader by surprise and encourages them to read on to find out why the author has this attitude.*

The text is written in the first person, which sounds as if the author is talking directly to the reader. Because the text is written as a first-hand account, it makes the author's experiences at the theme park seem more believable and relatable.

The author also tries to connect with the reader by using an informal register. The use of slang ("kids", "cash", "quid") and contractions ("That's", "didn't") creates a chatty voice, which sounds as though the writer is talking to the reader like a friend. Establishing this relationship makes the reader feel sympathy for the author. → *Use plenty of quotes.*

The author uses hyperbole to exaggerate their negative experience at the theme park. They say that the car parking space was "the size of a postage stamp",

Practice Questions

which creates the impression that the car parking space was very small. This use of exaggeration persuades the reader to think negatively about the writer's experience

Throughout the extract, the author employs a sarcastic tone. They say that it was a "mere 25-minute walk" to the entrance and that they "didn't think the day could get any better" when they encountered lots of problems in the park. The use of sarcasm creates humour, as it seems as though the writer is sharing a joke with the reader. This makes the reader sympathise with the author and their experiences at the theme park.

In conclusion, the author uses a number of techniques to convey their attitude towards the park. Most of these techniques are used to evoke sympathy from the reader in order to encourage the reader to agree with the writer's attitude towards theme parks. ⬅ *The conclusion summarises how the writer conveys their attitude.*

Practice Question

Time to have a go at analysing texts yourself. First up is fiction.

Read this extract and answer the question below.

> The tide was out; the beach was deserted; lazily flopped the warm sea. The sun beat down, beat down hot and fiery on the fine sand, baking the grey and blue and black and white-veined pebbles. It sucked up the little drop of water that lay in the hollow of the curved shells; it bleached the pink convolvulus* that threaded through and through the sand-hills. Nothing seemed to move but the small sand-hoppers. Pit-pit-pit! They were never still.
>
> Over there on the weed-hung rocks that looked at low tide like shaggy beasts come down to the water to drink, the sunlight seemed to spin like a silver coin dropped into each of the small rock pools. They danced, they quivered, and minute ripples laved* the porous shores. And how strong, how damp the seaweed smelt in the hot sun...
>
> The green blinds were drawn in the bungalows of the summer colony. Over the verandas, prone on the paddock, flung over the fences, there were exhausted-looking bathing-dresses and rough striped towels. Each back window seemed to have a pair of sand-shoes on the sill and some lumps of rock or a bucket or a collection of pawa* shells. The bush quivered in a haze of heat; the sandy road was empty except for the Trouts' dog Snooker, who lay stretched in the very middle of it. His blue eye was turned up, his legs stuck out stiffly, and he gave an occasional desperate-sounding puff, as much as to say he had decided to make an end of it and was only waiting for some kind cart to come along.
>
> * *convolvulus* — a type of flower   * *laved* — washed   * *pawa* — a type of pearly shell

Extract from *At the Bay* by Katherine Mansfield

1. Discuss how the author creates a relaxed mood in this extract.

Practice Question

Next up is a tasty non-fiction text to analyse...

Practice Question

Read the extract, then answer the question below.

CAVE AND CLIMB AT RANCHFORD CAVE!

With plenty of activities to suit all abilities and age groups, Ranchford Cave is the perfect adventure for all the family. You'll want to come back every day!

WHAT IS RANCHFORD CAVE?

Ranchford Cave is the best location for climbing and caving in the West Midlands. The ancient rock formations at Ranchford have enticed explorers for centuries. With the opportunity to both climb the exterior rock face, and cave down into the mysterious maze of caverns below, Ranchford combines two awesome adventures into one incredible day out.

CAN ANYBODY CLIMB?

- If you're a beginner, start off on our indoor climbing walls. Our friendly and experienced instructors will teach you how to climb in the comfort of our newly refurbished centre. This means you can build up your confidence before venturing outside. All our instructors are fully qualified mountaineers — you'll be as safe as houses.

- If you're an experienced climber, head straight out to the cave for an experience you'll never forget. You can climb the rock face to take in the breathtaking views at the top, or venture down into the cavernous depth of the cave — the choice is yours.

ADMISSION PRICES

Adults: £40 for an Outdoor Day Pass
            £60 for a Beginner Day Pass

Children: £20 for an Outdoor Day Pass
            £40 for a Beginner Day Pass

Beginner Day Pass includes 3 hours of indoor instruction prior to outdoor pursuits.

So what are you waiting for?
Call us now on 555 800 555

1. Discuss how the writer of the brochure tries to persuade the reader.

Revision Summary for Section Seven

Whoa, that was a lot of information to take in. When you're feeling ready to go, run through these questions. If any of them fox you, go back through this section until you find the answer.

1) Give three ways that a reader might learn about a character. ☐

2) Suggest two questions you could ask yourself to find out a character's purpose. ☐

3) Why is the setting of a text important? ☐

4) Why is dialogue useful for finding out what a character is like? ☐

5) Why might an author mention a certain object repeatedly? ☐

6) "In plots with a non-linear structure, the events happen chronologically." True or false? ☐

7) What is a turning point? ☐

8) Match the terms on the left with the correct definition on the right:
   limited narrator   knows what all characters think and feel
   omniscient narrator   knows what one character thinks and feels ☐

9) Why shouldn't you always trust the narrator? ☐

10) Give one reason why an author might choose to use a third-person narrator. ☐

11) How might an author use language to create a tense mood? ☐

12) What effect can writers create by using ellipsis? ☐

13) Name two layout features often found in newspaper articles. ☐

14) Decide whether the following texts would be written in the first, second or third person:
   a) A piece of writing in an advice column.
   b) A report on the increase of empty shops in town centres.
   c) An opinion piece about the benefits of meditating. ☐

15) How can you figure out what a writer's viewpoint is? ☐

16) What does it mean if a text is biased? ☐

Poetry Features

Poetry might seem tricky at first, but you'll get the hang of it. This page covers the basics of poetry.

There are **Different Types** of Poem

1) Poems are a type of fiction text. Poems tend to be shorter than novels or plays.

2) A poem is usually written to entertain, or to make a reader feel a certain way.

3) Poems have a different structure from other fiction texts. Poems can also look very different from each another. There are lots of different types of poem that you might come across — have a look at p.112.

A **Verse** is a **Section** of a poem

1) Poems are made up of lines, and a group of lines in a poem is called a verse.

2) Verses in a poem usually have different words, but they often follow the same rhyme scheme (see p.109).

3) Not all poems have multiple verses. Some types of poem, e.g. sonnets and limericks, are usually just one verse.

Verses can sometimes be called 'stanzas'.

Some poems **Rhyme**

There's more about rhyme on p.109.

1) A lot of poems rhyme. Rhyming words are words that sound the same.

> I wander thro' each charter'd street,
> Near where the charter'd Thames does flow,
> And mark in every face I meet
> Marks of weakness, marks of woe.
>
> *London — William Blake*

"Street" and "meet" rhyme with each other. The endings don't need to be spelt the same to rhyme — "flow" and "woe" rhyme with each other.

2) Not all rhymes are perfect. Here's an example:

> The fountains mingle with the river
> And the rivers with the ocean,
> The winds of heaven mix for ever
> With a sweet emotion;
>
> *Love's Philosophy — Percy Bysshe Shelley*

"river" and "ever" don't exactly rhyme. The sounds are similar, so they're known as half-rhymes.

3) Some poems don't rhyme at all.

KEY TERM

Get to grips with the basics first

You need to understand the terms on this page before you read on. Make sure you know what verses and stanzas are, as well as how to identify rhymes and half-rhymes.

Rhyme

Rhyme is an <u>important</u> poetic technique and it's used a lot. This page will help you to <u>spot</u> rhyme schemes and work out the <u>effect</u> that the poet is trying to create.

Work out the poem's **Rhyme Scheme...**

1) A poem's <u>rhyme scheme</u> is the <u>pattern</u> of the rhyming words. Rhyme schemes can be <u>regular</u> or <u>irregular</u> and some poems don't have one at all.

2) To work out the rhyme scheme, use <u>letters</u> to mark the words at the end of lines that rhyme with each other. Each time you come across a <u>different sound</u>, use a <u>new letter</u>.

> At evening when the lamp is <u>lit</u>, **A**
> Around the fire my parents <u>sit</u>; **A**
> They sit at home and talk and <u>sing</u>, **B**
> And do not play at <u>anything</u>. **B**

Put an 'A' next to "lit" since it's on the first line. "sit" rhymes with "lit", so put an 'A' next to "sit" too.

"sing" doesn't rhyme with "sit", so put a B next to it. "anything" rhymes with "sing", so put a B next to "anything".

The Land of Story-books — Robert Louis Stevenson

3) This poem has a <u>regular</u>, <u>AABB</u> rhyme scheme. The poem uses <u>rhyming couplets</u> — this is a term used to describe <u>a pair of lines</u> directly next to each other which <u>rhyme</u>. This rhyme scheme makes the poem seem quite <u>light-hearted</u> and <u>playful</u>.

... then comment on its **Effect**

> I look into my glass, **A**
> And view my wasting skin, **B**
> And say, 'Would God it came to pass **A**
> My heart had shrunk as thin!' **B**

The poet is looking at his reflection in the mirror. The <u>regular ABAB</u> rhyme scheme is <u>steady</u>, which helps to create a <u>thoughtful</u> tone.

I Look Into My Glass — Thomas Hardy

The rhyme scheme of this poem is <u>irregular</u> as there is <u>some</u> rhyming, for example the first and fourth lines. The poem is about <u>war</u>, so an irregular rhyme scheme could represent the <u>chaos</u> of war.

> He dropped, – more sullenly than wearily, **A**
> Lay stupid like a cod, heavy like meat, **B**
> And none of us could kick him to his feet; **B**
> – Just blinked at my revolver, blearily; **A**
> – Didn't appear to know a war was on, **C**
> Or see the blasted trench at which he stared. **D**

The Dead-Beat — Wilfred Owen

> Aboard, at a ship's helm,
> A young steersman, steering with care.
>
> A bell through fog on a sea-coast dolefully ringing,
> An ocean-bell — O a warning bell, rock'd by the waves.

This poem has <u>no rhyme scheme</u>. It sounds like the narrator is telling a <u>story</u>.

Aboard at a Ship's Helm — Walt Whitman

Rhyme is very important

To practise looking for rhyme, try starting with poems you know, such as nursery rhymes. Then you'll see that rhyme schemes are really not as difficult as they might seem.

Poetic Techniques

Poetry uses some <u>techniques</u> that you'll already be <u>familiar</u> with, but turn to pages 32-4 for a reminder.

Poems use a lot of **Imagery**

When you <u>read</u> a poem, pick out the techniques, then think about the <u>effect</u> they create. Here are a couple of verses from the poem *The Brook* by Alfred Lord Tennyson.

A 'brook' is a small stream.

The poem is written in the <u>first person</u> which makes the reader imagine that the brook is speaking. This is a form of <u>personification</u>. It makes the reader feel like they are on a <u>journey</u> along with the brook.

I chatter over stony ways,
In little sharps and trebles,
I bubble into eddying bays,
I babble on the pebbles.
[...]
I slip, I slide, I gloom, I glance,
Among my skimming swallows;
I make the netted sunbeam dance
Against my sandy shallows.

I murmur under moon and stars
In brambly wildernesses;
I linger by my shingly bars;
I loiter round my cresses;

"<u>chatter</u>" and "<u>babble</u>" are examples of <u>onomatopoeia</u>. They help the reader to imagine the <u>sounds</u> of the water.

This poem uses a lot of <u>alliteration</u> — for example "I gloom, I glance". It emphasises the <u>movement</u> of the brook.

Tennyson uses <u>imagery</u> to help the reader to picture the brook's <u>surroundings</u>. "brambly wildernesses" makes the brook seem <u>isolated</u> in places.

The image "under moon and stars" emphasises the <u>continuous movement</u> of the brook, day and night.

Repetition emphasises **Key Ideas**

Poets <u>repeat</u> words, <u>phrases</u> and even <u>whole lines</u>, in order to <u>emphasise</u> points in their poems. If you spot a word or phrase that's <u>repeated</u>, you can be sure that it's <u>important</u>.

My heart's in the Highlands, my heart is not here;
My heart's in the Highlands a-chasing the deer;

My Heart's in the Highlands — Robert Burns

The word "<u>heart</u>" is repeated three times in two lines. This suggests that the poet feels very <u>emotional</u>.

The poet repeats "<u>the Highlands</u>" — he is clearly <u>thinking</u> about this place <u>a lot</u>.

Poems are packed with figurative language

REVISION TASK

Find a copy of *The Brook* by Alfred Lord Tennyson online, and try to spot more examples of onomatopoeia, personification, alliteration and imagery, as well as any other techniques.

Rhythm

Working out the rhythm of a poem isn't always easy — it might help you to read the poem aloud.

A poem's **Rhythm** can be **Regular or Irregular**

1) The rhythm of a poem is how the beats are arranged within a line. It can be regular or irregular. Poems with a strict rhyme scheme usually have a regular rhythm.

2) The rhythm is created by the pattern of syllables in a line. This is called metre.

> Jack and Jill went up the hill
> To fetch a pail of water.

These two lines have 7 syllables each. This creates a regular rhythm.

A syllable is a word, or part of a word, which can be said in a single sound. E.g. in 'turnip', 'tur' and 'nip' are syllables.

3) The rhythm of a poem can affect its pace (speed) and mood. A fast rhythm can make a poem feel chaotic, whereas a regular, slow rhythm can create a sense of calm.

> I know that I shall meet my fate
> Somewhere among the clouds above;
> Those that I fight I do not hate,
> Those that I guard I do not love;

An Irish Airman Foresees His Death — W. B. Yeats

This poem has a regular rhythm as each line has 8 syllables and it has an ABAB rhyme scheme. The steady rhythm suggests the narrator is calm and accepts that he will die.

Punctuation can affect the rhythm of a poem

1) Punctuation is important in poetry — it's used in a different way from other fiction texts.

2) When a line ends, that isn't always the end of a sentence. You need to keep reading until you see a punctuation mark.

3) Poets often use punctuation to alter the pace of a poem, interrupt the rhythm or draw the reader's attention to something.

4) A caesura is when punctuation creates a pause somewhere in a line.

> I'm Nobody! Who are you?
> Are you — Nobody — too?

I'm Nobody! Who Are You? — Emily Dickinson

The exclamation mark creates a caesura in this line. It interrupts the flow of the poem, and draws the reader's attention to the question "Who are you?"

5) Enjambment is when a sentence flows from one line to another without any pause.

The enjambment here emphasises the clause "As if alive". This gives these lines a creepy undertone because the narrator is telling the reader that "she" is dead.

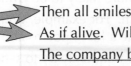

Then all smiles stopped together. There she stands
As if alive. Will't please you rise? We'll meet
The company below, then. I repeat,

There's enjambment here too.

My Last Duchess — Robert Browning

REVISION TASK

Practice makes perfect when it comes to rhythm

Rhythms can be tricky to work out at first, but if you practise, it'll get easier. Find a copy of *I Wandered Lonely as a Cloud* by William Wordsworth online, and work out whether the rhythm of the poem is regular or irregular and what rhyme scheme it uses.

Form and Structure

Take a look at this page to learn about different elements of a poem's structure and how they work.

A poem's **Structure** often **Depends** on its **Form**

1) Structure is the order of ideas on the page, and all the techniques used to do this.

2) A poem's line lengths, verses, rhyme scheme and rhythm all contribute to its structure.

3) The structure of a poem is often decided by its form (what type of poem it is). Here are some examples:

> HAIKUS: short poems that only have 3 lines and 17 syllables.
> BALLADS: poems that tell a story. They often have four-line verses and a chorus.
> SONNETS: usually 14 lines long, and have a special rhyme scheme.
> LIMERICKS: funny poems, with 5 lines and a strict rhyme scheme.

A chorus is just a verse that's repeated throughout a poem.

3) Some poems don't have a particular form. The poem below doesn't have a set form, but it does have a regular structure — it has a regular rhyme scheme, a steady rhythm and the stanzas are all four lines long.

4) This poem is about the loss the narrator feels after a loved one dies in the war.

> Now the sprinkled blackthorn snow
> Lies along the lovers' lane
> Where last year we used to go—
> Where we shall not go again.
> [...]
> Presently red roses blown
> Will make all the garden gay...
> Not yet have the daisies grown
> On your clay.

Spring in War-Time — Edith Nesbit

The poem has a regular ABAB rhyme scheme and a simple, steady rhythm. This rhythm emphasises the sadness of the narrator's words.

The stanzas and lines are all the same length in this poem, except the last line. By making the last line shorter, the poem finishes too soon, which mirrors the premature death of a loved one.

5) Free verse is another type of form — it doesn't rhyme or have a set line length, so it has an irregular structure. Free verse gives poets more freedom in their writing.

Don't forget about **Context** and **Themes**

1) Just like other types of writing, poetry is also affected by context — when and where it was written, as well as who the author was. There's more on context on pages 38-9.

2) For example, sonnets were a popular form of poetry about 400 years ago, but fewer sonnets are written today. Modern poetry is more likely to be written in free verse.

3) Poets are influenced by the world around them. For example, Wilfred Owen and Siegfried Sassoon served in the army and wrote a lot of poems about World War One.

4) Poems often have themes (see p.89) and poets frequently try to send a message to their readers. For example, a lot of Wilfred Owen's poems explore the theme of conflict, and his poems often express his anger towards the effects of war.

Wilfred Owen

REVISION TASK

Some types of poem have a very strict structure...

... whereas some poems don't seem to have much of a structure at all. Have a go at writing a haiku, limerick or sonnet, then have a go at writing a poem in free verse.

Answering Questions About Poetry

Time to put everything you've learnt about poems into practice...

Make sure you Understand the Question

Let's look at an example question and poem.

> Discuss how the poet creates a feeling of hope in the poem.

This question is about <u>hope</u>. All your points should refer to this.

You'll need to write about the <u>techniques</u> that the poet uses.

Here are some things that you should look for when analysing the poem below:

* What sort of <u>language</u> does the poet use?
* Have they used any special <u>techniques</u>?
* How is the poem <u>structured</u>? What is the <u>rhyme scheme</u> and <u>rhythm</u>?
* Does the poem have a <u>theme</u> or a <u>message</u>?

The <u>alliteration</u> of the 'l' sound emphasises that the rain is over.

The child has been unwell but he's well enough to get out of bed and look out of the window. This suggests that he's <u>getting better</u>.

The underlined words are really <u>positive</u>. This creates a hopeful tone.

The words "laughter" and "glee" create an <u>upbeat tone</u>.

The word "Gazing" suggests that the child is watching the other boys <u>intently</u>. This word conveys <u>more emotion</u> than "looking".

The rain was ending, and <u>light</u>
    <u>L</u>ifting the <u>l</u>eaden skies.
It shone upon ceiling and floor
    And dazzled a child's eyes.
Pale after fever, a captive
    Apart from his schoolfellows,
He stood at the high room's window
    With face to the pane pressed close,
And beheld an <u>immense glory</u>
    Flooding with fire the drops
Spilled on <u>miraculous</u> leaves
    Of the <u>fresh</u> green lime-tree tops.
Washed gravel <u>glittered</u> red
    To a wall, and beyond it nine
Tall limes in the old inn yard
    Rose over the tall inn sign.
And voices arose from beneath
    Of boys from school set free,
Racing <u>and</u> chasing each other
    With laughter <u>and</u> games <u>and</u> glee.
To the boy at the high room-window,
    <u>Gazing</u> alone and apart,
There came a wish without reason,
    A thought that shone through his heart.
I'll choose this moment and keep it,
    He said to himself, for a vow,
To remember for ever and ever
    As if it were always now.

The rain is ending and the weather is improving. This could be a <u>metaphor</u> for the child feeling better after his illness.

The poem has a <u>regular rhyme scheme</u> — every other line rhymes and a <u>steady rhythm</u>. It has a <u>regular structure</u>.

<u>Repetition</u> of the word "and" creates a sense of <u>excitement</u>.

These lines emphasise how <u>important</u> this moment is to the child.

How to Make a Memory — Laurence Binyon

Section Eight — Poetry

Answering Questions About Poetry

Time to turn those examples into impressive points...

Remember to Link your points back to the Question

This question is about how the poet creates a feeling of hope — so every point needs to link back to the question.

> At the start of the poem, the rain has ended which makes the poem seem hopeful. ✗

This point refers to hope but it doesn't develop the example.

> At the start of the poem, the rain has ended. The poet uses alliteration to emphasise this: "light / Lifting the leaden skies". The repetition of the "l" emphasises the hopeful tone and draws the reader's attention to these lines in the poem. ✓

This answer is good — it uses a technical term and links the point back to the question.

> At the start of the poem, the rain has ended. The poet uses alliteration to emphasise this: "light / Lifting the leaden skies". The repetition of the "l" sound draws the reader's attention to these lines. The end of the rain could be a metaphor for the child recovering from his illness, and the better weather suggests that the child's health is improving. This gives the poem a hopeful tone from the outset. ✓✓

This answer is really impressive. It makes a good point about the use of alliteration, but it also develops the point further.

Here's another example of how you might incorporate examples into an essay.

> The poem uses some positive words like "miraculous" which give the poem a hopeful tone. ✗

This point uses a quote from the poem, but it doesn't fully explain how the poet's use of language makes the poem seem hopeful.

> The poet uses the adjective "miraculous" to describe what the child sees. This suggests that the child is amazed by the view from his window and his excitement creates a hopeful tone. ✓

This answer is better — it explains how the language adds to the sense of hope.

> The child describes leaves covered in rain drops as "miraculous". The fact that the child describes something so simple as a miracle suggests that he sees beauty even in the most ordinary circumstances. This could be because he has recovered from a serious illness and is thankful that he is now well enough to appreciate the world around him. The child's positivity adds to the poem's hopeful tone. ✓✓

This answer is really good. It links the language to what has happened in the poem to create a really well-developed point.

Have a go at writing some points of your own

Look at some of the unused examples from the previous page (e.g. rhyme scheme, the use of the word 'Gazing'), and have a go at turning them into developed points like the ones above.

Worked Practice Questions

Right, let's see how much you've remembered from this section.
We're going to start things off with a worked practice question.

Worked Practice Questions

In this poem, Philip Gross writes about a travelling circus arriving in town.

For One Night Only

The deadbeat circus
rolls up on the hard edge of town.

They're sledge-hammering stakes in, raising
dust and thistledown.

Now they've run up the slack flounce of a tent.   5
A man barks at the moon.

They've nailed their colours to the sky
just as it darkens. Two bald clowns

come flatfoot, fly-postering everything
that can't get away. The show goes on   10

and on. Long past bedtime,
the stilt walker stalks through the streets,

face level with your bedroom window.
In the morning, someone will be gone.

---

1. In line 12, the writer uses a word to describe how the stilt walker moves.
   a) Write the word down.

   ....*stalks*...

   b) What effect does that word have?

   It makes the stilt walker sound menacing, as if he's hunting something...........

   > *You obviously don't have to use these exact words, but you have to get across the idea that the stilt walker sounds dangerous.*

---

2. Explain how the writer involves the reader in the last two lines of the poem.

   The writer involves the reader by saying "your bedroom window". Then when we

   read in the last line "someone will be gone", it seems like a direct threat to us.

   > *If a question asks "How?", use the word "by" in your answer.*

   > *The question asks you about the last two lines — so make sure you mention both.*

Worked Practice Questions

Mini-essay questions will expect you to make several different points and back them up with quotes. Take a look at how this example answer has used P.E.E.D. (point, example, explain, develop) to answer the question.

Worked Practice Question

> **First Ice** *by Andrei Voznesensky*
>
> In the telephone booth a girl
> is turning into ice.
> Huddled in a thin coat
> her face is tear-stained
> and smeared with lipstick.   5
>
> She wears earrings made out of glass
> and breathes on fingers that freeze.
> She will have to go home now.
> Alone along the icy street.
>
> First frost. A beginning of losses.   10
> The first frost of telephone phrases.
> Winter glistens on her cheek.
> The first frost of having been hurt.

1. How does the writer make us feel that the girl in the poem is unhappy?
   In your answer you should comment on:
   - the details he gives us
   - the language he uses
   - the way the poem is set out

   The answer covers all of these pointers.

   Every point is backed up with examples and then explained and developed.

   The writer implies that the girl in the poem is unhappy by using a mix of factual and descriptive details. The poem ends with the line "The first frost of having been hurt", which tells us that something has just caused her pain. The repetition of "first frost" could suggest that the girl will face further suffering.

   The language he uses links the coldness she is feeling inside with the coldness outside. In line 2 he says she "is turning into ice". This means that she is not only getting colder as she stands in the telephone booth but that what she has been told has made her emotionally frozen with shock.

   The poem is set out in short lines and stanzas, which makes it seem bleak and comfortless. Words like "Alone" and "hurt" are emphasised at the beginning or end of lines, reflecting the girl's loneliness and pain. The fact that the lines seem to stand alone implies that the girl has no-one to turn to.

Practice Questions

Read these two poems, then answer the questions on p.118.

These two poems are both about night.

Windy Nights

Whenever the moon and stars are set,
Whenever the wind is high,
All night long in the dark and wet,
A man goes riding by.
Late in the night when the fires are out,
Why does he gallop and gallop about?

Whenever the trees are crying aloud,
And ships are tossed at sea,
By, on the highway, low and loud,
By at the gallop goes he.
By at the gallop he goes, and then
By he comes back at the gallop again.

R. L. Stevenson

Meeting at Night

The grey sea and the long black land;
And the yellow half-moon large and low;
And the startled little waves that leap
In fiery ringlets from their sleep,
As I gain the cove with pushing prow,
And quench its speed i' the slushy sand.

Then a mile of warm sea-scented beach;
Three fields to cross till a farm appears;
A tap at the pane, the quick sharp scratch
And blue spurt of a lighted match,
And a voice less loud, thro' its joys and fears,
Than the two hearts beating each to each!

Robert Browning

Practice Questions

These questions are about the two poems on p.117.

Practice Questions

1. Find an example of personification in each poem.

    ....

    ....

2. Find two examples of repetition in 'Windy Nights'.

    ....

    ....

    ....

3. a) What effect is created by the rhythm in 'Windy Nights'?

    ....

    b) Compare your answer to part a) with the rhythm in 'Meeting at Night'.

    ....

    ....

4. Choose a word to describe the mood of each poem. Explain your choices.

    ....

    ....

    ....

    ....

5. Write a short essay about the similarities and differences in the way
    that the two poets deal with the theme of 'night'.
    You should compare the following in your answer:
    *   The poetry conventions the poets use, e.g. personification, repetition
    *   The structure of the poems, e.g. lines, verses, rhyme pattern, rhythm
    *   The overall mood of the poems

    *You don't have to write about all of these examples.
    Just make sure you cover the three bullet points.*

Revision Summary for Section Eight

Finished these pages on poems? Feeling ready to go? Then go ahead and run through these questions.
If any of them leave you scratching your head, make sure you flick back and check your answers.

1) Give two ways that a poem is different from a story.

2) What's a stanza?

3) A rhyming couplet is only made up of two lines. True or false?

4) Write down the rhyme scheme for this poem.

> To a bumblebee
> A bright scented flower
> Is as tall as a tower
> But not to you or me.

5) Repetition is an example of a technique found in poems. List three other techniques.

6) Why might a poet repeat a word in a line or verse?

7) What is metre?

8) What effect might a slow, regular rhythm have in a poem?

9) What is caesura?

10) Explain what enjambment is.

11) What is free verse?

12) Describe the structure that ballads often have.

13) Which of the following things should you look at when analysing a poem?
Circle the correct options.
a) the structure of the poem
b) how many letters are in each word
c) the poem's rhyme scheme
d) how many syllables are in each line

Play Features

Ready for some drama? This section will tell you everything you need to know about modern plays.

Plays are written to be Acted

1) Plays are works of fiction performed on stage by actors. Plays are different from novels but you still need to think about the effect that the play will have on the audience.

2) Much like stories, most plays feature a few main characters. There also tends to be a whole load of more minor characters. All the actors in a play are collectively referred to as the cast.

3) Plays have a different layout from other fiction texts. The text of a play is referred to as a script, and most of the words in a script are written to be read aloud by actors — these are known as lines.

4) Scripts also contain stage directions. Stage directions tell the actors what to do, when to enter and when to leave the stage. They can also give information about the set, the lighting, costumes and props. They are usually written in italics and/or brackets.

For more info on characters, turn to pages 122-23.

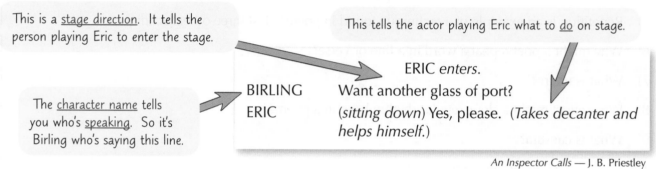

This is a stage direction. It tells the person playing Eric to enter the stage.

This tells the actor playing Eric what to do on stage.

The character name tells you who's speaking. So it's Birling who's saying this line.

ERIC *enters.*

BIRLING   Want another glass of port?
ERIC   *(sitting down)* Yes, please. *(Takes decanter and helps himself.)*

An Inspector Calls — J. B. Priestley

5) Sometimes, stage directions will tell the actors exactly how to say their lines, for example:

This stage direction tells the actor to say the lines very angrily. The tone of his voice helps the audience to understand how Parris feels.

PARRIS [*in a fury*]:   What are we, Quakers? We are not Quakers here yet, Mr Proctor.

The Crucible — Arthur Miller

6) Most playwrights don't give stage directions for every line, so it's usually up to the director to decide what the actors should do to help the audience understand what's going on.

A play is divided into Acts and Scenes

ACT   A play is usually divided into sections, called acts. Each act is like an episode of a TV series — plenty of things happen in it, but it's only part of the whole play.

SCENE   Acts can be divided up into smaller sections called scenes. Scenes can break up the story — a new scene can show that time has passed or that the story has moved to a different place.

Playwrights use the structure of acts and scenes to create tension. For example, Act Two of *An Inspector Calls* ends just as Mrs Birling realises that her son, Eric, is involved in the death of Eva Smith. Ending the scene with such a dramatic moment creates suspense.

There's more about staging plays on p.124.

 KEY TERM

Don't mix up acts and scenes

Make sure you know which is which when it comes to acts and scenes. Also make sure you can identify the stage directions — they're vital for understanding what's going on.

Play Features

There's a lot of talking in plays — this page will help you know your <u>dialogue</u> from your <u>monologues</u>.

Dialogue is when characters have a Conversation

1) The majority of a play's text is <u>dialogue</u>.
2) Dialogue in modern plays is usually written to sound like <u>normal speech</u>. This means that characters often speak using <u>non-Standard English</u> and that their language is not as descriptive as in prose.

Words like "Eh" and "Oh" make Helen's speech sound <u>realistic</u>.

HELEN   Eh? Oh! Yes, I did see a lad hanging around here when I called last week.

A Taste of Honey — Shelagh Delaney

© Alastair Muir/REX/Shutterstock

<u>Informal</u> language such as "lad" and "hanging around here" make Helen's speech sound <u>natural</u>.

A Monologue is when a character speaks for a Long Time

Monologues can give an insight into how a character is <u>feeling</u>, or can be used to tell other characters about something that's happened <u>off stage</u>.

MRS ERLYNNE   Believe what you choose about me. I am not worth a moment's sorrow. But don't spoil your beautiful young life on my account! You don't know what may be in store for you, unless you leave this house at once. You don't know what it is to fall into the pit, to be despised, mocked, abandoned, sneered at — to be an outcast!

Mrs Erlynne uses this monologue to <u>urge</u> another character to leave the house they are in. She uses <u>emotive language</u> such as "despised, mocked, abandoned" to try to <u>convince</u> her.

Lady Windermere's Fan — Oscar Wilde

Monologues are <u>different</u> from soliloquies (p.134). Other characters <u>can</u> hear monologues, but <u>not</u> soliloquies.

Characters use Asides when they Don't Want to be Overheard

Sometimes characters say their thoughts <u>aloud</u> to the <u>audience</u> when <u>other</u> characters are on the stage, but do it so that the other characters <u>can't hear</u>. This is called an <u>aside</u>. <u>Stage directions</u> should tell you when this is happening.

CECILY   May I offer you some tea, Miss Fairfax?
GWENDOLEN   [*With elaborate politeness*] Thank you. [*Aside*] Detestable girl! But I require tea!

"Aside" tells us that Cecily <u>can't hear</u> what Gwendolen says, but the aside lets the audience know that, although Gwendolen is polite to Cecily, she actually <u>dislikes</u> her.

The Importance of Being Earnest — Oscar Wilde

KEY TERM

Dialogue makes up the majority of a play's script

Monologues have lots of different effects, so think carefully about the information that the character includes in it. Asides let the audience know things that other characters don't.

Understanding Characters

Whether they're a villain, a hero or something in between, there's <u>plenty</u> to say about characters...

Characters are central to Every play

Characters <u>drive the action</u> and help the audience to <u>feel certain emotions</u>, so it's important that playwrights convey their characters well. They do this through:

- what characters <u>look like</u>
- what characters <u>say</u>
- how characters <u>behave</u>
- what other characters <u>say</u> about them
- how other characters <u>react</u> to them
- the play's <u>context</u>

Sometimes the playwright won't make things obvious, so you might have to make inferences, see p.28.

Learn about characters through their Appearance...

Actors wear <u>costumes</u> to reflect their character. These costumes will have been chosen <u>deliberately</u>.

The INSPECTOR ... creates at once an impression of massiveness ... He is ... dressed in a plain darkish suit

An Inspector Calls — J. B. Priestley

"an impression of massiveness" shows that the Inspector should have <u>authority</u> over the other characters.

© Alastair Muir/REX/Shutterstock

A "plain" suit makes the Inspector look <u>unremarkable</u>, but "darkish" makes the character more <u>mysterious</u>. This adds to the <u>uncertainty</u> surrounding the Inspector's identity in the play.

... what they Say...

MRS JOHNSTONE [*relieved*] Oh God, Mrs Lyons, never put new shoes on a table... You never know what'll happen.

Blood Brothers — Willy Russell

Mrs Johnstone <u>panics</u> when Mrs Lyons puts some new shoes on the table. This tells the audience that she's <u>superstitious</u>.

... the Way they Say things...

ABIGAIL [*tauntingly*] You come five mile to see a silly girl fly?

The Crucible — Arthur Miller

The word "tauntingly" suggests that Abigail is a <u>bold</u>, <u>playful</u> character.

Most characters aren't 100% good or 100% bad...

... they're usually somewhere in between, and have a mixture of positive and negative characteristics. Characters can also <u>change</u> (for better or for worse) over the course of the play.

Understanding Characters

... their **Body Language**...

MRS LYONS   Mrs J, nobody must ever know. Therefore
we have to have an agreement.
[...]
MRS JOHNSTONE *stands alone, afraid.*

Blood Brothers — Willy Russell

Facial expressions and body language show Mrs Johnstone's discomfort and fear.

... what **Other Characters** say about them...

Characters might talk about each other, but watch out — they might not always be completely honest.

MRS PEARCE   A young woman wants to see you, sir.
[...] She's quite a common girl, sir.

Pygmalion — George Bernard Shaw

Mrs Pearce says that the girl is of a lower class. This tells us a bit about the girl, but also that Mrs Pearce is a bit of a snob.

... how they **Behave** towards **Other Characters**...

THE FLOWER GIRL   Oh, if you're going to make a compliment of it —
HIGGINS [*thundering at her*] Sit down.

Pygmalion — George Bernard Shaw

Higgins treats the flower girl rudely. This suggests that he can be impatient and disrespectful.

... and **When** and **Where** the play is set

The context of the play will affect how the characters talk and behave. There's lots more on context on pages 38-9.

HALE   Let you sit, Goodwife Proctor.

The Crucible — Arthur Miller

The Crucible is set in America in the 1690s, but it was written in the 1950s. The playwright uses unusual syntax ("Let you sit" rather than "sit down") and old fashioned language such as "Goodwife" ("Mrs") to make the dialogue sound authentic. The costumes, props and set would also reflect the context of the play.

Characters are key to understanding the play

Take a play you're studying or a film you've seen and think about one or two of its main characters. Try to jot down a couple of points about their appearance, what they say and what they do. Think about how these things make you feel about the character.

Staging

Plays wouldn't be very exciting if there were just some actors talking on an empty stage. That's why you need to imagine what things like the set and lighting look like to get the full effect of the play.

Staging is how the play is presented Onstage

Staging refers to several different things, including:

THE SET — the scenery placed on stage which tells the audience where the action is happening.

PROPS — actors might use objects (called props) to make it clearer what they're talking about.

LIGHTING — lights can be used to draw the audience's attention to a certain place on stage.

MUSIC — music (as well as any other sound effects) can affect the mood of a scene.

Have a look at these Examples of Staging...

The dining-room of a fairly large suburban house, belonging to a prosperous manufacturer.

An Inspector Calls — J. B. Priestley

The whole play is set in a dining room. As only one room is used, it makes the play feel claustrophobic and intense.

© Jane Hobson/REX/Shutterstock

The playwright uses props such as the sandwiches and the empty plate to add humour to the play. The audience will have seen Algernon eat all the sandwiches throughout this scene.

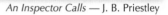

ALGERNON   *[Picking up empty plate in horror.]* Good heavens! Lane! Why are there no cucumber sandwiches?

The Importance of Being Earnest — Oscar Wilde

[...The lighting should be pink and intimate until the Inspector arrives, and then it should be brighter and harder...]

An Inspector Calls — J B Priestley

This lighting is very important in the play. The pink lighting in the beginning suggests the Birlings are wearing rose-tinted glasses — they look at their lives in an idealised way. The "brighter and harder" lighting makes them see their lives as they really are.

At the end of the play, several characters are executed. Their executions happen off-stage, but the drumroll signals their deaths to the audience. The sound of the drum creates tension.

The final drumroll crashes, then heightens violently.

The Crucible — Arthur Miller

You'll have to use your imagination...

...if you're only reading the play. If you don't think about what's onstage, you might miss something important. Read the playwright's directions carefully and think about the effect they were going for.

Answering Questions About Drama

Time to bring everything together. Here's how you might answer a question about drama.

Try to **Imagine** what the extract would look like **Onstage**

This extract is from a comedy called *The Importance of Being Earnest*. It was written in 1894. How does the playwright show the relationship between Cecily and Gwendolen in this extract?

You'll need to write about the techniques that the playwright uses.

This question is all about the characters.

Think about the context too.

Here are some things that you should look for when analysing the text below:
- What sort of language do the characters use? How do they behave towards each other?
- How do the stage directions add to the meaning?
- Does the relationship between the characters change over the course of the extract?

CECILY	[*Rather shy and confidingly.*] Dearest Gwendolen, there is no reason why I should make a secret of it to you. Our little county newspaper is sure to chronicle the fact next week. Mr. Ernest Worthing and I are engaged to be married.
GWENDOLEN	[*Quite politely, rising.*] My darling Cecily, I think there must be some slight error. Mr. Ernest Worthing is engaged to me. The announcement will appear in the *Morning Post* on Saturday at the latest.
CECILY	[*Very politely, rising.*] I am afraid you must be under some misconception. Ernest proposed to me exactly ten minutes ago. [*Shows diary.*]
GWENDOLEN	[*Examines diary through her lorgnette* carefully.*] It is certainly very curious, for he asked me to be his wife yesterday afternoon at 5.30. If you would care to verify the incident, pray do so. [*Produces diary of her own.*] I never travel without my diary. One should always have something sensational to read in the train. I am so sorry, dear Cecily, if it is any disappointment to you, but I am afraid I have the prior claim.
CECILY	It would distress me more than I can tell you, dear Gwendolen, if it caused you any mental or physical anguish, but I feel bound to point out that since Ernest proposed to you he clearly has changed his mind. [...]

[*Enter Merriman, followed by the footman. He carries a salver*, table cloth, and plate stand. Cecily is about to retort. The presence of the servants exercises a restraining influence, under which both girls chafe.*]

MERRIMAN	Shall I lay tea here as usual, Miss?
CECILY	[*Sternly, in a calm voice.*] Yes, as usual. [*Merriman begins to clear table and lay cloth. A long pause. Cecily and Gwendolen glare at each other.*]
CECILY	[...] May I offer you some tea, Miss Fairfax?
GWENDOLEN	[*With elaborate politeness.*] Thank you. [*Aside.*] Detestable girl! But I require tea!
CECILY	[*Sweetly.*] Sugar?
GWENDOLEN	[*Superciliously*.*] No, thank you. Sugar is not fashionable any more. [*Cecily looks angrily at her, takes up the tongs and puts four lumps of sugar into the cup.*]

*lorgnette — a magnifying glass
*salver — a tray
*superciliously — showing pride

The Importance of Being Earnest — Oscar Wilde

Cecily confides in Gwendolen at first. This suggests she trusts her.

Even though the characters are angry with each other, they try to remain polite — calling each other "darling" and "dearest". Politeness was very important in the 19th century.

Cecily now uses "Miss Fairfax" instead of "Gwendolen" — this shows that the relationship has become tense.

In an aside to the audience, Gwendolen calls Cecily "detestable" — she tells the audience what she really thinks.

Cecily ignores Gwendolen and puts sugar in her tea to annoy her.

Answering Questions About Drama

You should know the drill by now — time to turn these points into fully fledged answers.

Make sure you focus on the **Characters' Relationship**

The following answers look at how the characters' relationship <u>changes</u> over the course of the extract.

At the start of the extract, the characters seem like they are friends. By the end of the extract, they dislike each other. ✗

> Although this answer mentions how the characters' relationship <u>changes</u>, it doesn't go into enough detail.

At the start of the extract, Cecily talks to Gwendolen "confidingly" which suggests that she trusts her. However, by the end of the extract, the two women "glare" at each other which suggests that they are no longer friends. ✓

> This answer is <u>better</u> — it uses <u>quotes</u> from the extract to <u>back up</u> the point.

At the start of the extract, Cecily talks to Gwendolen "confidingly" which implies that she trusts her. However, the secret that Cecily confides to Gwendolen sours their relationship. Although outwardly the characters call each other "darling" and "dearest", which suggests that they are friends, their body language would tell the audience a different story — the women "glare" at each other, which hints that they are no longer friends. ✓✓

> This answer is really <u>good</u>. It <u>contrasts</u> the characters' <u>dialogue</u> with the <u>stage directions</u>.

Here's another example for you to get your teeth into.

Cecily puts sugar in Gwendolen's tea even though she doesn't want any. This suggests that Cecily is deliberately trying to annoy Gwendolen. ✗

> This point makes an <u>inference</u> about Cecily's behaviour, but it isn't fully developed.

At the end of the extract, the two women are struggling to be polite to each other. In Gwendolen's aside to the audience she calls Cecily "Detestable" and she talks to her "Superciliously". Cecily responds by putting sugar in Gwendolen's tea to annoy her. This suggests that there is a lot of tension between the characters. ✓

> This answer is <u>better</u> — it uses <u>quotes</u> and explains what the quotes suggest about the <u>characters' relationship</u>.

The play was written in 1894 at a time when politeness and manners were very important, especially amongst the upper classes. This convention is shown in the extract — although the women appear to dislike each other, they try to maintain an appearance of "elaborate politeness". However, this appearance of politeness starts to slip. Although Cecily talks to Gwendolen "Sweetly", Gwendolen's scornful reply causes Cecily to put sugar in Gwendolen's tea to deliberately annoy her. This suggests that there is a lot of tension between the two characters, but this tension creates humour, which the audience would find comical. ✓✓

> This answer is even <u>better</u> — it suggests how the <u>context</u> of the play affects the characters' behaviour and the <u>effect</u> that it would have on the audience.

Have a go at writing some points of your own

Pick out your own examples from the extract on p.125 and have a go at turning them into fully explained points like the ones above. As always, think about the <u>effect</u> on the audience.

Warm-Up and Worked Practice Questions

There's a lot to remember in the last few pages, but it'll be easier once you've done a few practice questions. Have a go at the next few pages before you move on.

Warm-up Questions

1) Give two things we can learn from reading stage directions.

2) Complete the following statement: "Plays can be divided into ____ and _____."

3) What is normally the reason for starting a new scene?

4) Are plays written to be:
   a) acted out,
   b) read, or
   c) sung?

You'll probably have to write about characters when studying plays. The example question below is based on *An Inspector Calls* by J B Priestley.

Worked Practice Question

Read the extract below. In this extract, Inspector Goole has just arrived at the Birling's house to investigate the tragic death of a young woman.

INSPECTOR:	I'd like some information, if you don't mind, Mr Birling. Two hours ago a young woman died in the Infirmary. She'd been taken there this afternoon because she'd swallowed a lot of strong disinfectant. Burnt her inside out, of course.
ERIC:	[*involuntarily*] My God!
INSPECTOR:	Yes, she was in great agony. They did everything they could for her at the Infirmary, but she died. Suicide, of course.
BIRLING:	[*rather impatiently*] Yes, yes. Horrid business. But I don't understand why you should come here, Inspector —
INSPECTOR:	[*cutting through, massively*] I've been round to the room she had, and she'd left a letter there and a sort of diary. Like a lot of these young women who get into various kinds of trouble, she'd used more than one name. But her original name — her real name — was Eva Smith.
BIRLING:	[*thoughtfully*] Eva Smith?
INSPECTOR:	Do you remember her, Mr Birling?
BIRLING:	[*slowly*] No — I seem to remember hearing that name — Eva Smith — somewhere. But it doesn't convey anything to me. And I don't see where I come into this.
INSPECTOR:	She was employed in your works at one time.
BIRLING:	Oh — that's it, is it? Well, we've several hundred young women there, y'know, and they keep changing.
INSPECTOR:	This young woman, Eva Smith, was a bit out of the ordinary. I found a photograph of her in her lodgings. Perhaps you'd remember her from that.

The extract continues on the next page.

Worked Practice Question

Worked Practice Question

> INSPECTOR *takes a photograph, about postcard size, out of his pocket and goes to* BIRLING. *Both* GERALD *and* ERIC *rise to have a look at the photograph, but the* INSPECTOR *interposes himself between them and the photograph. They are surprised and rather annoyed.* BIRLING *stares hard, and with recognition, at the photograph, which the* INSPECTOR *then replaces in his pocket.*
>
> GERALD: [*showing annoyance*] Any particular reason why I shouldn't see this girl's photograph, Inspector?
> INSPECTOR: [*coolly, looking hard at him*] There might be.

1. How does J B Priestley present the character of Inspector Goole in this extract?

When writing an essay, always start by writing a plan.
Below is an example of how you would plan an answer to this question.

PLAN

Try to divide your answer up into two or three logical parts

AUTHORITATIVE

* calm when talking about gory details — "Burnt her inside out, of course."

* controls the conversation, e.g. interrupting Mr Birling ("cutting through")

* won't let Gerald or Eric see the photograph until he's ready

INTELLIGENT

* knows a lot about Mr Birling already — "She was employed in your works..."

* asks questions to confirm what he already knows, not to get new info.

MYSTERIOUS

* how does Goole know so much about the Birlings already?

* doesn't make his intentions immediately clear — "There might be."

CONCLUSION: Goole commands the respect of the Birling family due to his authority and intelligence, but his true intentions remain mysterious.

Practice Question

Think you know your stuff? Time to prove it by having a go at this practice question.

Practice Question

The following extract is taken from the play *Death of a Salesman* by Arthur Miller. The play's main character, Willy Loman, has gradually been losing his mind despite the support of his wife, Linda, and his two sons, Biff and Happy. Not long before the start of the extract, he comes up with the idea of killing himself so that his family can benefit from the insurance money.

LINDA: [*calling*] Willy, you coming up?

WILLY: [*uttering a gasp of fear, whirling about as if to quiet her*] Sh! [*He turns around as if to find his way; sounds, faces, voices, seem to be swarming in upon him and he flicks at them, crying,*] 'Sh!, Sh!' [*Suddenly music, faint and high, stops him. It rises in intensity, almost to an unbearable scream. He goes up and down on his toes, and rushes off around the house.*] Shhh!

LINDA: Willy?

[*There is no answer. LINDA waits. BIFF gets up off his bed. He is still in his clothes. HAPPY sits up. BIFF stands listening.*]

LINDA: [*with real fear*] Willy, answer me! Willy!

[*There is the sound of a car starting and moving away at full speed.*]

LINDA: No!

BIFF: [*rushing down the stairs*] Pop!

[*As the car speeds off, the music crashes down in a frenzy of sound, which becomes the soft pulsation of a single cello string. BIFF slowly returns to his bedroom. He and HAPPY gravely don their jackets. LINDA slowly walks out of her room. The music has developed into a dead march. The leaves of day are appearing over everything. CHARLEY and BERNARD, sombrely dressed, appear and knock on the kitchen door. BIFF and HAPPY slowly descend the stairs to the kitchen as CHARLEY and BERNARD enter. All stop a moment when LINDA, in clothes of mourning, bearing a little bunch of roses, comes through the draped doorway into the kitchen. She goes to CHARLEY and takes his arm. Now all move toward the audience, through the wall-line of the kitchen. At the limit of the apron*, LINDA lays down the flowers, kneels, and sits back on her heels. All stare down at the grave.*]

*apron — part of a stage that sticks out into the audience

1. Death of a Salesman

In this extract, we see Willy Loman's last moments before his death.

How does Arthur Miller use stage directions to create an atmosphere before and after Willy Loman's death?
Support your ideas by referring to the extract.

Revision Summary for Section Nine

Reading plays can be a little intimidating — especially if you're not used to it. Just read this section and have a go, and you'll soon start to get the hang of it, bit by bit. Make sure you've learned this section well enough to answer all the questions below.

1) Fill in the missing word.
   "A novel tells a story by describing it to you. A play tells a story by _____ it to you."

2) What is the word for all of the actors who appear in a play?

3) How do you know who is supposed to be saying a line in a script?

4) Who might decide how the characters should say their lines?

5) Why might some lines in a play be written in non-Standard English?

6) What is a monologue?

7) What is an aside?

8) Give four ways you can learn about characters in a play.

9) Give two ways a director could suggest a play is set in the past.

10) What can the audience learn by looking at the set?

   a) how long the play is going to last
   b) where the action is taking place
   c) what the characters are thinking

11) What name is given to the objects used by actors while they perform?

12) What effect might music have in a play?

Background Information

On to Shakespeare now. You'll almost certainly study a Shakespeare play at KS3, so the stuff in this section is well worth knowing.

Shakespearean Scripts look Similar to Modern Scripts

1) William Shakespeare was a playwright who lived between 1564-1616.

2) Although he wrote his plays a long time ago, his scripts are set out in a similar way to modern scripts — the character's names are written down the left-hand side of the script, and their dialogue is written on the right-hand side.

3) Shakespeare uses stage directions too, but fewer than modern plays.

4) Like modern plays, Shakespeare's plays are broken down into acts and scenes.

Remind yourself about scripts on p.120.

Shakespeare wrote Three Kinds of Play

Shakespeare wrote three main kinds of play.

1) TRAGEDIES

These have serious plots and contain a lot of sadness. They often tackle big topics like love, war and death. Characters usually die at the end, e.g. *Macbeth* and *Romeo and Juliet*.

2) HISTORIES

These are based on real historical events. e.g. *Henry V* and *Richard III*.

3) COMEDIES

These are more funny and light-hearted. The characters and events are often exaggerated for comic effect. Characters usually get married at the end. e.g. *The Tempest, A Midsummer Night's Dream, Much Ado About Nothing, Twelfth Night.*

Some plays might fit into more than one genre — for example 'Julius Caesar' is a history and a tragedy.

Theatre was an Important Part of Shakespearean Society

There's more about context on p.141.

1) Shakespeare was writing more than 400 years ago so things were different back then.

2) The theatre was very popular in Shakespeare's time. There was no TV or internet — going to the theatre was one of the main forms of entertainment.

3) Both the rich and the poor went to the theatre — so Shakespeare's plays had to appeal to a wide audience.

4) Women weren't allowed to perform onstage — female roles were played by young men.

5) The stage was often quite bare, and actors relied on a few props rather than fancy scenery to help them tell the story.

Drawn by George Vielm

© Granger/REX/Shutterstock

Shakespearean theatre was enjoyed by all members of society

Many of the poorer members of Shakespearean society couldn't read, so theatres couldn't advertise their plays using posters. Instead, they'd fly a flag from the theatre to let people know a play would be performed that day — a white flag for a comedy, a black flag for a tragedy and a red flag for a history.

Shakespeare's Language

Shakespeare's language can be a bit <u>confusing</u> — there are lots of <u>unfamiliar words</u> which can make it tricky to know what's going on. Here are some tips to help you work out what's happening.

Look out for **Missing Letters**

1) Shakespeare often runs two words together and <u>misses out letters</u> to make them fit on one line.
2) There's usually an <u>apostrophe</u> to show where the missing letter should be.

GONZALO	— And were the king on't, what would I do?
SEBASTIAN	'Scape being drunk, for want of wine.
GONZALO	I'th' commonwealth I would by contraries

'on't' = 'on it'
"Scape' = 'escape'
'I'th" = 'In the'

The Tempest, Act 2, Scene 1

Shakespeare used different **Pronouns**

1) In Shakespeare's day, there were different words for '<u>you</u>'.
2) People used 'thou' for people they were more <u>familiar</u> or <u>friendly</u> with, and they used 'you' to be more <u>formal</u>.

thou = you   thy = your
thee = you   thine = your

LADY MACBETH	Against those honours deep and broad wherewith <u>Your</u> majesty loads our house

Lady Macbeth is speaking to King Duncan so she uses 'Your' to show <u>respect</u>.

Macbeth, Act 1, Scene 6

LADY MACBETH	Art <u>thou</u> afeard To be the same in <u>thine</u> own act and valour, As <u>thou</u> art in desire?

Lady Macbeth is speaking to her husband, Macbeth, so she uses the <u>less formal</u> pronouns 'thou' and 'thine'.

Macbeth, Act 1, Scene 7

Some **Unfamiliar Words** crop up a lot

1) Verbs often look a bit <u>different</u> too...

thou art = you are   thou wilt = you will
thou hast = you have   thou canst = you can

You usually just need to remove the 't' or 'st' from the end to make the verb look more familiar.

© Merrick Morton/20th Century Fox/Kobal/REX/Shutterstock

2) And here are some more words to <u>watch out for</u>:

hie = go quickly	wherefore = why	thence = from there	sooth = in fact
hither = to here	whence = from where	ere = before	prithee = please

REVISION TASK

When it comes to understanding Shakespeare, practice makes perfect

Grab a copy of the Shakespeare play you're studying and try to spot examples of all the things mentioned on this page. You'll be fluent in Shakespeare before you know it...

Shakespeare's Sentence Structure

It's not just the <u>unfamiliar words</u> that can make Shakespeare <u>tricky</u> to decipher — the sentences can be confusing too. But fear not, this page has it covered...

Characters speak in **Both Prose** and **Verse**

<u>Not all</u> of the characters in Shakespeare's plays speak <u>the same way</u>. In fact, you might notice that they speak in <u>three</u> different ways depending on the <u>situation</u>...

> Go back to pages 109 and 111 to remind yourself about rhyme and rhythm.

1) PROSE

<u>Prose</u> is just another word for <u>ordinary speech</u>. It follows no clear pattern of <u>rhyme</u> or <u>rhythm</u>.

2) BLANK VERSE

<u>Blank verse</u> is when words follow a set <u>rhythm</u> but <u>don't rhyme</u>. This sounds <u>grander</u> than prose and is often used by <u>posher</u> characters.

3) RHYMED VERSE

<u>Rhymed verse</u> is <u>even grander</u>. If the lines spoken by a character start to <u>rhyme</u>, you know what they're saying is <u>really important</u>.

When you're reading verse, <u>don't</u> stop just because you've reached the <u>end of a line</u>. Sentences can carry on for <u>multiple lines</u>, so only pause when you come to <u>punctuation</u> like a comma or full stop.

Different Rhythms can show **Different Emotions**

Shakespeare uses <u>sentence structure</u> and <u>punctuation</u> to change the <u>pace</u> and <u>rhythm</u> of dialogue.

ROMEO   News from Verona! How now, Balthasar!
         Dost thou not bring me letters from the Friar?
         How doth my lady? Is my father well?

Romeo and Juliet, Act 5, Scene 1

Romeo's dialogue is made up of <u>short exclamations</u> and <u>questions</u>. This <u>speeds up</u> the <u>pace</u> of the dialogue to show how <u>excited</u> he is to receive news from Balthasar.

MACBETH   Why do you show me this? — A fourth? Start, eyes!
           What, will the line stretch out to th'crack of doom?

Macbeth, Act 4, Scene 1

Shakespeare uses <u>punctuation</u> to <u>break up</u> the <u>rhythm</u> of the dialogue. This shows Macbeth's <u>fear</u> and <u>disbelief</u> at seeing Banquo's ghost.

Look out for words in a **Strange Order**

1) Another reason Shakespeare can be tricky to understand is the <u>long</u>, <u>complicated</u> sentences.

2) Sometimes the words can be in a <u>strange order</u>, too.

OLIVIA   What meanest thou, by that, Malvolio?

Twelfth Night, Act 3, Scene 4

Olivia says, 'What mean you, by that?' which is easier to understand when rearranged to, 'What do you mean by that?'

3) Occasionally the words are in an unusual order to <u>highlight</u> a particular word.

JULIET   Poison, I see, hath been his timeless end

Romeo and Juliet, Act 5, Scene 3

Putting the word 'Poison' at the <u>start</u> of the sentence gives it <u>extra emphasis</u>.

REVISION TASK

Don't be confused by strange sentence structures

Have a go at rewriting these sentences from *Twelfth Night* into modern English:
"What sayest thou?"   "Thou know'st not me."   "Hie thee."

Shakespeare's Techniques

On to techniques now. Here are two for you to learn — <u>soliloquies</u> and <u>dramatic irony</u>...

Sometimes characters **Talk** to **Themselves**

1) Characters sometimes <u>talk to themselves</u> so the audience can hear what they're <u>thinking</u> and <u>feeling</u>. They're talking for the <u>benefit</u> of the audience — so it's slightly different from a <u>monologue</u> (p.121).

2) When characters do this, it's called a <u>soliloquy</u>. Soliloquies are important because when characters talk to each other, they sometimes <u>lie</u> — but when they talk to themselves, they're saying what they <u>really</u> think.

ROMEO: O, she doth teach the torches to burn bright!
It seems she hangs upon the cheek of night
Like a rich jewel in an Ethiop's ear;
Beauty too rich for use, for earth too dear!
So shows a snowy dove trooping with crows,
As yonder lady o'er her fellows shows.
The measure done, I'll watch her place of stand,
And, touching hers, make blessed my rude hand.
Did my heart love till now? forswear it, sight!
For I ne'er saw true beauty till this night.

Romeo and Juliet, Act 1, Scene 5

Romeo isn't <u>actually</u> talking <u>to</u> anyone — he's just <u>overwhelmed</u> by Juliet's beauty. Because Romeo's talking to himself, it makes his feelings seem <u>genuine</u>.

Romeo's soliloquy is in <u>rhymed verse</u>. This gives more <u>significance</u> to what he's saying and makes his love for Juliet seem more <u>believable</u>.

Dramatic Irony can be used for **Different Effects**

1) <u>Dramatic irony</u> is when the audience knows something that the characters <u>don't</u>.

2) Dramatic irony can be used to create <u>humour</u>.

In *Twelfth Night*, Malvolio flirts with Olivia after he finds a love letter he thinks she's written to him. The audience knows that the love letter was actually a trick.

Malvolio is an <u>arrogant</u> character so the audience would find it <u>funny</u> that he'd been tricked into thinking that Olivia loved him.

3) It can also be used to create <u>tension</u>.

In *Romeo and Juliet*, Romeo thinks that Juliet is dead. The audience know that she's not really dead, she's just taken a sleeping potion.

Romeo visits Juliet's tomb. This increases the <u>suspense</u> — the audience hopes that Juliet wakes up before Romeo kills himself. The fact that Juliet isn't dead makes Romeo's suicide even more <u>tragic</u>.

 KEY TERM ## Dramatic irony and soliloquies crop up loads in Shakespeare...

... so make sure you can remember what they are and how to spell them. Have a go at finding an example of each in the play you're studying and think about the effect they have.

Shakespeare's Techniques

The dialogue in most modern plays is meant to sound as realistic as possible, so there are rarely any fancy techniques. Shakespeare's plays, on the other hand, are chock-full of 'em...

Shakespeare uses lots of Imagery

If you need a reminder about figurative language, have a look at pages 32-4.

Shakespeare uses imagery for different effects.

| MACBETH | Life's but a walking shadow |

Macbeth, Act 5, Scene 5

Macbeth has just found out his wife is dead. Shakespeare uses this metaphor to show how distressed Macbeth feels.

| JULIET | My bounty is as boundless as the sea, My love as deep; the more I give to thee The more I have, for both are infinite. |

Romeo and Juliet, Act 2, Scene 2

Juliet compares her love for Romeo to the sea using an epic simile. She does this to show just how much she loves Romeo.

An epic simile is an extended simile that runs over several lines.

| BENEDICK | She speaks poniards and every word stabs |

Much Ado About Nothing, Act 2, Scene 1

Benedick personifies Beatrice's words as daggers (poniards) which stab him. This emphasises how hurt Benedick is by what Beatrice says.

Puns are often used to create Humour

A pun is a word or phrase that's used deliberately because it has more than one meaning.

1) Shakespeare uses a lot of puns. Puns are used in comedies to add to the light-hearted tone.

| BOTTOM | this is to make an ass of me; |

A Midsummer Night's Dream, Act 3, Scene 1

Bottom has just has been given the head of a donkey. Bottom thinks that the other characters are making a fool of him, but 'ass' is another word for 'donkey'.

| ORSINO | That instant I was turn'd into a hart; And my desires, like fell and cruel hounds, E'er since pursue me. |

Twelfth Night, Act 1, Scene 1

Orsino compares falling in love to being hunted like a deer. A 'hart' is a male deer, but it also sounds like 'heart'.

2) ... and they're used in tragedies to provide a bit of dark humour.

| MERCUTIO | you shall find me a grave man |

Romeo and Juliet, Act 3, Scene 1

Mercutio has just been stabbed. He's making a pun on the word 'grave' which can mean both 'serious' and 'a place where a dead body is buried'.

3) Certain characters (like Mercutio in *Romeo and Juliet* and Beatrice in *Much Ado About Nothing*) use lots of puns — this is often a sign that a character is witty and intelligent.

4) Lower class characters often use puns to make crude jokes (like the Nurse in *Romeo and Juliet*) or to insult each another.

Make sure you know your metaphors from your similes

KEY TERM

Metaphors and similes are quite similar, so make sure you know the difference between them. Puns can be a bit hard to spot in Shakespeare, but that doesn't mean you shouldn't try.

Shakespeare's Techniques

Here are a few more techniques — <u>foreshadowing</u>, <u>oxymorons</u> and <u>rhetorical questions</u>. You should already be familiar with them, but flick back if you need a reminder.

Foreshadowing hints at things that are going to happen Later

1) Shakespeare uses quite a lot of <u>foreshadowing</u> (see p.92), especially in his <u>tragedies</u>.

2) Foreshadowing can have several <u>different effects</u>. For example, it can increase the <u>tension</u> in a play.

> MACBETH   Bloody instructions, which being taught, return
>   To plague th'inventor.
>
> *Macbeth, Act 1, Scene 7*

Macbeth comments that murderers often end up being killed themselves. This <u>foreshadows</u> his own <u>murder</u> — it increases suspense by hinting that something <u>bad</u> will happen to Macbeth.

3) Sometimes it can give the audience <u>information</u> that will help them to <u>understand</u> something that comes <u>later</u> in the play.

> FRIAR LAWRENCE   Within the infant rind of this small flower
>   Poison hath residence and medicine power
>
> *Romeo and Juliet, Act 2, Scene 3*

The Friar <u>explains</u> that plants can <u>kill</u>. This <u>foreshadows</u> the <u>deaths</u> at the end of the play.

Oxymorons are Contradictions

If you need a reminder about what oxymorons are, go to p.35.

1) Oxymorons can be used to create <u>humour</u>...

> THESEUS   A <u>tedious brief</u> scene of young Pyramus
>   And his love Thisbe, very <u>tragical mirth</u>.
>
> *A Midsummer Night's Dream, Act 5, Scene 1*

Theseus describes the play 'Pyramus and Thisbe' using <u>oxymorons</u> — "tedious brief" (which means 'long short') and "tragical mirth" (which means 'sad happiness'). The play itself is a bit of a <u>mess</u>, so the audience would find this <u>contradictory</u> description <u>amusing</u>.

2) ... or <u>mixed emotions</u>.

The Macbeths have just killed King Duncan in order to make Macbeth king. The Macbeths are <u>happy</u> they've got what they wanted, but the <u>oxymoron</u> "doubtful joy" suggests their happiness is tinged with <u>guilt</u>.

> LADY MACBETH   dwell in doubtful joy
>
> *Macbeth, Act 3, Scene 2*

Rhetorical Questions are questions that don't need an Answer

<u>Rhetorical questions</u> (see p.36) can show that a character is <u>confused</u>.

> HERMIA   Am not I Hermia? Are not you Lysander?
>
> *A Midsummer Night's Dream, Act 3, Scene 2*

Lysander has been <u>bewitched</u> and falls in love with someone else and Hermia can't understand what's happened. The rhetorical questions show her <u>confusion</u>.

KEY TERM

Learn how Shakespeare uses these techniques...

Spotting a technique is the first step. You've also got to think about the <u>effect</u> that it has on the audience. There are <u>loads</u> more effects than the ones mentioned on this page.

Structure

Right, now it's time to look at how Shakespeare's plays are structured...

The **Structure** of a play will have an **Effect** on the **Audience**

1) The structure is how the scenes are put together to reveal the plot.

2) Shakespeare didn't just put his scenes in a random order — he thought carefully about the structure of events and the effect they would have on the audience.

3) Most of Shakespeare's plays can be split into key scenes and minor scenes. Key scenes are usually about the main plot or characters, whereas minor scenes usually feature minor characters. They're used to develop a sub-plot, add humour or to increase the pace or tension.

A sub-plot is just a less important plot, for example, Caliban trying to murder Prospero in 'The Tempest'.

4) Key scenes tend to be quite long. Here's an example:

Act 2, Scene 2 in *Romeo and Juliet* is quite long. This scene is where Romeo and Juliet declare their love for each other and decide to get married. This scene has to be long enough for the audience to be convinced that the characters have fallen in love — it's the only time the two are alone for long. If this scene was short, it would make what happens in the rest of the play less believable.

5) Minor scenes are quite short. Here's an example:

Act 4, Scene 4 in *Romeo and Juliet* is very short. It's a light-hearted scene where Juliet's parents joke with each other — they're excited for Juliet and Paris's wedding. The scene ends with the Nurse being sent upstairs to get Juliet. This short scene increases the tension because the audience knows Juliet drank the sleeping potion in the previous scene, and her parents are about to find Juliet's lifeless body.

Most plays have a **Turning Point**

Some plays have more than one turning point.

A turning point is an important event which changes the direction of the plot. Usually the first part of a play will build up to a turning point, and the second half will deal with the consequences of the turning point.

Act 4, Scene 1 of *Much Ado About Nothing*, is a turning point — Claudio calls off his wedding to Hero because he's been tricked into thinking that she has been seeing other men. The remainder of the play focuses on Claudio learning the truth before being reunited with Hero.

The **Beginnings** and **Endings** are **Important** too

1) The scenes at the start of a play will often set the tone or introduce a key theme.

2) Act 1, Scene 1 of *Romeo and Juliet* introduces the feud between the Montagues and the Capulets. This sets a violent tone and introduces the theme of conflict.

3) The scenes at the end of a play are important too — they need to make the audience feel a certain emotion. Tragedies often leave the audience feeling sad, whereas comedies will end on a happy note.

© Alastair Muir/REX/Shutterstock

Don't ignore the structure

Take the Shakespeare play you're studying and find examples of key scenes, minor scenes and turning points. Make some notes about what effect they have on the plot and the audience.

Structure

Here's an example of how a play can be broken down into <u>key scenes</u>, <u>minor scenes</u> and <u>turning points</u>.

The first part is structured around Macbeth's **Rise To Power**

Key Scenes In Acts 1 and 2 the <u>key scenes</u> are focused on Macbeth becoming <u>King</u>. The plot gradually <u>builds up</u> until the <u>murder</u> of <u>Duncan</u> is discovered and Macbeth is <u>crowned</u>.

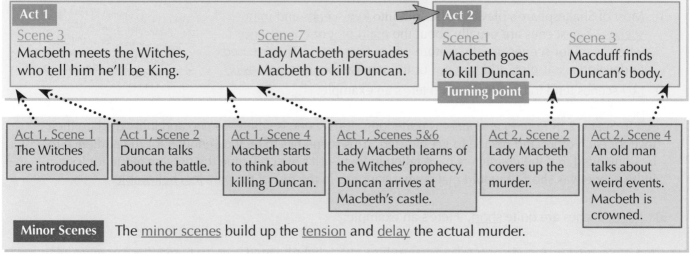

Act 1

<u>Scene 3</u>
Macbeth meets the Witches, who tell him he'll be King.

<u>Scene 7</u>
Lady Macbeth persuades Macbeth to kill Duncan.

Act 2

<u>Scene 1</u>
Macbeth goes to kill Duncan.
Turning point

<u>Scene 3</u>
Macduff finds Duncan's body.

<u>Act 1, Scene 1</u>
The Witches are introduced.

<u>Act 1, Scene 2</u>
Duncan talks about the battle.

<u>Act 1, Scene 4</u>
Macbeth starts to think about killing Duncan.

<u>Act 1, Scenes 5&6</u>
Lady Macbeth learns of the Witches' prophecy. Duncan arrives at Macbeth's castle.

<u>Act 2, Scene 2</u>
Lady Macbeth covers up the murder.

<u>Act 2, Scene 4</u>
An old man talks about weird events. Macbeth is crowned.

Minor Scenes The <u>minor scenes</u> build up the <u>tension</u> and <u>delay</u> the actual murder.

In the second part, **Things Fall Apart** for Macbeth

Key Scenes In Acts 3, 4 and 5, the other characters learn how <u>evil</u> Macbeth is, and start to <u>plot against him</u>. This builds up to the climactic <u>rebellion</u> in the final act.

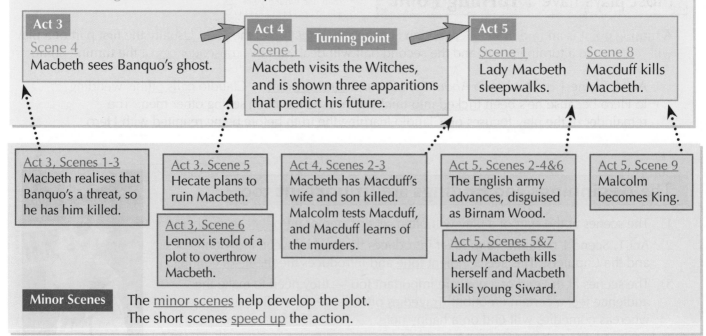

Act 3

<u>Scene 4</u>
Macbeth sees Banquo's ghost.

Act 4

<u>Scene 1</u>
Macbeth visits the Witches, and is shown three apparitions that predict his future.
Turning point

Act 5

<u>Scene 1</u>
Lady Macbeth sleepwalks.

<u>Scene 8</u>
Macduff kills Macbeth.

<u>Act 3, Scenes 1-3</u>
Macbeth realises that Banquo's a threat, so he has him killed.

<u>Act 3, Scene 5</u>
Hecate plans to ruin Macbeth.

<u>Act 3, Scene 6</u>
Lennox is told of a plot to overthrow Macbeth.

<u>Act 4, Scenes 2-3</u>
Macbeth has Macduff's wife and son killed. Malcolm tests Macduff, and Macduff learns of the murders.

<u>Act 5, Scenes 2-4&6</u>
The English army advances, disguised as Birnam Wood.

<u>Act 5, Scenes 5&7</u>
Lady Macbeth kills herself and Macbeth kills young Siward.

<u>Act 5, Scene 9</u>
Malcolm becomes King.

Minor Scenes The <u>minor scenes</u> help develop the plot. The short scenes <u>speed up</u> the action.

Make your own structure plan for the play you're studying

Using the structure plan above, make your own version for the play you're studying. You need to categorise the key scenes and the minor scenes and think about the effect on the audience.

Performance

On to performance now. There's plenty of info about sets, props, costumes and, of course, the actors.

Shakespeare uses Dialogue, Props and Sound Effects to set the scene

1) When Shakespeare's plays were first performed, the stage was often bare — there wasn't much scenery.

2) This meant that Shakespeare had to set the scene using dialogue, props and sound effects instead to give the audience a clear picture of where the action was taking place.

> Shakespeare uses sound effects to show that there is a storm. The characters (the Master = ship's captain, and Boatswain = deckhand) suggest that the action is taking place on a ship.

A tempestuous noise of thunder and lightning heard. Enter a MASTER and a BOATSWAIN

The Tempest, Act 1, Scene 1

Enter BEATRICE, who hides in the bower

Much Ado About Nothing, Act 3, Scene 1

> The actor playing Beatrice would use a leafy branch as a prop to show that the scene is set in an orchard and she is hiding amongst the trees.

3) In the 1600s, there wasn't any electricity. This meant that plays had to be performed in open-air theatres during the afternoon to allow enough light for the audiences and actors to see.

4) This meant if the action onstage was supposed to be happening at night, the actors' dialogue would have to communicate this to the audience rather than using lighting or special effects.

FIRST MURDERER   The west yet glimmers with some streaks of day

Macbeth, Act 3, Scene 3

> The first murderer says that the sun is setting which tells the audience that this scene is happening in the dark.

The audience could tell a lot about characters based on their Costumes

1) Unlike sets, costumes were very important to Elizabethan theatre companies.

2) The audience could tell a lot about a character just by looking at their clothes, so it was important to get the costumes right.

3) There were strict laws about what people could wear in Elizabethan times, and a person's clothes reflected their social status. Wealthy members of society would wear luxurious fabrics such as silk, velvet and lace, whereas the poorer members of society would wear simple fabrics, such as cotton. Shakespeare would have dressed his characters in clothes that matched their social status.

© Alastair Muir/REX/Shutterstock

4) Costumes could also give information about a character's occupation. For example, actors playing soldiers would have probably worn armour.

5) Because women weren't allowed to act on stage, all the female characters were played by men. This meant that actors used dresses, make up and wigs to look as convincing as possible.

6) Sometimes audience members had to use their imaginations though — characters might 'disguise' themselves just by putting on a different hat.

7) Shakespeare didn't usually specify what characters should wear in his stage directions, however there are some exceptions.

MALVOLIO   "Remember who commanded thy yellow stockings —"

Twelfth Night, Act 3, Scene 4

> Malvolio is tricked into wearing yellow stockings. It's an important part of the play, so the character playing Malvolio should wear yellow stockings.

Performance

Actors help plays to Come To Life

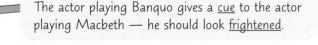

1) Shakespeare <u>didn't</u> include many stage directions — most just tell actors when to <u>enter</u> and <u>exit</u> the stage.

2) It's likely that Shakespeare didn't use many stage directions because he wrote his parts with certain actors <u>in mind</u>. He would have left the performance of these roles <u>up to the actor</u>.

3) Occasionally, Shakespeare included <u>cues</u> in the dialogue.

> BANQUO   why do you start and seem to <u>fear</u>
>
> *Macbeth, Act 1, Scene 3*

The actor playing Banquo gives a <u>cue</u> to the actor playing Macbeth — he should look <u>frightened</u>.

Actors use their Voices and Bodies to tell the story

1) Shakespeare, like modern directors, wanted the audience to <u>feel</u> a certain way during a performance. If it's a <u>comedy</u>, he wanted the audience to <u>laugh</u>. If it's a <u>tragedy</u>, he wanted the audience to be <u>moved</u>.

2) Actors can show these <u>different emotions</u> by saying their lines in a <u>certain way</u>...

Lady Capulet thinks Juliet is <u>dead</u>. The actor playing Lady Capulet would say these lines with a lot of <u>distress</u> to show how <u>distraught</u> she is.

> LADY CAPULET   O me, O me! My child, my only life,
> Revive, look up or I will die with thee!
>
> *Romeo and Juliet, Act 4, Scene 5*

3) ... by changing the <u>pace</u> of their speech ...

> BENEDICK   Well, you are a rare parrot-teacher.
> BEATRICE   A bird of my tongue is better than a beast of yours.
>
> *Much Ado About Nothing, Act 1, Scene 1*

Benedick and Beatrice exchange insults a lot in *Much Ado About Nothing*. The <u>pace</u> of their dialogue might be quite <u>quick</u> to show the speed of their <u>wit</u>.

4) ... or by using <u>facial expressions</u>, <u>actions</u> and <u>body language</u>.

Lady Macbeth is sleepwalking and trying to wash imaginary <u>blood</u> from her hands. The actor playing this part might <u>scrub</u> and <u>scratch</u> her hands <u>furiously</u> to show how <u>distressed</u> Lady Macbeth is.

> LADY MACBETH   Out, damned spot! Out, I say!
>
> *Macbeth, Act 5, Scene 1*

Some Scenes can be Interpreted in Different Ways

Because there are so <u>few</u> stage directions in Shakespeare's plays, modern directors have a lot of <u>flexibility</u> — they can interpret the <u>scenes</u> and <u>characters</u> in <u>different</u> ways.

In Act 4, Scene 2 of *Twelfth Night*, Maria and Feste lock Malvolio in a dark room and pretend that he has gone <u>mad</u>. This scene can be directed in a <u>comical</u> way (a silly <u>prank</u> played by Maria and Feste) or it can be performed in a much <u>darker</u> way (Maria and Feste are <u>tormenting</u> Malvolio by questioning his sanity).

© Donald Cooper/REX/Shutterstock

Lots to learn on these pages...

It's not enough to say that Shakespearean theatre was different to modern theatre — you must give examples.

Context

Shakespeare's plays were written over 400 years ago so things were quite different back then...

Life was **Different** in **Shakespearean Society**

Remember that things have changed a lot since Shakespeare was writing — plus he set some of his plays even further back in the past. It helps to know a bit more about what life was like when Shakespeare was writing his plays and how his audiences would have reacted.

CLASS

1) There was a very clear class structure in the 1600s — the king or queen at the top, followed by the aristocracy (dukes, earls etc), then wealthy landowners / merchants and commoners at the bottom.

2) Lots of Shakespeare's main characters are nobles — e.g. the Thanes in *Macbeth*, Prospero (the Duke of Milan) from *The Tempest* and Theseus (the Duke of Athens) from *A Midsummer Night's Dream*.

3) There are lower-class characters too, but they have smaller roles — Maria (*Twelfth Night*) is a servant, the Nurse from *Romeo and Juliet* and Balthasar (*Much Ado About Nothing*) is a footman.

WOMEN

1) Shakespearean women were expected to be quiet and obedient. Young girls were expected to obey their fathers, and then obey their husbands when they married. In *Romeo and Juliet*, Juliet's father demands that Juliet marries Paris. The fact that she defies her father to marry Romeo would have been very shocking to Shakespearean audiences.

2) Women were expected to be virgins when they got married — Hero is accused of not being a virgin during her wedding to Claudio and the wedding is called off.

3) Marriages between members of the upper classes were often treated like business deals — a marriage was an opportunity for families to gain more money or power.

4) However, Shakespeare liked to question gender roles and wasn't afraid to create strong, outspoken female characters such as Beatrice (*Much Ado About Nothing*) or Lady Macbeth (*Macbeth*). Shakespearean audiences may have found these characters surprising.

5) Queen Elizabeth I, who was only the second woman to rule England, was on the throne for much of Shakespeare's life, so she may have inspired his powerful female roles.

RELIGION

1) Religion was an important part of life in Shakespeare's day — almost everyone believed in God and went to church on Sunday. In *Romeo and Juliet*, the characters go to Friar Lawrence for advice — this shows the importance of the Church in everyday life.

2) Marriage ceremonies were religious affairs and were always conducted in a church. It wasn't unusual for couples to marry not long after meeting, so Shakespearean audiences wouldn't have found the marriages too sudden at the end of *Much Ado About Nothing* and *Twelfth Night*.

THE SUPERNATURAL

There's more about the theme of the supernatural on p.148.

1) People in the 1600s believed in the supernatural a lot more than today. Shakespearean audiences would've taken supernatural characters seriously.

2) These supernatural forces could be evil, like the Witches (*Macbeth*); mischievous like Puck (*A Midsummer Night's Dream*); or good like Ariel (*The Tempest*).

Make sure you know a bit about the context

Think about the Shakespeare plays you're studying and sort all the characters into the class categories mentioned above. Flick to pages 142-4 to learn about the different types of character.

Characters

Shakespeare's plays are full of different characters, but some of them share some similarities.

Romantic Heroes can be Passionate in different ways

1) Romantic heroes typically have something that makes them stand out from the other characters in the play — they usually go against society's conventions and have a strong sense of individuality.

2) Romeo from *Romeo and Juliet* is one of the clearest examples of a romantic hero in Shakespeare's plays. He goes against what is expected by falling in love with Juliet (who is a Capulet), and his love for her is incredibly passionate — they fall in love at first sight and they get married very quickly.

3) Romantic heroes often use exaggerated language and imagery to express their love or passionate feelings.

> ROMEO   But soft, what light through yonder window breaks?
>   It is the east and Juliet is the sun!

Romeo compares Juliet to the sun. This exaggeration makes it seem as though his entire world is lit up by her presence.

Romeo and Juliet, Act 2, Scene 2

4) Benedick from *Much Ado about Nothing* is a very different type of romantic hero. Unlike Romeo, he goes against conventions because he rejects the traditional ideas of love and marriage — he jokingly tells Don Pedro to shoot him if he ever falls in love. Despite this, he falls in love with Beatrice and they are engaged to be married by the end of the play.

Flawed Heroes have one or more key Weaknesses

1) Unsurprisingly, flawed heroes are characters that have considerable flaws or weaknesses.

2) These weaknesses are usually traits that we see a lot in real life — flawed heroes can be ambitious, impulsive, controlling etc.

3) However, these traits are often exaggerated in flawed heroes. Lots of people are ambitious, but Macbeth's "Vaulting ambition" leads him to commit terrible crimes, including murder, just so that he can become king.

4) Tragic flaws often lead to the death of the hero. Romeo's flaw is his impulsiveness — he doesn't think about the consequences of his actions. At the end of the play, Romeo hastily drinks the poison before he has time to realise that Juliet faked her own death.

5) A flawed hero doesn't always have to die. Throughout *The Tempest*, Prospero controls and manipulates the other characters on the island. However, by the end of the play, he realises that it's better to show mercy and kindness to his enemies.

© Donald Cooper/REX/Shutterstock

> PROSPERO   This airy charm is for, I'll break my staff,
>   Bury it certain fathoms in the earth,
>   And deeper than did ever plummet sound
>   I'll drown my book.

Prospero uses his magical staff to control and manipulate others. By breaking it, he shows that he understands this flaw — this realisation leads to his redemption rather than his death.

The Tempest, Act 5, Scene 1

Some characters might fit into more than one of these 'types'

Romeo is both a romantic and a flawed hero. His passionate love for his enemy's daughter makes him a romantic hero, but he also has an impulsive nature, which eventually leads to his downfall.

Characters

There's even more information about Shakespeare's characters on these pages.

Shakespeare created lots of **Strong Female Characters**

1) Shakespeare often used his plays to <u>question</u> the traditional <u>gender roles</u> of the time.

There's more about gender on p.141.

2) Shakespearean audiences would have expected women to be <u>obedient</u> and <u>reserved</u>, but Shakespeare created <u>strong</u> female characters that would have <u>surprised audiences</u>.

3) This strength comes in <u>different forms</u> — there isn't one type of strong female in Shakespeare's plays.

4) Some characters show their strength through their <u>kindness</u>:

> Titania in *A Midsummer Night's Dream* is a <u>proud</u> and <u>gracious</u> Queen. She showed <u>kindness</u> by adopting a young Indian prince when his mother died. When Oberon tries to take the prince away from her, Titania's feeling of responsibility leads her to <u>protect him</u> and she <u>refuses to give him up</u>.

5) Other characters show strength by <u>going against</u> what is <u>expected</u> of them:

> Viola in *Twelfth Night* goes against expectations by <u>dressing as a man</u> after the shipwreck — her strong will and quick-thinking allow her to <u>take control</u> of her future. Beatrice in *Much Ado About Nothing* doesn't do what's expected of her either — she <u>refuses to be married off</u>. She is out-spoken and witty, and although she falls in love with Benedick at the end of the play, she does so <u>on her own terms</u>.

6) Strength is also shown through a character's level of <u>power</u> and <u>control</u>:

> At the beginning of *Macbeth*, Lady Macbeth is in <u>control</u> of Macbeth's actions — she is presented as the <u>stronger</u>, more 'masculine' character. She mocks Macbeth for his lack of courage and even <u>persuades him</u> to murder Duncan.

These are just a few examples of strong female characters — there are lots more.

Shakespearean **Villains** are often complicated characters

1) Most Shakespeare plays have a <u>villain</u> — a character who performs <u>evil</u>, <u>cruel</u> or <u>immoral</u> acts.

2) The <u>majority</u> of these villains are <u>complex characters</u>. An exception is Don John from *Much Ado About Nothing* — even though he has a big impact on the play's plot, he's fairly <u>one-dimensional</u> — he's purely villainous without a lot of hidden depth.

> DON JOHN   I cannot hide what I am:

Don John knows he's a villain — he <u>can't hide</u> his <u>evil thoughts</u> and <u>actions</u>.

Much Ado About Nothing, Act 1, Scene 3

© Moviestore Collection/REX/Shutterstock

3) The level of <u>villainous behaviour</u> varies from play to play. For example, Don John's attempt to destroy Hero and Claudio's relationship in *Much Ado About Nothing* is villainous <u>in the context of the play</u>, but isn't that villainous when compared to the murders that Macbeth commits.

4) Sometimes identifying the villain of the play is more difficult. It's easy to see Caliban as the main villain in *The Tempest* because he's described as a "monster" and a "demi-devil", his language is full of <u>swearing</u> and he plots to <u>murder</u> Prospero with <u>no sign of guilt</u>.

5) However, Prospero could be described as a villain too — Caliban showed Prospero <u>kindness</u> when they first met, but Prospero <u>took over</u> Caliban's island and <u>locked him up</u> like a prisoner. This makes it easier to see Caliban as a <u>victim</u> rather than a <u>truly villainous</u> character.

Characters

Most of Shakespeare's <u>main characters</u> were members of the <u>nobility</u>, whereas his <u>fools</u> were often from the <u>lower classes</u>.

A lot of Shakespeare's characters are members of the **Nobility**

1) Noble characters are those at the top of the <u>class structure</u> (see p.141).
2) Examples include members of <u>high class families</u> (e.g. the Montagues and Capulets in *Romeo and Juliet*), <u>dukes</u> (e.g. Orsino in *Twelfth Night*) and <u>royalty</u> (e.g. Queen Titania in *A Midsummer Night's Dream*).
3) These characters usually have <u>status</u> and <u>power</u>, and are often <u>respected</u> members of society. Shakespeare included noble characters to <u>appeal</u> to the <u>noble members</u> of his <u>audiences</u>.
4) Noble characters often speak in <u>verse</u> — this makes them sound <u>grander</u> and more formal than the lower class characters, such as the fools (see below), who speak mainly in prose.
5) Shakespeare included noble characters in his <u>comedies</u> and his <u>tragedies</u>.
6) In some of his plays, Shakespeare uses noble characters to comment on abuse of <u>power</u>.

> For example, *Macbeth* looks at how different <u>kings</u> use their <u>power</u>. King Duncan uses his power in a <u>kind</u> and <u>generous</u> way, which makes him <u>popular</u>. Macbeth, however, murders Duncan to become king, and then uses his power in a <u>corrupt</u> and <u>ambitious</u> way, which leads to his <u>death</u>.

There are different types of **Fool**

1) Most Shakespeare plays have a <u>fool</u> — a character who adds to the <u>humour</u> of a play. Fools are often <u>minor characters</u>, and they're frequently of a <u>lower class</u>.
2) Fools often make <u>rude jokes</u> and <u>sexual innuendos</u> — these characters were designed to appeal to the <u>lower-class</u> members of Shakespeare's audience.
3) Traditionally, fools (or jesters) were people paid to behave ridiculously for the entertainment of the nobility. Shakespeare includes several <u>court jester</u> characters in his plays, for example Feste in *Twelfth Night* and Trinculo in *The Tempest*.
4) Although jesters were thought to be <u>idiotic</u>, Shakespeare's jesters can also be <u>intelligent</u> and <u>crafty</u>.

> VIOLA   This fellow is wise enough to play the Fool, ⬅ After talking to Feste, Viola realises that he's actually very <u>wise</u> and <u>witty</u>.
>
> *Twelfth Night, Act 3, Scene 1*

5) Sometimes the fool is just an <u>incompetent</u> character — someone who doesn't do their job very well. Dogberry in *Much Ado About Nothing* is a police chief, but he often gets <u>confused</u> and makes <u>mistakes</u>.
6) Although humorous characters are more typically found in <u>comedies</u>, fools appear in <u>tragedies</u> to <u>lighten the mood</u>. In *Macbeth*, the light relief is provided by the Porter in Act 2, Scene 3.
7) Although there isn't a traditional fool in *Romeo and Juliet*, the <u>Nurse</u> provides some <u>comic relief</u> during the play with her <u>rude jokes</u>.

Look at the characters in the plays you're studying

Write down a list of the main characters in each of the plays you've read, then make some brief notes next to each character — write about their character traits and the role they have in the play.

Theme — Deception and Disguise

Tricks, cross-dressing and deception — all the ingredients of a Shakespearean comedy.

Trickery causes lots of Funny moments in *Twelfth Night*

1) 'Twelfth Night' was a festival celebrating mischief and deception — men would dress as women or servants would dress as their masters. So from the title, Shakespeare's audiences would have expected the play to be full of trickery and disguise.

2) The main example of trickery in the play is Viola disguising herself as a man called Cesario. This deception affects almost everything that happens in the play.

> VIOLA   Then think you right: I am not what I am.
>
> *Act 3, Scene 1*

Viola (disguised as Cesario) says "I am not what I am" to Olivia. This is an example of dramatic irony — the audience know that Viola is a woman, but Olivia thinks she's a man.

3) Feste is the only character to see through Viola's disguise. Even though Feste is the 'fool' he's actually the smartest character in the play. This reinforces the theme that things aren't always what they seem.

4) Malvolio is tricked into thinking Olivia loves him after finding a letter supposedly from her. Although the letter is an obvious forgery, Malvolio is easily deceived because of his self-absorbed personality. This creates humour in Act 3, Scene 4 when Malvolio tries to flirt with Olivia.

5) Although every character in the play is affected by deception, it is presented in a light-hearted and comical way, and most of the characters have a happy ending.

Fairies Deceive people in *A Midsummer Night's Dream*

1) 'Midsummer Night' follows the longest day of the year — it's a night when the real and supernatural worlds are thought to overlap. This, and the word 'dream' in the title, suggest nothing is going to be as it seems.

2) The play includes magic and reality. Fairies influence and trick people, but they can't be seen by people.

3) Oberon orders Puck to use juice from flowers to deceive Titania into loving a ridiculous character. Titania falls in love with Bottom, a human whose head has been magically disguised as a donkey's — but her love wears off in the end.

4) Some characters are deceived into thinking the events they've experienced were dreams.

Demetrius is deceived by the fairies. The rhetorical question shows his confusion.

> DEMETRIUS   Are you sure
> That we are awake? It seems to me
> That yet we sleep, we dream.
>
> *Act 4, Scene 1*

5) At the end of the play, after the confusion has been resolved, Puck hints that there has been another deception. He suggests that the audience may have dreamt everything they've just seen in the play.

> PUCK   If we shadows have offended,
> Think but this, and all is mended:
> That you have but slumbered here,
> While these visions did appear.
>
> *Act 5, Scene 1*

Puck is speaking directly to the audience ("you"). He gives the ending a comic feel by seeming to reassure the audience — before telling them 'it was all a dream', which isn't reassuring at all. It casts doubt on everything that's happened.

In these plays, the audience often knows things the characters don't

In Shakespeare's day, the actor playing Viola in *Twelfth Night* would have been a man — so the audience would have watched a man, pretending to be a woman, pretending to be a man. Not confusing at all, then.

Theme — Love

Love is a fairly common theme in plays and stories. Love can be happy and light-hearted, like in *Much Ado About Nothing*, or it can be tragic, like in *Romeo and Juliet*.

There are two Different Attitudes to Love in *Much Ado About Nothing*

1) Love and relationships make up most of the play's action, which is typical of a Shakespearean comedy.

2) Claudio expresses his love for Hero using poetic language and they speak to each other using blank verse — this is a more formal way of speaking and suggests that their relationship is romantic and traditional.

> CLAUDIO   Can the world buy such a jewel?
>
> *Act 1, Scene 1*

Claudio uses poetic language to describe Hero. This metaphor suggests she's beautiful and precious.

3) Benedick and Beatrice's relationship is more unconventional. At the start of the play, they appear to dislike each other, and insult each other. This creates humour in the play.

> BEATRICE   I wonder that you will still be talking, Signor Benedick, nobody marks you.
> BENEDICK   What, my dear Lady Disdain! Are you yet living?
>
> *Act 1, Scene 1*

Benedick and Beatrice often talk to each other in prose. This is a more natural form of speech.

4) It takes time for Benedick and Beatrice to realise they love each other — this contrasts with Claudio who falls in love with Hero without even speaking to her.

5) Although both couples have different approaches to love, they all end up happy. This suggests that love doesn't have to be conventional to succeed.

Love is the most important theme in *Romeo and Juliet*

The prologue is the introduction to the play.

1) The prologue describes Romeo and Juliet as "star-cross'd lovers" — we know that the characters will fall in love before the audience even sees them onstage. This shows how central the theme of love is to the play.

2) At the very start of the play, Romeo is in love with another character, Rosaline, but he's miserable because she doesn't love him back.

> ROMEO   Feather of lead, bright smoke, cold fire, sick health!
> Still-waking sleep, that is not what it is!
> This love feel I, that feel no love in this.
>
> *Act 1, Scene 1*

Shakespeare uses oxymorons ("cold fire, sick health") to show how confused Romeo is about loving Rosaline — this presents love as something difficult and complicated.

3) Romeo falls in love with Juliet at first sight — their love is sudden, passionate and dramatic.

4) The language Romeo uses to talk about love changes after he sees Juliet.

Romeo is very certain of his love for Juliet. This contrasts with the uncertainty of his feelings towards Rosaline.

> ROMEO   Did my heart love till now? forswear it, sight!
> For I ne'er saw true beauty till this night.
>
> *Act 1, Scene 5*

5) Romeo and Juliet's love is destructive and makes them behave recklessly — they would rather die than live without one another. The couple's death is central to the tragic element of the play.

The theme of love was just as popular in the 1600s as it is today

Love has always been a popular theme with writers because it has lots of potential for drama — it can be funny, tragic or joyful. Take these two plays for example, they're both about love but they're very different.

Theme — Fate

Fate is the idea that characters can't control what happens to them — even if they had acted differently, the outcome would have still been the same.

Romeo and Juliet seem to be Doomed from the Start

1) The prologue tells the audience exactly what's going to happen in the play. Shakespeare wanted to make it clear from the start that the central characters are going to die.

'fatal' has two meanings — it can mean both 'deadly' and 'fateful'. Shakespeare uses this pun, as well as the alliteration of the 'f' sound, to draw attention to the characters' fate.

Romeo and Juliet are described as "star-cross'd". In Shakespeare's time, people thought that stars controlled their fate, so crossed by stars meant 'doomed'.

From forth the fatal loins of these two foes
A pair of star-cross'd lovers take their life;
Whose misadventured piteous overthrows
Doth with their death bury their parents' strife.

The prologue is written in rhymed verse. This emphasises the importance of the idea that Romeo and Juliet can't escape their fate.

2) Throughout the play, Shakespeare uses foreshadowing (see p.136) to remind the audience that Romeo and Juliet are going to die. This makes their fates seem inescapable.

JULIET   My grave is like to be my wedding bed

Act 1, Scene 5

Juliet links marriage with death. This is an example of dramatic irony — the audience knows that Juliet is fated to die because of her marriage to Romeo. This makes her line even more tragic.

3) But Shakespeare suggests that it wasn't entirely down to fate and that the characters are responsible for their own actions. Romeo and Juliet behave recklessly so they are partly to blame.

The Witches' Predictions are central to Macbeth's Fate

1) The Witches make predictions about Macbeth at the start of the play.
2) All of the predictions come true — it seems that Macbeth can't escape his fate.
3) At first, Macbeth is happy to let fate run its course...

MACBETH   chance may crown me,
             Without my stir.

Act 1, Scene 3

The Witches predict that Macbeth will become king. Macbeth doesn't think he has to do anything to make it happen — it's his fate.

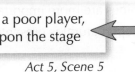

© Alastair Muir/REX/Shutterstock

4) ... but later, Macbeth tries to speed up fate by killing King Duncan so that he can become king. It's not clear whether the Witches are messengers of Macbeth's fate or whether they inspire him to do bad things.
5) The theme of fate reoccurs until the very end of the play.

MACBETH   a poor player,
             That struts and frets his hour upon the stage

Act 5, Scene 5

Macbeth uses a metaphor to compare his life to being an actor in a play. He thinks that he didn't have control over his actions — it was all down to fate.

Shakespeare's audiences believed in the power of fate

People in the 1600s were a superstitious lot — it's no surprise that the theme of fate crops up a lot.

Theme — The Supernatural

Not only did Shakespearean audiences believe in fate, they also believed in supernatural beings too, like witches, fairies and spirits. Spooky.

The **Supernatural** is presented as **Evil** in *Macbeth*...

© Gianni Dagli Orti/REX/Shutterstock

1) The Witches are the first characters onstage in *Macbeth*. This shows how important the theme of the supernatural is in the play.

2) They make prophecies which influence the events of the play. The prophecies eventually come true — this shows how powerful they are.

3) The Witches often speak in rhyme and use a distinctive rhythm. This sets them apart from the other characters and makes them sound sinister.

4) The Witches use dark, gruesome language which shows their wickedness.

> "hell-broth" links the Witches with hell and the Devil. Shakespearean audiences were very religious so this association would have made the Witches seem very evil.

| SECOND WITCH | Adder's fork, and blind-worm's sting, Lizard's leg, and owlet's wing, For a charm of powerful trouble, Like a hell-broth, boil and bubble. |

Act 4, Scene 1

5) When Macbeth decides to kill King Duncan, he sees a vision of a ghostly dagger. Later in the play, Macbeth sees Banquo's ghost. These visions show how much control supernatural forces have over him.

6) Macbeth is a tragedy, so it's not surprising that the supernatural elements in the play are dark and evil.

... but as **Mischievous** in *The Tempest*

1) At the start of the play, a storm conjured by magic causes a ship to wreck on an island. This shipwreck influences everything that happens in the play. This shows the importance of the supernatural.

2) Several characters have magical powers. Prospero is a magician and his servant, Ariel, is a spirit. Sycorax, a witch, is mentioned too, although she's never on stage.

3) Prospero controls Ariel who is the main source of his power. He often uses Ariel to manipulate others.

4) Although Prospero's magic isn't entirely good, it doesn't cause any lasting damage. Prospero sometimes uses his magic to keep other characters safe — although it's usually for his own benefit.

> Ariel is sent by Prospero to wake Gonzalo — he's about to get killed in his sleep. Prospero needs Gonzalo alive to keep his plan on track.

| ARIEL | My master through his art foresees the danger That you, his friend, are in, and sends me forth (For else his project dies) to keep them living. |

Act 2, Scene 1

5) In Act 3, Scene 3, Prospero sends Ariel dressed as a harpy (a half-woman, half-bird creature) to bring his enemies a message — he wants to punish them for stealing his dukedom. The appearance of the harpy adds to the supernatural tone of the play.

6) At the end of the play, Prospero gives up his magic so that he can return home. Shakespeare suggests that some things are more important than magical power.

7) *The Tempest* is a comedy, so the supernatural is presented in a light-hearted way.

The supernatural was a hot topic in Shakespeare's day

When Shakespeare was writing, lots of people believed in witches and magic. Between 1500 and 1700, hundreds of women were accused of being witches — some were even killed because of it.

Answering Questions About Shakespeare

Have you been paying attention? Let's find out with a practice question about Shakespeare...

Here's an example question — it focusses on the theme of the supernatural.

> How does Shakespeare present the theme of the supernatural in the following extract from *Macbeth*?

You'd need to write about the techniques that Shakespeare uses.

This question is all about the theme of the supernatural.

© Geraint Lewis/REX/Shutterstock

Here are some things that you should look for in the text below:

- What sort of language do the characters use?
- What do they say to each other?
- Do the characters speak in prose or verse?

SECOND WITCH	By the pricking of my thumbs, Something wicked this way comes. Open locks, whoever knocks. *Enter* MACBETH
MACBETH	How now, you secret, black, and midnight hags! What is't you do?
ALL THE WITCHES	A deed without a name.
MACBETH	I conjure you by that which you profess, However you come to know it, answer me. Though you untie the winds and let them fight Against the churches, though the yeasty waves Confound and swallow navigation up, Though bladed corn be lodged and trees blown down, Though castles topple on their warders' heads, Though palaces and pyramids do slope Their heads to their foundations, though the treasure Of nature's germens* tumble altogether Even till destruction sicken, answer me To what I ask you.
FIRST WITCH	Speak.
SECOND WITCH	Demand.
THIRD WITCH	We'll answer.
FIRST WITCH	Say, if thou'dst rather hear it from our mouths, Or from our masters'?
MACBETH	Call 'em, let me see 'em.
FIRST WITCH	Pour in sow's blood, that hath eaten Her nine farrow*; grease that's sweaten From the murderer's gibbet* throw Into the flame.
ALL THE WITCHES	Come high or low; Thyself and office deftly show.

The Second Witch speaks in rhymed verse. This makes her dialogue sound sinister.

The Second Witch refers to Macbeth as "Something". This makes him seem more like an animal than a man.

The Witches represent the supernatural in the play. Macbeth uses language with negative connotations to describe them.

Macbeth mentions some of the things that the Witches are capable of. This suggests that they are wicked and powerful.

The ingredients of the potion are gruesome.

The Witches speak in unison. This makes their dialogue sound unnatural.

Macbeth, Act 4, Scene 1

*nature's germens — the seeds of life
*farrow — piglets
*gibbet — a scaffold for hanging criminals

Answering Questions About Shakespeare

Let's turn those points into <u>dazzling</u> answers.

Make sure you focus on the **Theme** of the **Supernatural**

The following answers look at the <u>way</u> that the characters talk...

> The Witches speak in rhyme which makes their dialogue sound spooky. ✗

This answer needs to <u>link</u> the point back to the <u>theme</u> of the supernatural and add in a more <u>detailed</u> explanation.

> The Witches speak in rhymed verse, which makes their dialogue stand out from Macbeth's. The use of rhymed verse makes their dialogue sound sinister, as if they are casting a spell. This suggests that the supernatural is something to be feared in *Macbeth*. ✓

This answer is <u>better</u> — it uses <u>technical terms</u> and suggests how the theme of the supernatural is presented.

> The Witches are supernatural characters and the way that they speak sets them apart from the other characters in the play. In this extract, the Witches talk in rhymed verse which has a regular rhythm: this makes their dialogue sound sinister, as if they are casting a spell. They also speak in unison several times. This sounds unnatural, and as if they have the power to read each other's minds. The Witches' dialogue suggests that they are evil characters, and that the supernatural represents something to be feared in the play. ✓✓

This answer is really <u>good</u>. It makes a <u>clear</u> point about <u>rhymed verse</u>, and then <u>develops</u> it by mentioning how the Witches talk in <u>unison</u>.

These answers focus on the <u>language</u> that the characters use.

> Macbeth calls the Witches "secret, black... midnight hags" which suggests that they are evil characters. ✗

This point has used a good quote, but it's <u>too basic</u> and hasn't been fully explained.

> Macbeth describes the Witches as "secret, black... midnight hags". This suggests that Macbeth thinks that they are evil characters. Their evil nature is reinforced later in the scene when they use dark, gruesome language to describe the potion's ingredients, for example "blood" and "grease". This would form a horrifying picture in the audience's mind, and would emphasise the supernatural as something evil. ✓

This answer is <u>better</u> — it considers how the Witches are perceived by other <u>characters</u> as well as the <u>audience</u>.

> Macbeth describes the Witches as "secret, black... hags", which suggests that he thinks that the Witches are evil characters. Despite this, Macbeth still comes to the Witches to hear more about their predictions. He knows that the Witches are powerful: he thinks they can summon stormy weather, and he watches as they create a gruesome potion containing "blood" and "grease that's sweaten / From the murderer's gibbet". This language would form a horrible image in the audience's mind and suggests that the Witches are capable of truly wicked things, but Macbeth is not deterred. This suggests that although the Witches' supernatural abilities are evil, they are also incredibly powerful. ✓✓

This answer is really good. As well as saying that the theme of the supernatural is presented as <u>evil</u>, it also develops the point by saying that it is presented as something <u>powerful</u> too.

Remember to use PEED

If you need a reminder about how to structure an essay answer, turn to page 69 for some advice.

Warm-Up and Worked Practice Questions

Before you move on, it's well worth doing some practice questions to make sure you've understood everything from Section 10.

Warm-up Questions

1) Shakespeare's plays can be categorised into three main types. Name all three.

2) What usually happens at the end of...
   a) a comedy?
   b) a tragedy?

3) Why were the female roles in Shakespeare's plays filled by young boys?

4) Complete the sentence: "Blank verse follows a set _____, but doesn't _____."

5) True or false: "Lines written in rhymed verse are less important, so you shouldn't pay too much attention to them."

The example question below is about the theme of love, but you could also be asked to write an essay about characters, language or performance.

Worked Practice Question

1. **Romeo and Juliet**
   Act 1, Scene 1, lines 154-232
   Act 2, Scene 2, lines 10-84

   In both extracts, Romeo is talking about love, but his attitude in each of the two extracts is very different.

   How is Romeo's attitude to love changed by meeting Juliet?
   Support your ideas by referring to the extracts.

Always write a short introduction to your essay.

Love is a central theme in Shakespeare's "Romeo and Juliet", but the attitudes of some characters towards love change as the play goes on. Romeo is a good example of this, because his attitude towards love changes from the moment he meets Juliet.

When Romeo is introduced to the audience in Act 1 Scene 1, he says that "sad hours seem long". As a result, the audience's first impression of him is as a miserable character. The cause of Romeo's self-pity is soon

Link your answer back to the question.

revealed to be a girl called Rosaline. Romeo idealises Rosaline, describing her as "exquisite", but she does not love him back. This has a negative impact on Romeo's attitude towards love.

Worked Practice Question

Later in the same scene, a number of Romeo's lines shed even more light on his attitude towards love in the play's early stages. Firstly, he uses a series of contradictions — "feather of lead, bright smoke, cold fire, sick health" — to describe his feelings. These express how confusing Romeo finds love and how little he understands it. Secondly, he calls love a "madness most discreet" and compares himself to "a sick man". Romeo's attitude towards love at this point is so negative that it's like an illness to him.

Short quotes are best, so be sure to use them often.

However, meeting Juliet completely changes Romeo's attitude. In Act 2 Scene 2, his view of love is much more positive and passionate. This is probably because Romeo listens in on Juliet's soliloquy at the beginning of the scene and realises that she loves him back. He idealises Juliet even more than Rosaline, using religious imagery to compare her to a "bright angel" and a "wingèd messenger of heaven". This has a greater impact than using simple adjectives like "exquisite" in Act 1 Scene 1.

Use linking phrases to link your paragraphs together.

Furthermore, the idea that love is a form of madness or an illness is nowhere to be seen in Act 2 Scene 2. Instead, Romeo is much more upbeat, saying that:

Longer quotes go in a separate paragraph.

"For stony limits cannot hold love out,

And what love can do, that dares love attempt:

Therefore thy kinsmen are no stop to me."

His attitude towards love is now so positive that he believes nothing can stand in the way of his love for Juliet. Romeo uses an image of his love overpowering "stony limits" (walls) to suggest the strength of his feelings.

Your essay isn't complete without a short conclusion.

In conclusion, Romeo's attitude to love becomes much more positive when he meets Juliet. He goes from being very pessimistic to highly positive about love.

Practice Questions

Look at the practice questions below, and answer the question which relates to the play you've studied.

Practice Questions

1. **Macbeth** Act 1, Scene 7, lines 29-82; Act 5, Scene 1, lines 17-60

   In these scenes, we see different sides of Lady Macbeth.

   How do these extracts show how her character changes?
   Support your ideas by referring to the extracts.

2. **Romeo and Juliet** Act 2, Scene 2, lines 1-114; Act 3, Scene 5, lines 1-59

   In the first extract, Romeo and Juliet talk about how much they love each other. In the second extract, Romeo leaves Juliet's room in the morning so they don't get caught.

   How would you direct the actors playing Romeo and Juliet in these extracts?
   Support your ideas by referring to the extracts.

3. **Much Ado About Nothing** Act 2, Scene 3, lines 81-180; Act 3, Scene 1, lines 37-105

   In the first extract, Benedick is tricked into thinking Beatrice is in love with him.
   In the second extract, Beatrice is tricked into thinking Benedick is in love with her.

   How do these extracts show how language can be used to deceive people?
   Support your ideas by referring to the extracts.

4. **Twelfth Night** Act 2, Scene 5, lines 20-157; Act 3, Scene 4, lines 16-114

   In these extracts, Malvolio wants to marry Olivia in order to become a Count.

   How does Shakespeare explore the theme of ambition in these scenes?
   Support your ideas by referring to the extracts.

5. **The Tempest** Act 2, Scene 1, lines 194-295; Act 3, Scene 2, lines 87-146

   In these scenes, characters plan to betray and kill others.

   How does Shakespeare use language to create a threatening atmosphere in these scenes?
   Support your ideas by referring to the extracts.

6. **A Midsummer Night's Dream**
   Act 1, Scene 1, lines 128-179; Act 2, Scene 1, lines 132-172

   In the first extract, Lysander discusses love with Hermia.
   In the second extract, Oberon reveals his plan to put a love potion on Titania.

   How does Shakespeare explore the theme of love in these scenes?
   Support your ideas by referring to the extracts.

Revision Summary for Section Ten

If you've learnt all the information in this section, you should feel a lot more confident that
you can do some pretty great Shakespeare work. Go through all the questions on this page
to check you know everything. As always, if you get stuck, go back through the section
until you know all the answers.

1) In which year was Shakespeare born?

2) Which of these facts about Shakespearean theatre is incorrect?
a) The stage was usually bare.
b) Going to the theatre was very popular in Shakespeare's time.
c) Only rich people went to the theatre.

3) What do these words mean in modern English?
a) thine
b) prithee

4) Write a short definition of the following terms:
a) prose
b) blank verse
c) rhymed verse

5) What is a soliloquy?

6) What is dramatic irony?

7) If a character uses lots of puns, what does that suggest about them?

8) What effect do minor scenes have in a play?

9) Since plays were performed during the day in Shakespearean times,
how would the audience have known if a scene was taking place at night?

10) What could Shakespearean costumes tell you about a character?

11) "Shakespeare didn't include many stage directions in his plays." True or false?

12) Explain what the class structure was in Shakespearean times.

13) Name one romantic hero and one flawed hero from a Shakespeare play.

14) "Shakespeare created strong female characters which represented
how women were expected to act at the time." True or false?

15) Name two Shakespeare plays which feature trickery.

16) Very briefly describe how love is presented in:
a) *Much Ado about Nothing*
b) *Romeo and Juliet*

17) Give two ways that the supernatural is presented in Shakespeare's plays.

Spoken Language Tasks

Reading? Check. Writing? Check. Now have a look at the sorts of <u>speaking tasks</u> you might get.

There are **Different Speaking Tasks** you might do

There are a few ways your teacher might <u>test</u> your spoken English skills.

1) <u>Debates</u> and <u>discussions</u>
2) <u>Speeches</u> and <u>presentations</u>
3) Reading and performing <u>plays</u> and <u>poetry</u>

These might sound a bit daunting, but if you <u>practise</u> and <u>prepare</u> for them, it'll be easier than you think.

Do some **Research** about your topic

1) For tasks like <u>debates</u>, <u>speeches</u> and <u>presentations</u>, you might be <u>given</u> a topic to discuss or you might <u>choose</u> your own. It's important that you <u>know</u> your topic <u>really well</u>.

2) Think about what you can include in your preparation — research any <u>facts</u> or <u>statistics</u> that you can use to <u>support</u> your argument or add <u>interest</u> to your speech.

 If you spend too much time watching TV or using the computer, your grades will suffer. → This is quite <u>vague</u>, so it doesn't <u>support</u> the speaker's argument very well.

✓ *A recent study has shown that GCSE pupils who spend more than one hour a night watching TV or using the computer, will, on average, do worse in their exams.* → This uses <u>evidence</u> to <u>strengthen</u> the argument the speaker is making.

Respond to other people's points in **Debates** and **Discussions**

1) <u>Debates</u> and <u>discussions</u> focus on a certain topic.

2) In a debate, people are split into two sides — <u>for</u> and <u>against</u>.
Make sure you know <u>all</u> the points you could make to support your side.

3) For <u>both</u> discussions and debates, you'll be expected to <u>respond</u> to points that your classmates have made. Remember to back up your points with <u>evidence</u>.

4) In discussions, try to <u>acknowledge</u> what the other person has said, then <u>add</u> on your own point.

 Eating a balanced diet is the best way to improve your health. → <u>Mention</u> the previous point, then <u>add</u> your own. → *Eating healthily is very important, but so is exercising regularly.*

5) In debates, <u>disagree</u> with what the other side say and explain <u>why</u> you think they're <u>wrong</u>.

Some people spend too much time posting things on social media instead of enjoying their real lives. → Take the opposition's point and show <u>why</u> it's not correct. → *Social media allows people to share important moments in their lives with loved ones who live far away.*

You'll need to think quickly in discussions and debates

... that's why it's really important that you know your topic inside out. If you're well prepared, it'll be easy to respond to what other people say and make the audience see your point of view.

Speeches and Presentations

Giving a speech or presentation isn't as tricky as you might think. Just remember, preparation is key.

Speeches and Presentations are Similar

1) Speeches and presentations are pretty much the same thing
   — they both involve giving information on a subject.

2) You might talk about something you're interested in, like a sport or hobby, or a personal experience, like a holiday or childhood memory. You could also discuss an issue that concerns you, such as addiction to social media, or a current topic, e.g. a news story.

3) The important thing is that you give your opinion and ideas on the topic. You need to engage the audience — if you're not interested, there's no way the audience will be.

4) You might be asked questions at the end of your presentation. Make sure you do enough research to be really confident about your topic — the more you know about it, the better.

Think about what the Purpose of your Task is

1) Before you start writing, think about what the purpose of your talk is and how to achieve it. For example, the purpose of a presentation might be to give the audience information on something new to them.

> Writing a speech is like writing a non-fiction text — see pages 52-59 for more ideas.

2) You should choose your vocabulary carefully so that it helps you to achieve your purpose.

 International media conglomerates make the movie industry *monotonous*.

 → The vocabulary is too technical and makes the sentence hard to follow.

✓ *Large film companies* make the movie industry *bland*.

→ These words are simpler, so the sentence is easier to understand.

3) If you're trying to persuade your audience to agree with your point of view, you could use some rhetorical questions (see p.36).

Why waste your money on frivolous meals, parties and holidays? Don't you think you should be saving it for something important instead?

 → This uses rhetorical questions and the pronoun 'you' to persuade the reader by making them feel involved.

Structure your presentation so that it's Clear

You'll need to structure your speech or presentation clearly:

- Make sure you have a clear introduction stating the topic you've chosen. If you're putting across an argument, let the audience know your point of view.
- Plan what order to cover your points in. For example, if you're discussing a topic, you might give all your points for it, followed by all your points against.
- End with a strong conclusion — this could sum up the key points of your speech, or give your own opinion on the subject.

Make sure you stick to the point

If you're talking about a subject that you're really interested in, it's easy to get a bit carried away. Stick to your plan and make your points clearly — don't be tempted to go off topic.

Performing Plays and Poems

You might not have performed anything before, so here's a page packed with helpful information all about it.

You could perform a **Play** or a **Poem**

1) You might get to read or perform part of a play to practise your spoken English skills. Your teacher might just get you to read the script in class, or you might get the chance to act out the play.

2) You might also be asked to read a poem out loud in class.

3) You won't impress your teacher if you just read the words off the page like you're reading a shopping list. You need to think about what you're saying and how you're saying it.

Performing is **More** than just **Reading** the **Script**

1) If you're reading or performing a play, you'll be given a role to play.

2) When you're reading your lines, remember to think about the stage directions.

PROSPERO   [Aside] It goes on, I see,
As my soul prompts it. [to Ariel] Spirit, fine spirit,
I'll free thee
Within two days for this.

The Tempest — William Shakespeare

The words in brackets are stage directions that tell you who to speak to. At first, Prospero isn't speaking to anyone on stage, then he starts speaking to Ariel.

ROMEO   Here's to my love! [Drinks.] O true apothecary!
Thy drugs are quick. Thus with a kiss I die. [Dies.]

Romeo and Juliet — William Shakespeare

These stage directions are actions. You'd need to say the lines and act out the bits in brackets.

3) If you're acting out the play, think about what the character's actions might be. Use gestures and movements to make your performance more interesting.

4) Even if you're not talking, you still need to act. Think about what's going on around you and the mood of the scene.

Think about **How** you're reading the **Poem**

1) Reading the words on the page is just one part of performing a poem. You need to think about your intonation — how you read the words and the tone of your voice.

2) Here are some dos and don'ts for reading poetry:

DON'T read the poem in the same voice throughout.
DO vary your intonation. Use tone to draw attention to key words in the poem.

DON'T race through the poem as fast as you can.
DO look at the poem's punctuation. Use it as a guide to know when to pause during your reading. Speed up a little if the pace of the poem speeds up, and slow down if the poem does too.

Make sure you project when you're performing

It's no good knowing your lines if the audience can't hear you. Practise reading aloud to get the volume right. If you're on a stage, you might have to speak quite loudly.

Using Language Correctly

You can walk the walk, now it's time to talk the talk. Remember to speak <u>clearly</u> and use <u>Standard English</u>.

Make sure you **Speak Clearly**

1) If you're doing a presentation, for example, it needs to be easy for your audience to follow — make sure you <u>speak clearly</u> and <u>slowly</u>.

> Speak up and look around the room when you're talking — that way everyone can hear you.

2) Don't repeat yourself unless you're doing it for <u>effect</u>. Keep your points <u>concise</u> — saying them again in different words wastes valuable time.

> *We might succeed because we might be able to do what we need to, but we might also fail if we don't do what we need to. We'll only know once we succeed or fail.*

This is <u>waffly</u> and <u>repetitive</u>, which makes it sound <u>dull</u>.

> *Perhaps we'll succeed. Perhaps we'll fail. Only time will tell.*

Here, repetition is used for <u>effect</u> — it helps the speaker make a <u>strong, memorable point</u>.

3) Draw attention to the most important <u>facts</u> so the audience will remember them.

> *One and a half acres of forest is cut down every second — that's <u>the size of 66 football pitches</u>.*

Linking a statistic to something the audience <u>can relate to</u> makes it more <u>memorable</u>.

Use **Standard English**

<u>Standard English</u> is the type of English that everyone agrees is correct. You'll probably need to use Standard English during your speaking task.

> There's more on Standard English on p.10.

1) Don't use <u>slang</u> or <u>local dialect</u> words that some people might not understand.

✗ *Local residents were <u>gutted</u> at the decision.* ➡ "Gutted" is a <u>slang</u> term.

✓ *Local residents were <u>disappointed</u> with the decision.* ➡ The <u>formal</u> wording is more appropriate.

2) Use <u>correct grammar</u>.

✗ *The issue <u>aren't</u> high on the political agenda.* ➡ This sentence is <u>grammatically incorrect</u>.

✓ *The issue <u>isn't</u> high on the political agenda.* ➡ The word 'isn't' is correct here.

3) Think about the <u>formality</u> of your language too. You'll probably want to avoid being too <u>informal</u>.

✗ *Some people are, like, "P.E. is completely pointless".* ➡ This is too <u>informal</u> and <u>familiar</u>.

✓ *Some people maintain that P.E. is completely pointless.* ➡ This is much better.

Don't rush when you're speaking

The thought of speaking in front of people might seem a bit scary, but don't race through what you have to say. Take your time, speak clearly and make eye contact with the audience.

Revision Summary for Section Eleven

You should be ready and raring to tackle any speaking tasks that come your way now. This section has covered quite a lot of information, so have another read over any bits that you're not so sure about. When you're ready, have a go at the questions below to make sure you've taken it all in. If you get any of them wrong, go back over them until you're 100% comfortable.

1) Give three different speaking tasks that you might have to do. ☑

2) How well should you know the topic you're speaking about? ☑

3) "In a debate, just disagree with the opposition and say they're wrong." True or false? ☑

4) Write down five points for and five points against the following statement: "School uniforms make life easier. You don't need to think about what to wear in the morning." ☑

5) Write down three topics you might choose for a speech or presentation. ☑

6) Kaya says, "Using lots of technical vocabulary will show your audience that you know what you're talking about". Is she right? Explain why or why not. ☑

7) What technique could you use to persuade your audience to agree with you? ☑

8) You've been asked to give a presentation on your favourite hobby. Write a brief plan covering what you would say. Include a short introduction and conclusion. ☑

9) Now think of three questions that people might ask you at the end of your presentation. ☑

10) In a play, what do you call the words in brackets that tell an actor what to do? ☑

11) When acting out a play, what should you be doing when you don't have any lines?
   a) Listening to the other actors.
   b) Staying in character.
   c) Reacting to what's going on around you.
   d) All of the above. ☑

12) What is intonation? ☑

13) "Punctuation isn't important in poetry. Focus on the words instead." True or false? ☑

14) When can you repeat yourself in a speech or presentation? ☑

15) How can you get your audience to remember your key facts? ☑

16) Henry says, "If you're just having an informal discussion in class, you can speak like you're talking to your friends". Is Henry right? ☑

17) Read the sentences below. Rewrite any that are grammatically incorrect.
   a) Smoking and drinking alcohol is damaging for your health.
   b) My favourite sports are tennis and volleyball.
   c) Advertising junk food to children isn't a good idea.
   d) A few small changes isn't enough. More needs to be done. ☑

Mixed Practice Test

You've worked through the book, so hopefully you're feeling pretty confident about your English skills, but is it time to dive into the Practice Exam? There's only one way to find out — have a go at these Mixed Practice Tests first.

- Jot down your answers to the questions. When you've answered all of them, correct your answers (see pages 192-3). Tick the box next to each question you got right. Put a cross in the box if you got it wrong.

- If you're getting 7 or more right on these tests, you should be ready for the Practice Exams on pages 168-187.

- If you're getting less than that, go back and do some more revision. Have another go at the Section Summaries — they're the best way to find out what you know and what you've forgotten.

Test 1

✓ / ✗

1. What is enjambment?

2. Which of the following is an example of a metaphor?

   A Justin's face was as red as a tomato.
   B The wind whistled through the trees.
   C Ahmed's eyes were overflowing pools of water.
   D The silence in the room was deafening.

3. If a Shakespearean character speaks in rhymed verse, this often means that...

   A ... they're very angry.
   B ... they're speaking only to the audience.
   C ... they're declaring their love for someone.
   D ... they're saying something important.

4. Why are first person narrators sometimes unreliable?

5. When a writer hints at what will happen later in the story, this is called...

   A ... a flashforward.
   B ... a turning point.
   C ... foreshadowing.
   D ... a flashback.

6. Give an example of onomatopoeia.

7. What is an anecdote?

8. A formal letter should not include...

   A ... contractions.
   B ... impressive vocabulary.
   C ... the date.
   D ... the name of the addressee.

9. A text which addresses the reader as "you" is written in which person?

10. Which punctuation mark is used to show direct speech?

Total (out of 10):

Mixed Practice Test

Test 2

1. Who is the protagonist of a story?

2. Which of the following is written in Standard English?

   A   They wasn't dressed properly for the occasion.
   B   They weren't dressed proper for the occasion.
   C   Them weren't dressed properly for the occasion.
   D   They weren't dressed properly for the occasion.

3. "He will win the competition". What tense is this sentence written in?

4. What is an aside?

5. Which of the following is <u>not</u> part of the 'A Forest' mnemonic used to persuade or argue?

   A   Statistics
   B   Alliteration
   C   The magic three
   D   Oxymorons

6. When quoting from a poem, when should you use a '/'?

7. The rhythm of a poem is...

   A   ... the way that it rhymes.
   B   ... the number of syllables in each line.
   C   ... how the beats in a line are arranged.
   D   ... the type of poem it is, e.g. a sonnet.

8. Give an example of one type of play that Shakespeare wrote.

9. Which of the following is an example of a generalisation?

   A   Studies suggest 70% of pupils enjoy science lessons.
   B   Studies suggest 30% of pupils do not enjoy science lessons.
   C   Almost all pupils enjoy science lessons.
   D   Approximately 7 out of 10 pupils enjoy science lessons.

10. What is the name of the technique where a character talks to themselves in a play?

Total (out of 10):

Mixed Practice Test

Test 3

✓ / ✗

1. Who went to the theatre in Shakespearean times?

   A Royalty and the rich
   B Everyone
   C Men
   D The poor

2. To make an inference, you have to...

   A ... evaluate how effective the text is.
   B ... work out if the text is formal or informal.
   C ... decide who the audience of the text is.
   D ... look for clues that tell you what the writer thinks.

3. What is dramatic irony?

4. What does P.E.E.D. stand for?

5. Suggest one way that the audience can learn about the characters in a play.

6. What is register?

7. What is the context of a text?

   A The feeling created by the text.
   B The reason why the text was written.
   C The type of text it is.
   D Where and when the text was written.

8. What is a caesura?

9. Give an example of how you might recognise a piece of biased writing.

10. Which of the following is an example of personification?

   A Nina let out a lion-like roar.
   B The sweets rolled off the counter like a waterfall.
   C The cat jumped onto the chair.
   D The long grass danced in the breeze.

Total (out of 10):

Mixed Practice Test

Test 4

✓ / ✗

1. What is a turning point?

☐

2. Which of the following features is least likely to appear in an informal text?

   A Contractions
   B Humour
   C Slang
   D Impersonal language

☐

3. What does the word "thou" mean in Shakespeare's plays?

☐

4. What is irony?

   A When a writer mocks someone.
   B When a writer puts two contradicting words together.
   C When a writer means the opposite of what they say.
   D When a writer exaggerates for effect.

☐

5. What is a connotation?

☐

6. Texts that inform should always include...

   A ... rhetorical questions.
   B ... the author's opinion.
   C ... facts.
   D ... suggestions.

☐

7. How many lines does a sonnet have?

☐

8. What is the difference between an act and a scene?

☐

9. Which of the following could be a reason why an author has used subheadings?

   A To make the text more descriptive.
   B To make the text more emotive.
   C To make the text more factual.
   D To split the text up into smaller sections.

☐

10. What does it mean if a plot has a linear structure?

☐

Total (out of 10): ☐

Mixed Practice Test

Test 5

✓ / ✗

1. Name four purposes a text could have.

☐

2. What is hyperbole?

☐

3. Which of the following is an example of a simile?

    A He stretched and yawned like a cat.
    B The moon smiled at the couple below.
    C The reckless runner raced onwards.
    D His heart was a lump of lead.

☐

4. In a play, why might a character's dialogue contain informal language?

    A To make it easier to understand.
    B To make it sound more believable.
    C To make it sound more tense.
    D To make it sound more emotive.

☐

5. What is alliteration?

☐

6. First-person narrators...

    A ... have a more direct relationship with the reader.
    B ... aren't very involved with the story.
    C ... can always be trusted.
    D ... know everything that's going on in the story.

☐

7. What is tone?

    A The type of language used by the writer.
    B The feeling created by the text's language.
    C The way that the whole text is put together.
    D The reason why the text was written.

☐

8. Name two things that stage directions tell actors to do.

☐

9. Sometimes writers end a chapter with an exciting event. What is this technique called?

☐

10. Why were plays performed during the day in Shakespeare's time?

☐

Total (out of 10):

☐

Mixed Practice Test

✓ / ✗

1. What is a stanza?

    A A verse in a poem.
    B A poetic form.
    C When a sentence flows across multiple lines in a poem.
    D When one line of a poem rhymes with the next line.

2. What is a monologue?

3. Name three layout features a non-fiction text may have.

4. When two seemingly contradictory words are used together, this is called...

    A ... sarcasm.
    B ... an oxymoron.
    C ... hyperbole.
    D ... an aside.

5. Name four examples of figurative language.

6. What is a sub-plot?

7. What is free verse?

8. When comparing texts in an essay, you should...

    A ...only discuss how the texts are different.
    B ...talk about each text separately.
    C ...talk about both texts at the same time.
    D ...focus on the similarities.

9. When writing to argue or persuade, why should you keep your criticisms impersonal?

10. What is a flashback?

    A When the writer gives clues about what will happen in the story.
    B When the action of a story jumps back in time.
    C When a character talks about something that happened in the past.
    D When the events of the plot don't take place chronologically.

Total (out of 10):

Mixed Practice Test

✓ / ✗

1. What is a half rhyme?

2. Give an example of when you would start a new paragraph.

3. Give an example of a text you would write in an informal style.

4. When you use your own words to explain what happens in a story, this is known as...

    A ... persuading.
    B ... embedding.
    C ... quoting.
    D ... paraphrasing.

5. In Shakespeare's time, his plays were often performed without...

    A ... much dialogue.
    B ... many actors.
    C ... an audience.
    D ... much scenery.

6. Which of the following contains an imperative verb?

    A If you were to throw litter on the floor, it would be wrong.
    B He threw the litter on the floor.
    C Throwing litter on the floor is wrong.
    D Don't throw litter on the floor.

7. Which sentence gives you the impression that Marcus is angry?

    A Marcus stormed to school.
    B Marcus sauntered to school.
    C Marcus traipsed to school.
    D Marcus ambled to school.

8. Give two examples of when you would use commas.

9. Why were female characters played by male actors in Shakespeare's day?

10. What is a rhyming couplet?

Total (out of 10):

Mixed Practice Test

✓ / ✗

1. What is a cliché?

2. What is a syllable?

3. The term 'staging' refers to which of the following?

    A   The set
    B   The lighting
    C   The props
    D   All of the above

4. In poetry, what is metre?

    A   The pattern of syllables in a line.
    B   The way that punctuation is used in the poem.
    C   The number of lines in each verse.
    D   The number of lines in the poem.

5. Name two layout features you might find in a newspaper article.

6. How is sarcasm different from irony?

7. Which of the following is written in the passive?

    A   He walked along the path that led towards the village.
    B   Charles had been hiding in the garage all along.
    C   It'll take a while, but it will be worth the effort.
    D   Lola was taken to the vets by her owner.

8. Symbolism is when...

    A   ... authors set their novels in the past.
    B   ... authors include images or graphics in their texts.
    C   ... authors repeat key words or ideas to emphasise their importance.
    D   ... authors use made up words to make their characters come to life.

9. In a play script, how can you tell the dialogue from the stage directions?

10. Name two non-fiction texts which would be written in a formal style.

Total (out of 10):

CGP

Key Stage 3 English Practice Exam English Language

Paper 1: Fiction

Instructions

- The test is 1 hour and 45 minutes long.
- Write your answers in **black** ink or ball-point pen.
- Cross out any rough work that you do not want to be marked.
- You should **not** use a dictionary.
- Check your work carefully before the end of the test.

Advice

- You should spend about 15 minutes reading through the source and the five questions that follow.

Score: ☐ **out of 80**

This extract comes from the opening chapter of a novel by Chinua Achebe, set in Nigeria and published in 1958.

Things Fall Apart

Okonkwo was well known through the nine villages and even beyond. His fame rested on solid personal achievements. As a young man of eighteen he had brought honour to his village by throwing Amalinze the Cat. Amalinze was the great wrestler who for seven years was unbeaten, from Umuofia to Mbaino. He was called the Cat because his back would never touch the earth. It was this man that
5 Okonkwo threw in a fight which the old men agreed was one of the fiercest since the founder of their town engaged a spirit of the wild for seven days and seven nights.

The drums beat and the flutes sang and the spectators held their breath. Amalinze was a wily craftsman, but Okonkwo was as slippery as a fish in water. Every nerve and every muscle stood out in their arms, on their backs and their thighs, and one almost heard them stretching to breaking point. In
10 the end Okonkwo threw the Cat.

That was many years ago, twenty years or more, and during this time Okonkwo's fame had grown like a bush-fire in the harmattan*. He was tall and huge, and his bushy eyebrows and wide nose gave him a very severe look. He breathed heavily, and it was said that, when he slept, his wives and children in their out-houses could hear him breathe. When he walked, his heels hardly touched the ground
15 and he seemed to walk on springs, as if he was going to pounce on somebody. And he did pounce on people quite often. He had a slight stammer and whenever he was angry and could not get his words out quickly enough, he would use his fists. He had no patience with unsuccessful men. He had had no patience with his father.

Unoka, for that was his father's name, had died ten years ago. In his day he was lazy and
20 improvident* and was quite incapable of thinking about tomorrow. If any money came his way, and it seldom did, he immediately bought gourds of palm-wine, called round his neighbours and made merry. He always said that whenever he saw a dead man's mouth he saw the folly of not eating what one had in one's lifetime. Unoka was, of course, a debtor, and he owed every neighbour some money, from a few cowries* to quite substantial amounts.

25 He was tall but very thin and had a slight stoop. He wore a haggard and mournful look except when he was drinking or playing on his flute. He was very good on his flute, and his happiest moments were the two or three moons after the harvest when the village musicians brought down their instruments, hung above the fireplace. Unoka would play with them, his face beaming with blessedness and peace. Sometimes another village would ask Unoka's band and their dancing *egwugwu** to come and stay with
30 them and teach them their tunes. They would go to such hosts for as long as three or four markets, making music and feasting. Unoka loved the good fare and the good fellowship, and he loved this season of the year, when the rains had stopped and the sun rose every morning with dazzling beauty. And it was not too hot either, because the cold and dry harmattan wind was blowing down from the north. Some years the harmattan was very severe and a dense haze hung on the atmosphere. Old
35 men and children would then sit round log fires, warming their bodies. Unoka loved it all, and he loved the first kites that returned with the dry season, and the children who sang songs of welcome to them. He would remember his own childhood, how he had often wandered around looking for a kite sailing leisurely against the blue sky. As soon as he found one he would sing with his whole being, welcoming it back from its long, long journey, and asking it if it had brought home any lengths of cloth.

Glossary
*harmattan — a season characterised by a dry, dusty wind
*improvident — reckless
*cowries — a form of West African currency
*egwugwu — tribal leaders with a key role in certain rituals

Section A: Reading

*You should spend about 45 minutes answering **all** of the questions in this section.*

1   Read **lines 1 to 6** of the extract.

    Give **four** things from these lines that tell you about Okonkwo and Amalinze.

    (4 marks)

2   Read **lines 7 to 18** of the extract.

    How does the writer use language in these lines to describe Okonkwo?

    You might want to refer to the writer's use of:
    •   specific words and phrases
    •   language techniques
    •   sentence structure.

    (8 marks)

3   Now think about the **whole extract**.

    This extract is from the opening chapter of a novel.

    How has the writer structured the text to hold the reader's attention?

    You might want to refer to:
    •   how the extract begins
    •   how and why the focus of the extract changes as it goes on
    •   any other elements of the structure that you find interesting.

    (8 marks)

4   Read from **line 19** to **the end of the extract**.

    "The writer presents the reader with a strongly negative view of Unoka.
    He is clearly a flawed character with very few redeeming qualities."

    How far do you agree with this statement?

    You should include:
    •   your own perceptions of Unoka
    •   the techniques the writer has used to influence your perceptions
    •   evidence from the text to support your ideas.

    (20 marks)

Section B: Writing

You should spend about 45 minutes answering the question in this section.

Only complete ONE of the tasks below.

*There are 24 marks available for the content of your writing,
and for structuring your ideas in a clear and organised way.*

*There are a further 16 marks available for the technical accuracy of your writing, including
spelling, punctuation and grammar.*

You are advised to plan your answer.

5 You have decided to enter a creative writing competition.

A panel of published authors will judge your writing.

Either:

Write a description inspired by this picture:

Or:

Write a story about people who have different levels of success.

Or:

Write a story that uses **one** of the following titles:

a) The Village

b) Letting Go

c) The Sandstorm

(40 marks)

[End of Test]

CGP

Key Stage 3 English Practice Exam English Language

Paper 2: Non-Fiction

Instructions

- The test is 1 hour and 45 minutes long.
- Write your answers in **black** ink or ball-point pen.
- Cross out any rough work that you do not want to be marked.
- You should **not** use a dictionary.
- Check your work carefully before the end of the test.

Advice

- You should spend about 15 minutes reading through the sources and the five questions that follow.

Score: out of **80**

Source A

The following abridged letters were written by Charles Dickens to his sons, Plorn and Harry, in 1868.

My dearest Plorn,

I write this note to-day because your going away is much upon my mind, and because I want you to have a few parting words from me to think of now and then at quiet times. I need not tell you that I love you dearly, and am very, very sorry in my heart to part with you. But this life is half
5   made up of partings, and these pains must be borne. It is my comfort and my sincere conviction that you are going to try the life for which you are best fitted. I think its freedom and wildness more suited to you than any experiment in a study or office would ever have been; and without that training, you could have followed no other suitable occupation.

What you have already wanted until now has been a set, steady, constant purpose. I therefore
10   exhort you to persevere in a thorough determination to do whatever you have to do as well as you can do it. I was not so old as you are now when I first had to win my food, and do this out of this determination, and I have never slackened in it since.

Never take a mean advantage of anyone in any transaction, and never be hard upon people who are in your power. Try to do to others, as you would have them do to you, and do not be
15   discouraged if they fail sometimes.

I hope you will always be able to say in after life, that you had a kind father. You cannot show your affection for him so well, or make him so happy, as by doing your duty.

Your affectionate Father.

My Dear Harry,

20   Now, observe attentively. We must have no shadow of debt. Square up everything whatsoever that it has been necessary to buy. Let not a farthing be outstanding on any account, when we begin together with your allowance. Be particular in the minutest detail.

It appears to me that an allowance of two hundred and fifty pounds a year will be handsome for all your wants, if I send you your wines. I mean this to include your tailor's bills as well as every
25   other expense; and I strongly recommend you to buy nothing in Cambridge, and to take credit for nothing but the clothes with which your tailor provides you.

Whatever you do, above all other things keep out of debt and confide in me. If you ever find yourself on the verge of any perplexity or difficulty, come to me. You will never find me hard with you while you are manly and truthful.

30   As your brothers have gone away one by one, I have written to each of them what I am now going to write to you. You know that you have never been hampered with religious forms of restraint, and that with mere unmeaning forms I have no sympathy. But I most strongly and affectionately impress upon you the priceless value of the New Testament, and the study of that book as the one unfailing guide in life.

35   Ever your affectionate Father.

Source B

The following abridged letter was published in an article by CNN reporter Deborah Mitchell in 2014.
It was written to her son before he went to university.

Already the days are getting shorter, nature's signal that everything must come to an end and
begin again. It's almost here — the freedom you have longed for all year and the day I've
dreaded for months, perhaps, even, since the day you were born. As a parent, you quickly
realize that life is one long series of letting go: watching your kid crawl, then walk, then run and

5   then drive away.

In less than a month, I'll release you, like a falcon, into the future. Where and how high you
fly will be completely up to you. You won't see me cry — I won't burden you. But I can barely
write this now without laying my head down on my desk and crying for all the happy childhood
memories that will never be experienced again and for all the things we meant to do but didn't.

10   Watching you learn and grow has been one of the greatest experiences of my life. Now you
will have one of the greatest experiences of your life, and I hope that you will remember these
unofficial commandments for the journey ahead of you:

Take chances. As parents, we spend so much time and effort trying to protect our kids that
we take away the chance to learn from mistakes, to grow from failure and to build confidence

15   through success. For years, I've told you to be careful, but I was wrong. So start now — it's not
too late. Take flying lessons. Start that business. Ask out the girl in class, even if you're afraid of
rejection.

You are in no way obligated to follow in the footsteps of either parent. Although I've brought you
up free of religion, as you make your way through college and learn more about science and

20   history and philosophy, you may find that life with God is better than life without. The choice will
be yours. I will be proud of you no matter where you land on the spectrum of belief.

If you use a credit card, pay it off every month without fail. Continue to tithe to* your future by
setting aside $10 or $20 a week. Stick to your rule of waiting three days to make a purchase,
which has helped you avoid emotional or impulse purchases. This will be important as you

25   continue through college because these next few years will be some of your leanest, yet this is
the time in your life when you can also build self-control and financial security.

Don't expect life to be fair, for things to even out in the end or to get your just desserts. You're
not entitled to anything except respect from others. You will have both home runs and strikes.
Don't quit. Life does not reward natural talent or intelligence or beauty. You will be rewarded for

30   a positive attitude, for your competence, but most of all, for your grit.

The underpinnings of treating others well is treating ourselves well, too, for we cannot give love
and respect that we do not have. Don't hurt yourself with too much food or drink. Be the man
who does the right thing, who is fair but also be fair to yourself.

I know you'll be searching for your own answers, but if you ever need an ear or a shoulder, have

35   a question or a problem, I'm here. Always — no matter how far you go in distance or time.

*tithe to — prepare financially for

Section A: Reading

*You should spend about 45 minutes answering **all** the questions in this section.*

1   Read **lines 1 to 12** of **source A**.
    There are **four correct statements** in the list below.
    Shade in the boxes of the statements that are **true**.

    A   Charles Dickens will miss Plorn when he leaves.   ☐

    B   He wants Plorn to think about the contents of the letter.   ☐

    C   Charles Dickens believes that we spend most of our lives saying goodbye. ☐

    D   He doesn't think that Plorn is doing the right thing.   ☐

    E   He would have preferred Plorn to work in an office.   ☐

    F   Plorn has been looking for purpose in his life.   ☐

    G   He thinks Plorn should put more effort into achieving his goals.   ☐

    H   Charles Dickens has worked hard to provide for himself and his family.   ☐

                                                                        (4 marks)

2   Refer to **both sources** for this question.
    Using evidence from **both** sources, summarise the similarities
    in the advice given by the authors.

                                                                        (8 marks)

3   Refer **only** to **source B, lines 13-33** for this question.
    Deborah Mitchell is trying to persuade the reader to follow her advice.
    How does she do this?
    You should write about:
    •   what she says
    •   her language and tone.

                                                                        (12 marks)

4   Refer to **the first letter in source A (lines 1-18)** and **source B** for this question.
    Both texts are about children leaving home. Compare the writers' views on this subject.
    You should write about:
    •   the writers' attitudes to their children leaving home
    •   the methods they use to communicate their attitudes.

                                                                        (16 marks)

Section B: Writing

You should spend about 45 minutes answering the question in this section.

*There are 24 marks available for the content of your answer,
and for structuring your ideas in a clear and organised way.*

*There are a further 16 marks available for the technical accuracy of your answer,
including spelling, punctuation and grammar.*

You are advised to plan your answer.

5 "Children should move out of their parent or guardian's house
once they turn 18 and learn to look after themselves."

Write an article for a newspaper in which you
argue for or against this statement.

(40 marks)

[End of Test]

CGP

Key Stage 3 English Practice Exam English Literature

Paper 1: Unseen Poetry

Instructions

- The test is 45 minutes long.
- Write your answers in **black** ink or ball-point pen.
- Cross out any rough work that you do not want to be marked.
- You should **not** use a dictionary.
- Check your work carefully before the end of the test.

Score: ☐ **out of 32**

Unseen Poetry

Read the following two poems and answer questions 1 and 2.

You should spend about 45 minutes on this paper.

Read the poem below.

Aftermath

Have you forgotten yet?...
For the world's events have rumbled on since those gagged days,
Like traffic checked while at the crossing of city-ways:
And the haunted gap in your mind has filled with thoughts that flow
5   Like clouds in the lit heaven of life; and you're a man reprieved to go,
Taking your peaceful share of Time, with joy to spare.
But the past is just the same — and War's a bloody game...

Have you forgotten yet?...
Look down, and swear by the slain of the War that you'll never forget.

10   Do you remember the dark months you held the sector at Mametz* —
The nights you watched and wired and dug and piled sandbags on parapets?
Do you remember the rats; and the stench
Of corpses rotting in front of the front-line trench —
And dawn coming, dirty-white, and chill with a hopeless rain?
15   Do you ever stop and ask, 'Is it all going to happen again?'

Do you remember that hour of din before the attack —
And the anger, the blind compassion that seized and shook you then
As you peered at the doomed and haggard faces of your men?
Do you remember the stretcher-cases lurching back
20   With dying eyes and lolling heads — those ashen grey
Masks of the lads who once were keen and kind and gay?

Have you forgotten yet?...
Look up, and swear by the green of the spring that you'll never forget.

Siegfried Sassoon

> * Mametz — an area in France where a battle
> during the First World War took place

1   Discuss the poet's attitude to war in *Aftermath*.

(24 marks)

Read the poem below. In both *Aftermath* and *For the Fallen*, the poets write about remembering those who died during the First World War.

For the Fallen (abridged)

They went with songs to the battle, they were young,
Straight of limb, true of eye, steady and aglow.
They were staunch to the end against odds uncounted,
They fell with their faces to the foe.

5   They shall not grow old, as we that are left grow old:
Age shall not weary them, nor the years condemn.
At the going down of the sun and in the morning
We will remember them.

They mingle not with their laughing comrades again
10   They sit no more at familiar tables of home;
They have no lot in our labour of the day-time;
They sleep beyond England's foam.

But where our desires are and our hopes profound,
Felt as a well-spring that is hidden from sight,
15   To the innermost heart of their own land they are known
As the stars are known to the Night;

As the stars that shall be bright when we are dust,
Moving in marches upon the heavenly plain,
As the stars that are starry in the time of our darkness,
20   To the end, to the end, they remain.

Laurence Binyon

2 What are the similarities and differences in the way these poems present the theme of death?

(8 marks)

[End of Test]

CGP

Key Stage 3 English Practice Exam English Literature

Paper 2: Shakespeare and 19th-Century Prose

Instructions

- The test is 1 hour and 50 minutes long.
- Write your answers in **black** ink or ball-point pen.
- Cross out any rough work that you do not want to be marked.
- You should **not** use a dictionary.
- Check your work carefully before the end of the test.

Score: ☐ out of 80

Section A: Shakespeare

Answer **one** question from this section.

You should spend about 55 minutes on this section.

William Shakespeare: *Romeo and Juliet*

1 Read the extract below, then answer the question.

What does Juliet's reaction to the news of Tybalt's death tell the audience about her feelings towards Romeo?

(35 marks)

(+5 marks for spelling, punctuation and grammar)

From Act 3, Scene 2. *In this scene, Nurse informs Juliet of Tybalt's death.*

NURSE:		Tybalt is gone and Romeo banishèd,
		Romeo that killed him, he is banishèd.
JULIET:		O God, did Romeo's hand shed Tybalt's blood?
NURSE:		It did, it did, alas the day, it did!
5	**JULIET:**	O serpent heart, hid with a flowering face!
		Did ever dragon keep so fair a cave?
		Beautiful tyrant, fiend angelical!
		Dove-feathered raven, wolvish-ravening lamb!
		Despisèd substance of divinest show!
10		Just opposite to what thou justly seem'st,
		A damnèd saint, an honourable villain!
		O nature, what hadst thou to do in hell
		When thou didst bower the spirit of a fiend
		In mortal paradise of such sweet flesh?
15		Was ever book containing such vile matter
		So fairly bound? O that deceit should dwell
		In such a gorgeous palace.
	NURSE:	There's no trust,
		No faith, no honesty in men, all perjured,
		All forsworn, all naught, all dissemblers.
20		Ah, where's my man? Give me some aqua vitae.
		These griefs, these woes, these sorrows make me old.
		Shame come to Romeo!
	JULIET:	Blistered be thy tongue
		For such a wish! He was not born to shame:
		Upon his brow shame is ashamed to sit;
25		For 'tis a throne where honour may be crowned
		Sole monarch of the universal earth.
		O what a beast was I to chide at him!

William Shakespeare: *Macbeth*

2   Read the extract below, then answer the question.

What does this exchange between Macbeth and Banquo tell the audience about
Macbeth's ambition?

(35 marks)

(+5 marks for spelling, punctuation and grammar)

From Act 1, Scene 3. *Macbeth and Banquo discuss*
the predictions made to them by the Witches.

	MACBETH:	Do you not hope your children shall be kings,
		When those that gave the Thane of Cawdor to me
		Promised no less to them?
	BANQUO:	That, trusted home,
5		Might yet enkindle you unto the crown,
		Besides the Thane of Cawdor. But 'tis strange,
		And oftentimes, to win us to our harm,
		The instruments of darkness tell us truths,
		Win us with honest trifles, to betray's
10		In deepest consequence.
		Cousins, a word, I pray you.
	MACBETH:	(Aside) Two truths are told,
		As happy prologues to the swelling act
		Of the imperial theme. — I thank you, gentlemen.
		Aside
15		This supernatural soliciting
		Cannot be ill, cannot be good. If ill,
		Why hath it given me earnest of success,
		Commencing in a truth? I am Thane of Cawdor.
		If good, why do I yield to that suggestion,
20		Whose horrid image doth unfix my hair
		And make my seated heart knock at my ribs
		Against the use of nature? Present fears
		Are less than horrible imaginings.
		My thought, whose murder yet is but fantastical,
25		Shakes so my single state of man that function
		Is smothered in surmise, and nothing is,
		But what is not.
	BANQUO:	Look how our partner's rapt.
	MACBETH:	(Aside) If chance will have me king, why, chance may crown me,
		Without my stir.

William Shakespeare: *Much Ado About Nothing*

3   Read the extract below, then answer the question.

What does this exchange between Benedick and Claudio tell the audience about Benedick's feelings towards love?

(35 marks)

(+5 marks for spelling, punctuation and grammar)

From Act 1, Scene 1. *Claudio has just asked Benedick for his opinion of Hero, who Claudio has fallen in love with.*

	BENEDICK:	Do you question me, as an honest man should do, for my simple true judgment; or would you have me speak after my custom, as being a professed tyrant to their sex?
	CLAUDIO:	No; I pray thee speak in sober judgment.
5	**BENEDICK:**	Why, i' faith, methinks she's too low for a high praise, too brown for a fair praise and too little for a great praise: only this commendation I can afford her, that were she other than she is, she were unhandsome; and being no other but as she is, I do not like her.
10	**CLAUDIO:**	Thou thinkest I am in sport: I pray thee tell me truly how thou likest her.
	BENEDICK:	Would you buy her, that you inquire after her?
	CLAUDIO:	Can the world buy such a jewel?
15	**BENEDICK:**	Yea, and a case to put it into. But speak you this with a sad brow? or do you play the flouting Jack, to tell us Cupid is a good hare-finder and Vulcan a rare carpenter? Come, in what key shall a man take you, to go in the song?
	CLAUDIO:	In mine eye she is the sweetest lady that ever I looked on.
20	**BENEDICK:**	I can see yet without spectacles and I see no such matter: there's her cousin, an she were not possessed with a fury, exceeds her as much in beauty as the first of May doth the last of December. But I hope you have no intent to turn husband, have you?
25	**CLAUDIO:**	I would scarce trust myself, though I had sworn the contrary, if Hero would be my wife.
30	**BENEDICK:**	Is't come to this? In faith, hath not the world one man but he will wear his cap with suspicion? Shall I never see a bachelor of three-score again? Go to, i' faith, an thou wilt needs thrust thy neck into a yoke, wear the print of it and sigh away Sundays.

William Shakespeare: *The Tempest*

4 Read the extract below, then answer the question.

What does this extract tell the audience about the
relationship between Prospero and Caliban?

(35 marks)
(+5 marks for spelling, punctuation and grammar)

From Act 1, Scene 2. *Prospero is looking for his servant, Caliban.*

PROSPERO: Thou poisonous slave, got by the devil himself
Upon thy wicked dam, come forth!

Enter **CALIBAN**

CALIBAN: As wicked dew as e'er my mother brush'd
With raven's feather from unwholesome fen
5 Drop on you both! A south-west blow on ye
And blister you all o'er!

PROSPERO: For this be sure tonight thou shalt have cramps,
Side-stitches that shall pen thy breath up. Urchins
Shall, for that vast of night that they may work,
10 All exercise on thee. Thou shalt be pinch'd
As thick as honeycomb, each pinch more stinging
Than bees that made 'em.

CALIBAN: I must eat my dinner.
This island's mine by Sycorax my mother,
Which thou tak'st from me. When thou cam'st first
15 Thou strok'st me and made much of me; wouldst give me
Water with berries in't, and teach me how
To name the bigger light and how the less,
That burn by day and night; and then I lov'd thee,
And show'd thee all the qualities o'th'isle,
20 The fresh springs, brine pits, barren place and fertile —
Curs'd be I that did so! All the charms
Of Sycorax, toads, beetles, bats light on you!
For I am all the subjects that you have,
Which first was mine own king, and here you sty me
25 In this hard rock, whiles you do keep from me
The rest o'th'island.

William Shakespeare: *Twelfth Night*

5   Read the extract below, then answer the question.

What does this extract tell the audience about Orsino's attitude to love?

(35 marks)

(+5 marks for spelling, punctuation and grammar)

Abridged extract from Act 1, Scene 1. *Orsino proclaims his love for Olivia.*

ORSINO:	If music be the food of love, play on,	
	Give me excess of it; that, surfeiting,	
	The appetite may sicken and so die.—	
	That strain again;—it had a dying fall;	
5	O, it came o'er my ear like the sweet south,	
	That breathes upon a bank of violets,	
	Stealing and giving odour.—Enough; no more;	
	'Tis not so sweet now as it was before.	
	O spirit of love, how quick and fresh art thou!	
10	That, notwithstanding thy capacity	
	Receiveth as the sea, nought enters there,	
	Of what validity and pitch soever,	
	But falls into abatement and low price	
	Even in a minute! so full of shapes is fancy,	
15	That it alone is high-fantastical.	
CURIO:	Will you go hunt, my lord?	
ORSINO:		What, Curio?
CURIO:		The hart.
ORSINO:	Why, so I do, the noblest that I have:	
	O, when mine eyes did see Olivia first,	
	Methought she purg'd the air of pestilence;	
20	That instant was I turn'd into a hart;	
	And my desires, like fell and cruel hounds,	
	E'er since pursue me. (...)	
	O, she that hath a heart of that fine frame	
	To pay this debt of love but to a brother,	
25	How will she love when the rich golden shaft	
	Hath kill'd the flock of all affections else	
	That live in her; when liver, brain, and heart,	
	These sovereign thrones, are all supplied and fill'd,—	
	Her sweet perfections,—with one self king!—	
30	Away before me to sweet beds of flowers:	
	Love-thoughts lie rich when canopied with bowers.	

186

William Shakespeare: *A Midsummer Night's Dream*

6 Read the extract below, then answer the question.

What does the extract tell the audience about Hermia's character?

(35 marks)

(+5 marks for spelling, punctuation and grammar)

From Act 1, Scene 1. *Egeus, Hermia's father, is telling Theseus how Lysander has stolen Hermia's heart. She has subsequently refused to marry Demetrius, her father's choice.*

	EGEUS:	With cunning hast thou filch'd my daughter's heart,
		Turn'd her obedience, which is due to me,
		To stubborn harshness: and, my gracious duke,
		Be it so she; will not here before your grace
5		Consent to marry with Demetrius,
		I beg the ancient privilege of Athens,
		As she is mine, I may dispose of her:
		Which shall be either to this gentleman
		Or to her death, according to our law
10		Immediately provided in that case.
	THESEUS:	What say you, Hermia? be advised fair maid:
		To you your father should be as a god;
		One that composed your beauties, yea, and one
		To whom you are but as a form in wax
15		By him imprinted and within his power
		To leave the figure or disfigure it.
		Demetrius is a worthy gentleman.
	HERMIA:	So is Lysander.
	THESEUS:	In himself he is;
20		But in this kind, wanting your father's voice,
		The other must be held the worthier.
	HERMIA:	I would my father look'd but with my eyes.
	THESEUS:	Rather your eyes must with his judgment look.
	HERMIA:	I do entreat your grace to pardon me.
25		I know not by what power I am made bold,
		Nor how it may concern my modesty,
		In such a presence here to plead my thoughts;
		But I beseech your grace that I may know
		The worst that may befall me in this case,
30		If I refuse to wed Demetrius.

Section B: 19th-Century Prose

You should spend about 55 minutes on this section.

Bram Stoker: *Dracula*

1   Read the extract below from Chapter 1, then answer the question.

Discuss how the author creates a menacing atmosphere in the following extract.

(40 marks)

In this extract, Jonathan Harker is on the way to Dracula's castle.
He is accompanied by a mysterious coachman who works for Dracula.

...just then the moon, sailing through the black clouds, appeared behind the jagged crest of
a beetling*, pine-clad rock, and by its light I saw around us a ring of wolves, with white teeth and
lolling red tongues, with long, sinewy limbs and shaggy hair. They were a hundred times more
terrible in the grim silence which held them than even when they howled. For myself, I felt a sort

5   of paralysis of fear. It is only when a man feels himself face to face with such horrors that he can
understand their true import*.
    All at once the wolves began to howl as though the moonlight had had some peculiar effect
on them. The horses jumped about and reared, and looked helplessly round with eyes that rolled
in a way painful to see; but the living ring of terror encompassed them on every side; and they

10   had no choice but to remain within it. I called to the coachman to come, for it seemed to me that
our only chance was to try to break out through the ring and to aid his approach. I shouted and
beat the side of the calèche*, hoping by the noise to scare the wolves from that side, so as to
give him a chance of reaching the trap. How he came there, I know not, but I heard his voice
raised in a tone of imperious command, and looking towards the sound, saw him stand in the

15   roadway. As he swept his long arms, as though brushing aside some impalpable* obstacle, the
wolves fell back and back further still. Just then a heavy cloud passed across the face of the
moon, so that we were again in darkness.

    * beetling — projecting, or overhanging
    * import — importance, or significance
    * calèche/trap — a type of horse-drawn carriage
    * impalpable — unable to be felt by touch

[End of Test]

Answers

Section Three — Improving Your Style

Page 23 — Warm-up Questions

1) Any one or more from the following: use commas, full stops and semicolons; change the word order or use alternative connectives.
2) E.g. gasped, grumbled
3) a) sang happily
   b) sobbed uncontrollably
   c) muttered grumpily
4) False
5) Sentences b), c) and e)
6) a) She smiled like a crocodile with a good dentist.
   b) It made a sound like two trumpets and a sick donkey.
   c) He was as lazy as a toad at the bottom of a well.
   d) It tasted like a biscuit and a cake in one.
7) Version a), because it uses a mix of short and long sentences.
8) a) E.g. Since
   b) E.g. although
   c) E.g. While

Section Four — Understanding Fiction and Non-Fiction

Page 41 — Warm-up Questions

1) E.g. 'He disliked the present.'
2) Any three from: chatty language/slang, personal language, humour, contractions and short sentences.
3) Any five from: alliteration, exaggeration, metaphors, similes, personification, onomatopoeia and imagery.

Page 43 — Practice Questions

1) E.g. The characters' dialogue, e.g. "I am much obliged to you", reflects the formality of society in the 1800s.
2) Lady Dalrymple seems to have a high social status — she has her own carriage and a servant, who she sends into the shop instead of going in herself.
3) It reflects how society was divided by class, as some people were upper-class like Lady Dalrymple and had lots of money, while others were lower-class like the servant, who has to work.

Page 44 — Practice Questions

E.g. Layout feature 1: Heading
Effect: The bold blue heading grabs the reader's attention and makes it clear what the text is about.
E.g. Layout feature 2: Photo of fruit and vegetables
Effect: The colourful photo makes the text seem appealing, and illustrates the subject by showing a range of fruit and vegetables.
E.g. Layout feature 3: Coloured boxes
Effect: The two boxes separate the information so it is clear. The colours are also attractive and make the meal plans more eye-catching.

Page 45 — Practice Questions

1) a) Any two from: dentition, milliseconds, interlocking design, pores.
   b) Using technical language suggests that the writer knows a lot about piranhas.
2) The writer uses similes such as "snapping shut like a steel trap" to imply that there is no escape from the speed of a piranha attack, which makes them sound more dangerous.
3) The writer addresses the reader directly, for example: "you suddenly feel an unspeakable pain". This makes the reader feel as if they are personally at risk from a piranha attack.

Section Five — Writing Fiction and Non-Fiction

Page 61 — Warm-up Questions

1) True
2) c), a), b), d)
3) True

Page 63 — Practice Questions

1) Answers need to follow the layout, tone and style expected of a formal letter. Language techniques should be used to persuade the reader to change their mind, and your answer should be well-organised and clear with correct spelling, punctuation and grammar. Here are some techniques you could include:
   - Formal language: I'm sure you will agree that the whole school does not deserve to be punished for the disgraceful actions of a small minority.
   - Emotive language: Restricting Year 11 pupils' access to the library at lunchtimes could negatively impact on their GCSE studies, which is detrimental not only to the pupils, but to the school as well.
   - List of three: If we manage to agree on these proposals we will have a school that is cheerful, comfortable and a productive place for staff and students.
2) Answers need to reflect purpose and audience using suitable vocabulary and language techniques. Writing needs to be well-organised and clear with correct spelling punctuation and grammar. Here are some techniques you could include:
   - Clear introduction and conclusion: I will explain how choosing to walk or cycle to school can benefit your health, ease congestion and reduce the risk of accidents.
   - Facts: Walking and cycling to school will help to reduce pollution levels and improve pupils' health.
   - Proving the opposition wrong: Those who prefer to drive their children to school may be concerned about their children being at risk from strangers if they walk on their own. However, if more children walk to school, there is safety in numbers and they can walk together in a group.
   - Impersonal criticisms: The increase in the number of cars is causing high levels of pollution, which is damaging to our health. Congestion in the roads by the school gates creates a higher risk of children being involved in road accidents.

Section Six — Essay Writing

Page 80 — Warm-up Questions

1) E.g. 'Tanya felt very uneasy on the way upstairs to her room. It didn't help that it was so dark.'

2) c)

3) E.g. 'Although the ghost disappears, Tanya's feeling that she "hadn't seen the last" of it implies that it will come back later in the story.'

Page 83 — Practice Questions

1) a) E.g. "Say Lord strike you dead if you don't!"
   b) E.g. "eluding the hands of the dead people"
   c) E.g. "ran home without stopping"
   d) E.g. "The marshes were just a long black horizontal line"

2) Your plan should include the main points of your essay and quotes/examples to support your points. Here are some things you could include in your plan:
   - First person narrator tells us Pip is afraid and finds the atmosphere menacing — "ran home without stopping".
   - Threatening language used by the convict — "Say Lord strike you dead if you don't!"
   - Desolate setting — "graves" and presence of the "gibbet". Pip struggles to see what's around him — can only "faintly" see the beacon and the gibbet.
   - Imagery associated with death — "eluding the hands of the dead people" and "as if he were the pirate come to life".

Page 84 — Practice Question

1) Your answer should offer an opinion on the statement. It should comment on the techniques used to create tension, using relevant examples and terminology to support each point. Here are some things you could mention:
   - I agree that the author makes this extract very tense. Dusk is personified and it "advanced" on the character, which shows how the darkness is fast approaching, establishing an eerie setting.
   - Short sentences such as "Then the faces began" are repeatedly used to introduce new threats to the character. They control the direction of the narrative, as each sentence is followed by a description of how the threat frightens the character, which builds tension in the extract. These sentences are also on separate lines from the rest of the text. This creates a pause before and after the line, which makes them seem more dramatic.
   - The author's use of punctuation emphasises the character's fear. The uncertainty about what he sees is shown by "— yes! — no! — yes!". The dashes create pauses, building the tension as the character tries to determine if he imagined the face or whether it was real. The use of punctuation also increases the pace of the text, which adds to the build up of tension.
   - Lists of three are also used to create tension. The faces the character sees are "hard-eyed and evil and sharp", emphasising how terrifying they are. The character himself is described as "alone, and unarmed, and far from any help", which highlights how vulnerable he is.

Page 85 — Practice Questions

1) Dickens makes us dislike **Scrooge** by portraying him as cruel and **obsessed** with money. The first way in which he does this is by using ~~of~~ a series of adjectives such as "squeezing", "scraping", "clutching" and "covetous" to describe Scrooge. All of these **words** have similar meanings, but Dickens uses **multiple** words instead of just one to emphasise his point further. // Another way in which Dickens emphasises Scrooge's cruelty is the description of how he **treats** the staff in **his** counting house. We are told that one clerk works in a "dismal little cell" with no coal for the fire. This shows how **badly** he is treated, especially as it is the **winter**. // Finally, Scrooge is made to seem cruel in the way he speaks to his nephew, Fred. When **he / Fred** comes to Scrooge's counting house to wish him a merry Christmas, Scrooge replies only "bah!" followed by **"Humbug!".**

Section Seven — Analysing Fiction and Non-Fiction

Page 102 — Warm-up Questions

1) When authors use objects to represent ideas.

2) a) flashbacks — when the story moves to events in the past
   b) foreshadowing — when clues are given about later events
   c) flashforwards — when the story temporarily moves to events in the future

3) False

4) a) emotive
   b) impersonal
   c) figurative

Page 105 — Practice Question

1) All your points should use relevant examples and terminology, and comment on the effect of the language used. Here are some things you could mention:
   - The author creates a relaxed setting in the extract. Images of a "deserted" beach and the sea flopping "lazily" establish a peaceful atmosphere. The repetition of "beat down" suggests that the "haze of heat" is so overpowering that all there is to do is relax.
   - The author uses alliteration in the phrases "prone on the paddock" and "flung over the fences". The repetition of the soft 'p' and 'f' sounds adds to the relaxed tone.
   - The author personifies the bathing-dresses as "exhausted-looking". She suggests that they're resting, which creates a sense of relaxation. The fact that the dresses are exhausted suggests that the people who were wearing them have gone to relax too.
   - The author uses several long sentences in the extract which create a slow and relaxed pace for the reader.

Page 106 — Practice Question

1) All your points should use relevant examples and terminology, and comment on the techniques the author uses to persuade the reader. Here are some things you could mention:

- The opening sentence explains that Ranchford Cave has something for everyone as it's suitable for "all abilities and age groups". This suggests that it has a wide appeal and would be suitable for anyone reading the advert.
- The brochure directly addresses the reader and engages them through statements such as "the choice is yours". Referring to the reader as "you" makes the information feel personalised to the individual.
- The writer uses hyperbole such as "You'll want to come back every day!" to entice the reader. The experience is made to sound thrilling and memorable through statements like "an experience you'll never forget".
- Alliteration is used to highlight the main attractions of Ranchford Cave. The caverns are described as a "mysterious maze" and the writer describes the "awesome adventures" the reader could have there. It draws the reader's attention to the main selling points of the brochure and makes them more memorable.

Section Eight — Poetry

Page 118 — Practice Questions

1) 'Windy Nights' — "the trees are crying aloud"
   'Meeting at Night' — "startled little waves that leap / In fiery ringlets from their sleep"

2) Any two from: Whenever / gallop / By.

3) a) The rhythm creates the effect of the man galloping along on his horse.
   b) This poem has a slower rhythm than 'Windy Nights', which creates a sense of calm.

4) 'Windy Nights' — E.g. spooky — The poet keeps the identity of the rider hidden, and asks direct questions about him ("Why does he gallop and gallop about?"), which makes him a more threatening figure. The trees are also "crying" and there is a lack of light ("dark and wet", "the fires are out").
   'Meeting at Night' — E.g. romantic — The phrase "two hearts beating" makes us think of love, and the description of the beach appeals to the reader's senses of sight, smell and touch: "a mile of warm sea-scented beach".

5) For this question, you have to think about how the theme of 'night' is presented in the two poems and the similarities and differences in how the theme is handled. Make sure you comment on the techniques, structure and mood of the poems and how these affect the theme. Here are some points you could make:

- The conventions that R. L. Stevenson uses in 'Windy Nights' present night as frightening, e.g. personification of the trees "crying". By contrast, Robert Browning uses personification to present night as a pleasant time, e.g. "startled little waves that leap / In fiery ringlets from their sleep" — the waves sound like small children, playful and unthreatening.

- The rhythm in 'Windy Nights' mimics the rider galloping along on his horse, forcefully and loudly. In 'Meeting at Night', the rhythm is more gentle and creates the effect of tides gently rising and falling. Stevenson presents night as a time for adventure, whereas night is presented as a much calmer and quieter time in Browning's poem.
- The mood of 'Windy Nights' is spooky, because the identity of the rider is unknown. Stevenson asks "Why does he gallop and gallop about?", which makes him a mysterious figure. The mood of 'Meeting at Night' is far more romantic — the phrase "two hearts beating" makes us think of love, and the beach is "warm" and "sea-scented", which is sensual.

Section Nine — Drama

Page 127 — Warm-up Questions

1) Any two from: who's on stage, what action the character is doing, how actors should say their lines and how the stage is set up.
2) "Plays can be divided into acts and scenes."
3) Time has passed or the story has moved to a new location.
4) a)

Page 129 — Practice Question

1) All your points should use relevant examples and terminology, and comment on the effects of the stage directions. Here are some things you could mention:

- The stage directions describing Willy's actions indicate his panicked state. They show how he is hearing and seeing "sounds, faces, voices" which are making him agitated. His actions are erratic as he "rushes off around the house". This creates a tense atmosphere and builds suspense as the audience anticipates his death.
- Linda calls for Willy "with real fear", which heightens the tension as the audience anticipates what Willy is going to do.
- A "frenzy of sound" is used to suggest that Willy's car has crashed. Because the audience doesn't see the accident on stage, the sound effects convey what has happened.
- The "soft pulsation" of a cello string reflects how the atmosphere has shifted from panic to sadness as they mourn Willy's death.
- After Willy's death, Miller relies on the stage directions to show the audience what is happening, rather than using dialogue. The fact that the characters don't have any lines is unusual. This creates an eerie silence punctuated by the occasional sound effect, which reflects the sombre mood.

Section Ten — Shakespeare

Page 151 — Warm-up Questions

1) histories, comedies and tragedies
2) a) There's a wedding.
   b) A character dies.
3) E.g. Because women weren't allowed to perform in plays.
4) "Blank verse follows a set rhythm, but doesn't rhyme."
5) False

1) All your points should use relevant examples and terminology, and analyse how Lady Macbeth's character is different in the two extracts. Here are some things you could mention:

- In the first extract, Lady Macbeth is unafraid and forceful. She mocks Macbeth for being a "coward" in order to push him into killing Duncan. She is also the driving force behind the plan — she comes up with the idea of framing Duncan's guards for the crime. This shows that she is intent on carrying out the murder and has no concerns about it. This highlights her forceful personality.

- In the second extract, however, Lady Macbeth has become overwhelmed by guilt. The Doctor describes how she looks like she is trying to wash her hands when she is sleepwalking. This action symbolises her feelings of guilt by suggesting that she is trying to wash the blood from the murders off her hands. It shows how far her character has changed from earlier in the play, when she didn't appear to show any guilt or remorse about the things she and Macbeth were doing.

- Lady Macbeth's speech in the second extract is written in prose rather than blank verse. She speaks incoherently, saying "Come, come, come, come, give me your hand". This represents how her mind has become very disturbed, because it is a less formal and less controlled way of speaking. Unlike in earlier scenes, Lady Macbeth is no longer in control and is not the cunning, scheming person she once was.

2) All your points should use relevant examples and comment on how the actors playing Romeo and Juliet might be directed in these scenes. Here are some things you could mention:

- In the first extract, Romeo has broken into the Capulets' garden and is trying not to be noticed — he says "But soft" in line 2 to tell himself to be quiet. To show how he wants to stay hidden, you could direct the actor to speak quietly, and perhaps crouch down. This would make it clear to the audience that Romeo is sneaking into the garden.

- At the start of the first extract, Romeo and Juliet haven't seen each other, so they shouldn't be looking in each other's direction. When Juliet hears Romeo speaking and realises he has heard her "counsel", she could be directed to peer through the darkness, to show how she is trying to spot him.

- In the second extract, Romeo thinks he needs to leave, warning that he must go or "stay and die". However, Juliet doesn't want him to go, trying to persuade him that it is not yet "daylight". To show her desperation for Romeo to stay, the actress could use a pleading voice or even cling onto him to try and stop him leaving. Romeo, in contrast, could be trying to pull away and move towards the edge of the balcony so he can climb down it.

3) All your points should use relevant examples and terminology, and analyse how language is used to trick Benedick and Beatrice. Here are some things you could mention:

- In both extracts, the deceivers praise Benedick and Beatrice to make them sound attractive. In the first, Don Pedro describes Beatrice as "excellent sweet" and "virtuous", while in the second, Hero says that Benedick has an "excellent good name". These compliments encourage Benedick and Beatrice to think of each other romantically by highlighting their respective good features.

- In both extracts, the deceivers warn what will happen if Benedick and Beatrice let themselves remain apart. In Act 2, Scene 3, Claudio says that Beatrice "will die" without Benedick, while in Act 3, Scene 1, Hero warns that Benedick will "Consume away in sighs" soon. This urges Benedick and Beatrice, listening to these speeches, to start a relationship with each other to prevent this suffering.

- In the second extract, Ursula and Hero trick Beatrice in order to encourage her love for Benedick. Hero states that she will "devise some honest slanders / To stain my cousin with" so that Benedick will fall out of love with her. Hero intends for the fear of losing Benedick's love to spur Beatrice into revealing that she loves him. The fact that Hero has no intention of inventing "honest slanders" suggests that Beatrice is strong-willed, as deceiving her is the only way to make her see the truth.

4) All your points should use relevant examples and terminology, and link closely to the theme of ambition. Here are some things you could mention:

- In the first extract, Malvolio is shown to be ambitious for a higher social status. He imagines a scene where he sits in a throne and wears a "velvet gown". This reveals that he desires a high social position and luxury. However, in this imagined scene, he also treats other people badly. He tells them to know their "place" and imagines their "curtsies" to him. This suggests that he wants to be better than other people, rather than wanting equality for everyone.

- Because he is ambitious, Malvolio is easily tricked. For example, he chooses to believe that "M.O.A.I." in Olivia's letter refers to himself, even though he has to "crush" the letters to make this possible. This scene is an example of dramatic irony as the audience also knows that Fabian and Sir Toby are actually deceiving Malvolio. The fact that Malvolio is so easily fooled suggests that ambition can cause someone to become 'blind' to the ways things actually are.

- Malvolio's humiliation in the second extract, in which he wears yellow stockings, suggests that Shakespeare wants to criticise Malvolio's selfish desires. His costume makes him look ridiculous and turns him into a comic figure for the audience, 'punishing' him for his selfishness. However, the audience may also pity him, because his reason for wanting a better social position is due to a sense of inequality, as he was not born wealthy. This suggests that people's ambitions, even if they are selfish, can sometimes be a reflection of social problems.

5) All your points should use relevant examples and terminology, and analyse how language is used to create a threatening atmosphere. Here are some things you could mention:

- Antonio's lack of concern about killing Alonso in the first extract creates a disturbing atmosphere. He asks "where lies that?" in response to Sebastian's comment about his conscience, stating that he doesn't "feel" anything about the plan to murder. This makes the audience feel uneasy, as it suggests Antonio will definitely carry out his plan.

- Caliban's language in the second extract also causes a threatening atmosphere. He describes how Stephano and Trinculo could kill Prospero, using violent verbs such as "brain", "batter", "paunch" and "cut". These gruesome descriptions build an unpleasant mood in the scene, and make the audience feel worried for Prospero.

- The language used about Miranda reinforces this uneasy atmosphere. Caliban explains to Stephano and Trinculo that "most deeply to consider is / The beauty of his daughter", suggesting that Miranda will belong to them if they kill Prospero. Stephano states that he and Miranda will be "king and queen". This emphasises that Miranda could be forced to marry Stephano if her father is killed, and the men pose a threat to her freedom.

6) All your points should use relevant examples and terminology, and link closely to the theme of love. Here are some things you could mention:

- In the first extract, Shakespeare presents love as difficult. Lysander states that "The course of true love never did run smooth", giving a list of reasons for this including differences in social status, age and the objections of others. Each of these explanations is presented as another obstacle to a successful relationship. This emphasises how unlikely love is and how hard it is to make it work.

- Love is also presented as temporary. Lysander uses several similes to describe how love can be easily lost, including "momentary as a sound", "swift as a shadow", "short as any dream" and "Brief as the lightning". These similes emphasise how easily love is stopped and therefore how rare it is for love to succeed. The similes also suggest that love is beautiful. The things love is compared to — sounds, shadows, dreams and lightning — can all be magical and mysterious, partly because they are so brief. Shakespeare therefore suggests that the often temporary nature of love can be what makes it so beautiful.

- In the second extract, Oberon's plan to use a love potion highlights how love can be false. He describes seeing Cupid's arrow hit a flower and explains how he will "drop the liquor" of the flower on Titania's eyes, causing her to love "The next thing then she waking looks upon." The way that love can be so easily faked suggests that it can be difficult to know for sure when love is genuine. This again emphasises how rare and unusual true love is.

Section Twelve — Exam Practice

Page 160 — Test 1
1) When a sentence in a poem flows from one line to another without any pause.
2) C
3) D
4) E.g. they tell the story from their point of view, so they might not be entirely truthful.
5) C
6) E.g. crash / pop / clatter / zoom
7) A short story about a real event.
8) A
9) The second person
10) inverted commas

Page 161 — Test 2
1) The main character
2) D
3) simple future
4) When a character tells the audience their thoughts without the other characters onstage hearing them.
5) D
6) To show where a new line begins.
7) C
8) Any one from: history / tragedy / comedy.
9) C
10) soliloquy

Page 162 — Test 3
1) B
2) D
3) When the audience knows something that the characters don't.
4) Point, Example, Explain, Develop
5) Any one from: their appearance / what they say / how they say things / their body language / what other characters say about them / how they behave towards other characters / the context of the play.
6) The vocabulary a writer uses in a text.
7) D
8) When punctuation creates a pause in a line of poetry.
9) Any one from: e.g. opinions that are made to sound like facts / emotive language / generalisations / exaggeration.
10) D

Page 163 — Test 4
1) An important event that changes the course of a text.
2) D
3) you
4) C
5) An impression you get from a word on top of its actual meaning.
6) C
7) 14
8) E.g. A scene is a small section of a play. Several scenes make up an act, which is a larger section of a play.
9) D
10) The events of the plot happen in chronological order.

Page 164 — Test 5

1) Any four from: to entertain / to inform / to advise / to explain / to argue or persuade.

2) exaggeration / When something is made out to be much better or much worse than it really is.

3) A

4) B

5) When words that are close to each other begin with the same sound.

6) A

7) B

8) Any two from: when to enter / when to leave / how to say their lines / what actions to do.

9) cliffhanger

10) E.g. There was no electricity back then, so the actors and audience needed daylight to be able to see.

Page 165 — Test 6

1) A

2) When a character in a play speaks for a long time.

3) Any three from: e.g. titles / headings and subheadings / columns / boxes / lists / images / graphs / tables.

4) B

5) Any four from: exaggeration / metaphors / similes / personification / alliteration / imagery / onomatopoeia.

6) A less important plot in a play or novel.

7) A form of poetry which doesn't have a rhyme scheme or a set line length / has an irregular structure.

8) C

9) E.g. So you don't sound angry or cause people who are neutral to side with the opposition.

10) B

Page 166 — Test 7

1) When words don't rhyme perfectly, but still sound similar.

2) Any one from: when you make a new point in an essay / when a story moves to a different time / when a story moves to a different place / when you talk about a new person / when a new person speaks / to introduce direct speech in a sentence.

3) E.g. a letter to a friend / a review of a product / an agony aunt column / a magazine article for children.

4) D

5) D

6) D

7) A

8) Any two from: to separate items in a list / to add extra information / to separate the adverbial from the rest of the sentence / to make the meaning of a sentence clearer / to introduce direct speech in a sentence.

9) E.g. because women weren't allowed to act onstage.

10) When a line of poetry rhymes with the next line.

Page 167 — Test 8

1) A figure of speech which has been used so much that it's lost its effect.

2) A word or part of a word which can be said in a single sound.

3) D

4) A

5) Any two from: e.g. a headline / headings and subheadings / columns / photos.

6) E.g. sarcasm is angrier than irony.

7) D

8) C

9) Stage directions are usually written in italics or in brackets.

10) Any two from: e.g. a job application / a letter of complaint / a newspaper article / a report.

Practice Papers — English Language

Pages 170-171 — English Language: Paper 1

1) 1 mark for each valid response given, up to a maximum of four marks. Answers might include:

- Okonkwo was eighteen years old when he beat Amalinze the Cat.
- Okonkwo beat Amalinze.
- Winning the fight brought honour to Okonkwo's village.
- Amalinze was a good fighter.
- Amalinze was unbeaten for seven years.
- Amalinze was known as the Cat.
- The fight was one of the fiercest anyone had seen.

2) Your points should use relevant examples and terminology, and comment on the effects of the language used. Here are some things you could mention:

- The author uses figurative language to describe Okonkwo. One simile, "as slippery as a fish in water", tells us that Okonkwo is very agile. The reader is also told in another simile that Okonkwo's fame grew "like a bush-fire in the harmattan" after he defeated Amalinze. This suggests that Okonkwo's victory very quickly earned him the respect of his tribe.

- Okonkwo is described as "tall and huge". Using two synonymous words emphasises how imposing Okonkwo is.

- The writer uses the phrase "it was said that" when describing Okonkwo. This suggests that Okonkwo is something of a legend in the area, because people talk about him.

- Strong emphasis is placed on how quickly Okonkwo turns to violence. The author repeats the word "pounce", which reinforces the idea Okonkwo can be violent. The word "pounce" has connotations of an animal hunting and evokes an image of a swift act of violence to kill prey. This reinforces the speed with which Okonkwo becomes violent.

- Changing sentence length has a significant impact on the reader's perception of Okonkwo. The sentences at the beginning of this section are relatively long, but the last two ("He had no patience with unsuccessful men. He had had no patience with his father.") are quite short. This reflects the shortness of Okonkwo's temper.

3) Your points should use relevant examples and terminology, and comment on the effects of the structural features used. Here are some things you could mention:

- The extract begins in very dramatic fashion with a fight between Okonkwo and Amalinze. Jumping straight into the action immediately grabs the reader's attention.

- Throughout the extract, there are several shifts in time. For example, after describing the fight between Okonkwo and Amalinze, the narrative jumps forward around twenty years to the description of Okonkwo in the present day. Soon after, it jumps back again to a time when Okonkwo's father was still alive. This has the effect of holding the reader's attention because the reader isn't sure what the narrative will describe next.

- Placing the description of Unoka immediately after the description of Okonkwo encourages the reader to make a direct comparison between these two characters, and draw their own conclusions about how different the two characters are.

- The way the extract ends is completely at odds with the way it begins, because Unoka's childhood is described as very laid back and cheerful. While this isn't necessarily as gripping as the fight scene that opens the novel, the change of pace effectively reflects the content and holds the reader's attention.

4) Your answer should offer an opinion on the statement. It should comment on the techniques the writer uses to portray the character of Unoka, using relevant examples and terminology to support each point. Here are some things you could mention:

- I agree in some ways that Unoka is a "flawed character". The reader's immediate impression of him is that he was "lazy", "improvident" and "quite incapable of thinking about tomorrow." This either suggests that he doesn't think about the future or can't be bothered to prepare for it, neither of which is a very good quality for someone to have.

- The extract goes on to explain that Unoka was careless with money, because he "made merry" and drank away what little money he had with his neighbours. Worse still, the reader finds out that the money he spent in this way was borrowed from other people. He owed "a few cowries to quite substantial amounts" to various people. This portrays Unoka as a reckless and selfish person.

- Unlike his son, Unoka was also physically unimpressive. He is described by the author as being "tall but very thin", with "a slight stoop" and "a haggard and mournful look". This should also be viewed as a flaw in a society that clearly favoured the athleticism of people like Okonkwo.

- However, the image of Unoka presented to the reader is not completely negative. He was "very good on his flute" to the point where his talents were in demand from other villages, and he seems to have been well-liked in spite of his debts to many of his neighbours.

- Unoka is also shown to be more appreciative of the smaller pleasures in life, like the "dazzling beauty" of the sunrise or the return of the kites during the dry season. The fact that he is at one with nature in this way makes him a more sympathetic character to the reader.

- The image of Unoka presented to the reader is therefore more balanced than the statement suggests. He is without doubt "a flawed character", but it would not be accurate to say that he has "very few redeeming qualities".

5) Whether your answer is a story or a description, it needs to use an appropriate tone, style and register to match the purpose, form and audience. Your writing needs to be well-organised, clear and technically accurate. Here are some techniques you could include:

In a description:

- Figurative language: The dense foliage glinted green in the sun like a polished emerald.

- Interesting descriptive words and phrases: The luscious fronds swayed in the breeze as a tendril of dust was whipped up into the air.

In a story:

- Descriptive language that sets the scene: The sun rose gradually over the village, the shadows slowly shortening until everything was bathed in a pale gold light.

- Direct address to the reader: If only you knew what I've been through, you would understand exactly why I can't just let go.

- A dramatic, unexpected event: The endless wall of dust was upon us before we could do anything about it.

Pages 175-176 — English Language: Paper 2

1) 1 mark for shading each of the following statements:
   A — Charles Dickens will miss Plorn when he leaves.
   B — He wants Plorn to think about the contents of the letter.
   F — Plorn has been looking for purpose in his life.
   H — Charles Dickens has worked hard in life to provide for himself and his family.

2) Answers should use relevant quotes from both texts to summarise several similarities in the advice given. Here are some things you could mention:

- The authors give advice on many different areas of life, but there is some overlap in the issues they discuss. For example, both authors address the subject of debt. Charles Dickens explains to Harry that "We must have no shadow of debt". Similarly, Deborah Mitchell gives the same advice but in a 21st century context by explaining that her son should pay off his credit card "every month without fail".

- Dickens and Mitchell both explain to their sons that they are there to help them if needed. They explain that there is no shame in adults asking for help. Dickens reassures that "You will never find me hard with you" as long as his son is honest. Mitchell tells her son that "I'm here. Always" if he needs her.

- Both writers address religion in their advice, but they do not force anything on their children. Instead, they let them choose which path they follow in life. Deborah Mitchell is more open than Charles Dickens as she explains "The choice will be yours". On the other hand, Dickens explains that Harry has not been "hampered with religious forms of restraint", but is more specific with his advice by emphasising "the priceless value of the New Testament".

3) All your points should use relevant examples and terminology, and comment on the effects of the language used, focusing on how it is used to influence the reader. Here are some things you could mention:

- Deborah Mitchell speaks to her son in her letter. But as she never mentions his name and refers to "you" throughout, her advice is addressed not just to her son, but to anyone who reads her letter. By inviting all readers to take her advice, it makes the letter more persuasive to a wider audience.

- The tone of her letter is very encouraging and light-hearted. She uses lots of commands such as "Start that business" which address the reader directly. Her commands vary from serious advice, like "Be the man who does the right thing", to more fun suggestions like "Take flying lessons". The use of commands creates a more direct connection between the reader and the author, which is effective in making the letter more persuasive.

- Although some examples she gives are more specific to her son and his life, on the whole the author's advice is very broad and applies to most people. Advice such as "Don't quit" and "Start that business" could be taken by people at any stage in their life, not just starting university. By giving advice that can be applied to many different situations, the reader is more likely to take the author's advice and use it in their own life.

4) Answers should clearly compare the different attitudes and techniques in each text, using quotations to support points. Here are some things you could mention:

- Both authors explain that they have been thinking about the day when their children will leave home. Charles Dickens addresses this at the beginning of his letter to Plorn, saying "your going away is much upon my mind". Expressing this at the beginning of the letter emphasises how much the author has been thinking about it. Similarly, Deborah Mitchell refers to it as "the day I've dreaded... since the day you were born". Unlike Dickens, Mitchell also looks at the day from her son's point of view and how for him it is "the freedom you have longed for all year". The words "longed for" and "dreaded" contrast starkly with each other and show that children and parents have very different emotions towards leaving home.

- Both Dickens and Mitchell are sad to see their children go and tell them just how much they care for them. Dickens tells Plorn "I love you dearly" and repeats the word "very" to express just how sad he is to see Plorn leave. Mitchell similarly expresses her love for her son by explaining that raising him "has been one of the greatest experiences of my life". Although Dickens refers to the "pains" of saying goodbye, Mitchell expresses more emotion. She tells her son "I won't burden you" with seeing her cry. However, by telling him that she will cry, she lets him know just how much she cares for him and how difficult she finds the experience.

- The two writers accept that letting children go is a part of life. They express the same point, but use slightly different words. Charles Dickens explains that life "is half made up of partings", while Deborah Mitchell explains that "life is one long series of letting go". Both authors make this point despite writing their letters over 150 years apart. This reiterates that children leaving home is something that all parents face and that it is a rite of passage in parenthood.

5) Answers need to use an appropriate tone, style and register to match the purpose, form and audience. Writing needs to be well-organised, clear and technically accurate. Here are some techniques you could include:

- Anecdote: My cousin Siobhan was 18 when she left home. She was racked by nerves for months beforehand, but she now recognises how character-building the experience was for her, and she got a huge sense of satisfaction out of being so independent.

- Magic threes: Continuing to live at home after you turn 18 has many advantages. You can avoid paying high rent prices, build up your savings and have a larger deposit when you come to buy a house.

- Rhetorical questions: Does anyone really want to be a twenty-something professional whose mother still does their laundry?

- Facts and statistics: Although unemployment rates among young people are falling, 16-24-year-olds are the age group most at risk of unemployment. Renting their own property is not financially viable for many young people.

- Direct address: Turning 18 is a rite of passage — you're young, free and independent, learning how to survive on your own two feet. You have to seize the opportunity to fly the nest and start enjoying your adulthood.

Practice Papers — English Literature

Page 178-179 — English Literature — Paper 1: Unseen Poetry

1) For this question, you have to think about what the poet says about his attitude to war and how he presents this attitude. Be sure to comment on how form, structure and language are used to present feelings and ideas in the poem. Here are some points you could make:

- *Aftermath* is about Sassoon's experiences of the war and the need to remember the sacrifice of those who weren't fortunate enough to survive as he did. Line 15 ("Do you ever stop and ask, 'Is it all going to happen again?'") is the best indicator of what Sassoon's concern is — if we allow ourselves to forget this war, more might follow.

- Sassoon also makes the war out to be pointless, referring to it as "a bloody game". The word "bloody" has a double meaning — it refers to the bloodshed involved in war, but is also a swear word to express Sassoon's frustration at the needless loss of life he has witnessed.

- The poem's first stanza talks about the post-war period, when "the world's events have rumbled on". This means that many people's lives are starting to return to normal, but Sassoon is unable to move on from his experience of the war, saying that "the past is just the same". The remaining stanzas mainly reflect back on what Sassoon saw during the war, such as the "ashen grey / Masks" of his fellow soldiers. The "Masks" dehumanise the soldiers and obscure how "kind and gay" their faces once were. The "ashen grey" colour shows how the young men have been robbed of their youth and their vitality, which emphasises how tragic the war is.

- The poem is quite irregular in structure: the length of the stanzas and lines within each stanza varies, and although there is a rhyme scheme, it is not consistent. For example, the third stanza is made up of three rhyming couplets, but the fourth stanza follows an ABBACC rhyme scheme. This variation in the rhyme scheme reflects the unpredictable nature of war. The inconsistent structure also gives the poem quite a chaotic look on the page, which reflects the chaos of war itself.

- In the first stanza, Sassoon uses a fairly innocent simile to describe life returning to normal: "the world's events have rumbled on since those gagged days, / Like traffic checked while at the crossing of city-ways". However, as the poem progresses and Sassoon starts to address the horrors of war, the imagery becomes graphic and matter-of-fact. He evokes in the reader's mind "the rats; and the stench / Of corpses rotting in front of the front-line trench". Rather than hiding behind similes or other techniques, Sassoon describes the war exactly as he remembers it to emphasise how awful it really was.

- Sassoon also presents war as very wearisome. This is apparent in line 11: "The nights you watched and wired and dug and piled sandbags on parapets". The repeated use of the word "and" makes the sentence seem endless. Including multiple verbs emphasises the long list of responsibilities the soldiers had and the exhaustion they must have felt.

- Two rhetorical questions are repeated throughout the poem. The first — "Have you forgotten yet?..." — implies that there is a strong chance of the war being forgotten at some point in the future, which is exactly what Sassoon wants to avoid. He uses another rhetorical question, "Do you remember...?", to remind the reader what he and other soldiers went through, therefore making it harder to forget.

2) For this question, you have to think about how the theme of death is presented in the two poems. You are asked to make a comparison, so think about the similarities and differences in form, structure and language and how the poet uses these to present feelings and ideas in the poems. Try to compare both poems in every paragraph, rather than writing about one poem followed by the other. Here are some examples of points you could make:

- *Aftermath* and *For the Fallen* both discuss the importance of remembering those who died during the First World War, but the poets approach this subject in different ways. *Aftermath* reads almost like a warning — Sassoon thinks that if we don't remember the dead and learn from their sacrifice, there's a good chance it will all "happen again". Binyon is much more confident that the dead will not be forgotten, saying that "At the going down of the sun and in the morning / We will remember them."

- In Binyon's poem, each stanza contains four lines: three longer lines followed by a shorter line. The second and fourth lines always rhyme with each other (e.g. "aglow" and "foe", "condemn" and "them"). This lends the poem a gentle rhythm and mirrors the "steady" and "staunch" way in which young men went to their almost certain deaths. In contrast, *Aftermath* is quite irregular in terms of line length, stanza length, rhyme and its appearance on the page. The rhythm is also interrupted by a number of caesuras (e.g. "But the past is just the same — and War's a bloody game"). Sassoon's poem therefore gives the reader a more realistic impression of how chaotic war really was, with death being a constant possibility.

- In *For the Fallen*, the dead are described in idealised terms. Those who died were "young, / Straight of limb, true of eye, steady and aglow", and the reader is told that "They shall not grow old, as we that are left grow old." This couldn't be more different from Sassoon's graphic recollections of the dead, with their "dying eyes and lolling heads" and faces compared to "ashen grey / Masks". Even those still alive in *Aftermath* are described as "doomed and haggard".

- The way Binyon describes soldiers falling "with their faces to the foe" presents being killed in action as an honourable and even glorious way to die. There is no suggestion in *For the Fallen* that the lives of these young soldiers were wasted. Sassoon, on the other hand, shows his frustration in *Aftermath* that so many "lads who once were keen and kind and gay" died in the name of little more than "a bloody game". The death of young men is made even more tragic by the fact that it seems to be for nothing.

- *For the Fallen* ends by comparing the memory of the dead to the stars in the night sky, which suggests that it will remain in people's minds "to the end". Sassoon is more doubtful of how long people will continue to remember the dead, which is why he finishes his poem by making the reader swear that they'll "never forget". While both poets agree that the dead need to be remembered long-term, Binyon is much more positive than Sassoon about how easy this will be to achieve.

<u>Page 181-186 — English Literature — Paper 2:</u>
<u>Section A (Shakespeare)</u>

1) For this question, you'll need to pay close attention to the language used in the extract. Close analysis of the language is the best way to get a good impression of how a character is feeling. Remember to back up each of your points with quotes from the extract. Here are some points you could make in your answer:

- Juliet's immediate reaction to the news of Tybalt's death is very conflicted. She uses a number of contradictory images to describe Romeo, including "fiend angelical", "damnèd saint" and "honourable villain". This shows that she is caught between her love for Romeo and her anger and shock at what he has done.

- During Juliet's monologue, there is a strong focus on her physical attraction to Romeo. One of the main sources of shock for her seems to be that someone so beautiful could do something so awful: "Was ever book containing such vile matter / So fairly bound? O that deceit should dwell / In such a gorgeous palace!" This suggests that her feelings towards Romeo are still quite shallow.

- Juliet's contradictory reaction to the news that Romeo has killed Tybalt contrasts with that of her Nurse. The Nurse is in no doubt that Romeo is to blame and doesn't hesitate to express her anger: "Shame come to Romeo!" This is the reaction you might expect to see from a member of Tybalt's own family, so the fact that Juliet doesn't react in the same way highlights how intense her feelings for Romeo really are.

- When the Nurse starts to criticise Romeo, Juliet makes up her mind and starts to defend him. The Nurse's words ("Shame come to Romeo!") are met with a furious response from Juliet: "Blistered be thy tongue / For such a wish!" These are very strong words for Juliet to use to someone who has looked after her since she was a baby, and so are a good indicator of how strongly she feels about Romeo.

- In the last line of the extract, Juliet feels guilty for having doubted Romeo: "Oh what a beast was I to chide at him!" Her initial indecision about her feelings for Romeo has given way to a certainty that she still loves him — she feels like "a beast" for even thinking of criticising him.

2) For this question, you'll need to consider what the extract tells you about a character's emotions. Analysing two different characters discussing the same event is a good way to understand how a character might be feeling (in comparison with another). Remember to back up each of your points with quotes from the extract. Here are some points you could make in your answer:

- The exchange between Macbeth and Banquo shows the audience that Macbeth is ambitious for power and a high status in society. Macbeth asks Banquo "Do you not hope your children shall be kings?" The fact that he assumes Banquo will "hope" for this to happen suggests that Macbeth values having power and a high status in society, and expects others to feel the same.

- Macbeth sees the predictions that have come true so far as a good thing. He describes the two correct predictions that the witches have made as "happy prologues" to the "swelling act / Of the imperial theme". This shows how glad he is that they have come true and suggests that he views them as leading the way to him becoming king. This implies to the audience that Macbeth views the predictions in a broadly positive way and is focused on how they can help him achieve his ambition.

- Macbeth's feelings about the witches' predictions contrast with those of Banquo. Banquo is suspicious about the predictions and expects them to cause "harm" and "deepest consequence". This makes the audience aware that the witches' predictions could be dangerous. In contrast, Macbeth's lack of suspicion about the predictions emphasises his strong sense of ambition, because it has made him less aware of the dangers of the predictions.

- Macbeth is presented as being overwhelmed by his ambitious thoughts. Banquo describes him as "rapt", suggesting he is in a trance. This highlights how Macbeth can't stop thinking about becoming king. It also suggests that Macbeth is becoming detached from reality, showing how strongly his ambition is affecting him.

- However, Macbeth seems scared by his own ambition and the murderous thoughts it has given him. He describes the idea of murdering the king as a "horrid image" that causes his heart to "knock" at his ribs. His knocking heart indicates that it is beating fast and therefore that he is very scared. This suggests that Macbeth is horrified and frightened by his murderous thoughts. Macbeth's fear suggests that, at this stage in the play, his ambition is not completely all-consuming, as he is still disturbed by the idea of murdering the king.

3) For this question, you'll need to consider what the extract tells you about a character's feelings about love. Analysing two different characters discussing the same topic is a good way to understand how a character might be feeling (in comparison with another). Remember to back up each of your points with quotes from the extract. Here are some points you could make in your answer:

- The exchange between Benedick and Claudio suggests that Benedick doesn't take love seriously. When Claudio asks Benedick to give his view of Hero, he plays on words instead of giving a proper answer, saying that Hero is, for example, "too low for a high praise". The use of the contrasts "low" and "high" suggests that Benedick is enjoying using words in interesting ways rather than answering Claudio's question. This indicates that Benedick does not take love as seriously as Claudio.

- Benedick deliberately undermines Claudio's romantic language. Claudio uses a metaphor to describe Hero as a "jewel", suggesting that she is beautiful and precious. However, Benedick then states that you could also buy a "case" for the jewel. This makes the jewel seem ordinary, by describing it as something that could be bought and contained, making Claudio's image of Hero as a jewel seem a lot less romantic. Benedick's undermining of Claudio's romantic language suggests that he claims not to believe in romantic love.

- Benedick seems afraid to talk about romantic love in an honest way. He needs the reassurance of Claudio that he is asking his question in a serious romantic "key" to answer it honestly. Benedick's fear of discussing love suggests that he might have been spurned in love in the past. Benedick's difficulty talking about love and his unromantic opinions may therefore be consequences of his past experiences, and may not reflect how he really feels.

- Benedick's view of Hero suggests to the audience that he is quite shallow. He doesn't agree with Claudio's view that she is "the sweetest", instead seeing "no such matter" and claiming that Beatrice "exceeds" Hero in beauty. Benedick's emphasis on beauty could imply that he is shallow, by focusing on her appearance, and incapable of talking directly about love. However Benedick's view that Beatrice is beautiful suggests that he may be secretly in love with her. This implies his true feelings of love and hints to the audience the events that are to come between Benedick and Beatrice.

- Yet Benedick has a very negative view of marriage. He describes marriage as a "yoke" around a married person's neck. His idea of marriage as a restraint like the sort used to hold animals shows how poorly he views marriage. This makes the audience wonder whether his view will change during the rest of the play, especially since he seems to be attracted to Beatrice.

4) For this question, you'll need to pay close attention to the language used in the extract. Close analysis of the language used is the best way to get a good impression of how two characters feel about each other. Remember to back up each of your points with quotes from the extract. Here are some points you could make in your answer:

- The extract shows that Prospero and Caliban have a very poor relationship, seeming to hate each other. Prospero verbally abuses Caliban, calling him "poisonous" and "got by the devil himself", and Caliban curses Prospero in return. The extensive use of exclamation marks in this exchange, for example, "And blister you all o'er!", shows how angry the characters are. The exchange makes the audience wonder what happened to cause such hatred between them.

- Prospero threatens pain as a punishment on Caliban, showing how Caliban is his "slave". He promises Caliban "cramps" and to be "pinch'd / As thick as honeycomb". This simile is extreme and suggests that Prospero especially wants to hurt Caliban. This emphasises how negatively Prospero thinks of him. However, it also seems harsh, highlighting how their relationship is very unbalanced, because Prospero has the upper hand.

- Caliban describes how Prospero helped him when they first met. Prospero "strok'st" and cared for him; gave him "Water with berries in't"; and taught him how to speak, seeming to take on a parental role for Caliban. This implies that Prospero may at one point have held affection for Caliban. This indicates that their relationship wasn't always so bad, and makes their transition into master and slave more shocking.

- Caliban is presented as feeling betrayed by Prospero. He exclaims "Curs'd be I that did so!", demonstrating his unhappiness that Prospero took his island, and regret that he showed him courtesy. Monosyllabic words highlight Caliban's bitterness and the position of "Curs'd" at the start of the sentence emphasises that Caliban feels Prospero took advantage of his actions and brought about his misfortune.

- Caliban suggests that Prospero is an unfair ruler of the island. He describes Prospero as a "king" and himself as one of Prospero's "subjects". This suggests that Prospero rules without listening to other people and thinks he is better than them. It also emphasises how Prospero has more control than Caliban and how Caliban feels he has been badly treated. The criticism further shows how poor Prospero and Caliban's relationship has become.

5) For this question, you'll need to pay close attention to the language used in the extract. Close analysis of the language used is the best way to get a good impression of a character's attitude about love. Remember to back up each of your points with quotes from the extract. Here are some points you could make in your answer:

- The extract suggests to the audience that Orsino has a very romantic attitude to love. In the opening lines, Orsino tries to use music to get rid of his feelings of love, hoping that it may cause them to "sicken and so die". However, he still can't help thinking romantic thoughts, describing the music as "the sweet south" breeze that "breathes upon a bank of violets". This image of soft wind and flowers is very romantic and beautiful. This suggests that Orsino tends to think of love in a romantic way.

- However, Orsino also seems to believe that love can become a negative thing. His desire for music to make his love go away suggests that love can be unpleasant when experienced excessively. This shows that Orsino understands that love can have a negative side and implies that his attitude towards love is more complex than being completely romantic.

- Orsino's consideration of whether love is actually just about the imagination implies that he is unsure about love. He states that "fancy" is "so full of shapes" that it is "high-fantastical", linking love ("fancy") with the "fantastical" imagination. This shows that he is aware that feelings of love are not always real and implies that he has concerns his own feelings of love may only be imaginary.

- Orsino appears to view love as inescapable. When Curio asks him to go hunting, he describes himself as a "hart" and his desires as hounds chasing him. Thinking of himself as a hunted animal shows that he feels helpless to love and sees himself as a victim. It also suggests that he views love as unavoidable, because he cannot fight back against his desires and is bound to be caught by them eventually. This indicates that he believes love is very strong and that falling in love is inevitable and unavoidable.

- Yet at the end of the extract, Orsino still seems romantic and enjoys being in love. He states that he wants to lie on "sweet beds of flowers" to think "Love-thoughts". The slightly silly image and the fact that he is once again thinking of flowers, as he did at the start of the extract, shows that he is still very romantic, despite his worries about love. It also suggests that he likes thinking about love and wants to do it more. This implies to the audience that he may, ultimately, be more in love with the feeling of being in love than with Olivia herself.

6) For this question, you'll need to consider what the extract tells you about a character. Analysing a character helps you to understand their behaviour. Remember to back up each of your points with quotes from the extract. Here are some points you could make in your answer:

- The extract shows that Hermia used to be very obedient. Egeus claims that Lysander has "Turn'd her obedience", indicating that she used to be very polite and dutiful. Hermia also expresses surprise herself that she is now so confident, stating "I know not by what power I am made bold". This suggests that she was especially obedient before and that her current behaviour is now very different.

- Hermia is defiant in opposing her father's choice of husband. She states bluntly "So is Lysander" when Theseus describes Demetrius as "worthy". The shortness of the sentence makes her view seem strong and shows how she is confidently standing up to her father. She appears especially bold because she is going against the social expectations of the time, when daughters were expected to obey their fathers and marry whoever they were told to. For example, Theseus says that Hermia ought to see her father "as a god", the simile showing how women were expected to follow orders. Hermia's refusal to do so therefore emphasises her defiance.

- Hermia comes across to the audience as brave in the extract. Egeus threatens her with "death" if she doesn't marry Demetrius. However Hermia still stands up to him even after hearing this. This shows how brave she is as well as how strongly she feels about Lysander, because she is prepared to die for their love.

- Hermia is presented as a reasonable person. She wishes that her father would consider her perspective — "I would my father look'd but with my eyes". This suggests that she wants to have a good relationship with her father by politely asking him to take into account her point of view. This makes the audience feel more on her side, as she seems very fair in her request.

- Hermia's request that Egeus sees with her "eyes" also emphasises how she believes that her own view is as important as her father's. This is unlike Theseus, who says that she should look only with Egeus' "judgment" and follow his orders. Again, this shows how Hermia is going against the normal social expectations of women at the time by valuing her own opinion, emphasising how she is a brave and determined character.

Page 187 — English Literature — Paper 2: Section B (19th-Century Prose)

1) For this question, you have to write about how the author creates a menacing atmosphere in a given extract, so you need to pick out the bits that contribute to this atmosphere and relate them back to the question. Don't forget to use plenty of quotes and examples from the extract in order to discuss the question in detail. Here are some examples of points you could make:

- The extract starts in darkness ("the moon, sailing through the black clouds, appeared...") and ends in darkness ("a heavy cloud passed across the face of the moon..."). Harker only spots the wolves when the moon appears, which means they have surrounded the carriage unseen. This adds to the sense of Harker's vulnerability and therefore the menacing atmosphere of the extract.

- Stoker uses a lot of vocabulary relating to fear throughout the extract. The words "terrible", "fear" and "horrors" all appear in the space of a few lines, which emphasises Harker's own feelings about the situation he is in.

- The vivid description of the wolves plays an important role in the creation of a menacing atmosphere. Firstly, they are terrifying to look at, with their "white teeth", "lolling red tongues" and "shaggy hair". Furthermore, Stoker describes how they sound: they stand in "grim silence" at the start, but soon begin to howl. Perhaps surprisingly, Harker finds the silence "a hundred times more terrible" than the howling. Appealing to two of the reader's senses — sight and hearing — instead of just one is much more effective in creating a menacing atmosphere.

- Stoker compares the wolves to a "living ring of terror" encompassing the carriage and its horses "on every side". The idea that there is no possibility of escape (at least until the coachman arrives) adds to the menacing atmosphere.

- Despite getting rid of the wolves and apparently saving Harker's life, Dracula's coachman himself contributes to the creation of a menacing atmosphere. When he first appears in this extract, Harker says "How he came there, I know not", which hints at there being something supernatural about him. The fact that the coachman is able to scare off the wolves so easily also suggests that he is in some way even more "terrible" than they are.

Glossary

alliteration	When words that are <u>close together</u> start with the <u>same sound</u>. E.g. "the <u>b</u>eat of the <u>b</u>and".
anecdote	A <u>short</u> story that describes a <u>real</u> event or person.
aside	When a <u>character</u> in a play makes a <u>short comment</u> that reveals their <u>thoughts</u> to the <u>audience</u>, and no other character can hear it.
audience	The <u>person</u> or <u>group of people</u> that read or listen to a text or that watch a play.
biased writing	Writing that gives <u>more support</u> to one point of view than to another.
blank verse	Lines from a play or poem that are written in a <u>set rhythm</u> and <u>don't rhyme</u>.
caesura (plural <u>caesurae</u>)	A <u>pause</u> in a line of poetry. E.g. the full stop in "Over the drifted stream. My father spins" ('Eden Rock' by Charles Causley).
characterisation	The way that an author <u>creates</u> or <u>presents</u> a fictional character.
chronological	When events are arranged in the <u>order</u> in which they <u>happened</u>.
clause	Part of a sentence that has a <u>subject</u> and a <u>verb</u>. <u>Main clauses</u> make sense on their own.
clichés	Words and phrases that are so <u>commonly</u> used that they've <u>lost their effect</u>, e.g. "She was as fit as a fiddle."
connotations	The <u>suggestions</u> that words can make <u>beyond</u> their obvious meaning. E.g. 'stroll' means 'walk', but it has connotations of moving slowly.
context	The <u>background</u> to something, or the situation <u>surrounding</u> it, which affects the way it's understood. E.g. the context of a text from 1915 would include the First World War.
dialogue	A <u>conversation</u> between <u>two or more</u> people in a <u>play</u> or a <u>novel</u>. Dialogue is shown with <u>inverted commas</u> in a novel, but not in a play.
direct address	When a narrator or writer <u>speaks directly</u> to another character or to the reader, e.g. "you might recall..."
dramatic irony	When the reader or audience <u>knows something</u> that a character <u>does not know</u>.
emotive	Something that makes you <u>feel</u> a particular <u>emotion</u>.
enjambment	When a sentence or phrase runs over from <u>one line</u> or <u>stanza</u> to the <u>next</u>.
figurative language	Language that is used in a <u>non-literal</u> way to create an effect, e.g. personification.
first person	A <u>narrative viewpoint</u> where the narrator is one of the <u>characters</u>, written using words like 'I', 'me', 'we' and 'our'.
flashback	A technique where a scene shifts from the <u>present</u> to an event in the <u>past</u>.
flashforward	A technique where the scene temporarily shifts from the <u>present</u> to an event in the <u>future</u>.
foreshadowing	A literary device where a writer <u>hints</u> or <u>gives clues</u> about a <u>future event</u>.
form	The <u>type</u> of text (e.g. a letter, a speech) or poem (e.g. a sonnet or a ballad).
free verse	Poetry that <u>doesn't rhyme</u> and has <u>no regular rhythm</u> or <u>line length</u>.
generalisation	A statement that gives an <u>overall impression</u> (sometimes a misleading one), without going into details. E.g. "children today eat too much junk food."
half-rhymes	Words that have a <u>similar</u>, but not identical, <u>end sound</u>. E.g. "plough" and "follow".

Glossary

hyperbole	When exaggeration is used to have an effect on the reader.
imagery	Language that creates a picture in your mind, e.g. metaphors, similes and personification.
imperative verb	A verb that gives orders or directions, e.g. "run away" or "stop that".
impersonal tone	A tone of writing that doesn't try to directly engage with the reader.
inference	A conclusion reached about something, based on evidence. E.g. from the sentence, "Yasmin wrinkled her nose at the lasagne", you could infer that Yasmin doesn't like lasagne.
irony	When words are used to imply the opposite of what they normally mean. It can also mean when there is a difference between what people expect and what actually happens.
limited narrator	A narrator who only has partial knowledge about the events or characters in a story.
linear structure	A type of narrative structure that tells the events of a story in chronological order.
list of three	Using three words (often adjectives) or phrases together to create emphasis.
metaphor	A way of describing something by saying that it is something else, e.g. "his feet were blocks of ice".
metre	The way syllables are arranged to create rhythm in a line of poetry.
monologue	One person speaking alone for a long period of time in a play.
mood	The general feel or atmosphere of a text, e.g. humorous, peaceful, fearful.
narrative	Writing that tells a story or describes an experience.
narrative viewpoint	The perspective that a text is written from, e.g. first-person point of view.
narrator	The voice or character speaking the words of the narrative.
non-linear structure	A type of narrative structure that tells the events of a story in a non-chronological order.
omniscient narrator	A narrator who knows the thoughts and feelings of all the characters in a narrative.
onomatopoeia	A word that imitates the sound it describes, e.g. 'whisper'.
oxymoron	A phrase which appears to contradict itself, e.g. "pale darkness".
pace	The speed at which the writer takes the reader through the events in a text or poem.
paraphrasing	Describing or rephrasing something in a text without including a direct quote.
personification	Describing a non-living thing as if it's a person. E.g. "The sea growled hungrily."
prose	Any kind of writing which doesn't have a set rhyme or rhythm.
protagonist	The main character in a text, e.g. Pip is the protagonist in 'Great Expectations'.
pun	A word or phrase that's deliberately used because it has more than one meaning, often for humorous effect.
purpose	The reason someone writes a text, e.g. to persuade, to argue, to advise, to inform.

Glossary

register	The specific language used to match the piece of writing to the social situation.
rhetorical question	A question that doesn't need an answer but is asked to make or emphasise a point, e.g. "Do you think the planet is worth saving?"
rhyme scheme	A pattern of rhyming words in a poem, e.g. if a poem has an ABAB rhyme scheme, this means that the first and third lines in each stanza rhyme, and so do the second and fourth lines.
rhymed verse	Lines from a play or poem that are written in a set rhythm which rhyme.
rhyming couplet	A pair of rhyming lines that are next to each other.
rhythm	A pattern of sounds created by the arrangement of syllables.
sarcasm	Language that has a scornful or mocking tone, often using irony.
second person	A narrative viewpoint that is written as if the reader is one of the characters, usually using the pronoun "you".
simile	A way of describing something by comparing it to something else, usually using the words 'like' or 'as'. E.g. "The apple was as red as a rose".
slang	Words or phrases that are informal, and often specific to one age group or social group.
soliloquy	When a single character in a play says their thoughts out loud in a speech, usually for the benefit of the audience, but no other characters can hear them.
stage directions	Written instructions in a play that describe how the play should be staged or performed.
staging	How a play appears on the stage, including the set, costumes and where the actors stand.
Standard English	English that is considered to be correct because it uses formal, standardised features of spelling and grammar.
stanza	A group of lines in a poem, also known as a verse.
structure	The order and arrangement of ideas in a text. E.g. how it begins, develops and ends.
subject	The person (or thing) that performs the action described by the verb. E.g. in "Billy ate a sandwich", Billy is the subject.
syllable	A single unit of sound within a word. E.g. "all" has one syllable, "always" has two.
symbolism	When an object stands for something else. E.g. a cross symbolises Christianity.
theme	A reoccurring idea in a play, novel or poem.
third person	A narrative viewpoint where the narrator remains outside the events of the story, written using words like 'he' and 'she'.
tone	The feeling created by the language of a piece of writing, e.g. happy, sad, serious, light-hearted.
unreliable narrator	A narrator who might not be trustworthy or might present things from their own point of view.
verse	A group of lines in a poem, also known as a stanza.
viewpoint	The attitude and beliefs that a writer is trying to convey.
voice	The characteristics of the person narrating a poem or text.

Index

A

acts 120, 138
adjectives 19, 21, 68
adverbs 10, 18
advise (writing to) 26, 58, 59
'A Forest' 52
alliteration 34, 52
anecdotes 52
apostrophes 6, 132
argue (writing to) 26, 52-57
asides 121
audience 26, 27, 29, 131

B

background (context) 39
bias 98, 99
blank verse 133, 146
body language 123, 140
brackets 8
bullet points 40

C

caesura 111
capital letters 1, 7
characters 87, 88, 120, 122, 123, 140, 142-144
clauses 2
clichés 18, 48
cliffhangers 92
colons 4
comedies 131, 135, 137, 144
commas 3
comparisons
  of texts 76
  to describe 19
conclusions 69
conjunctions 2, 22
connotations 28
context 38, 39, 89, 112, 123, 141
contractions 30
costumes 122, 139
criticism 57

D

dashes 8
debates 155
dialogue 87, 90, 121, 122, 139
discussions 155
drama 25, 120-126
dramatic irony 134

E

ellipses 94
ellipsis 40
embedding quotes 72
emotive language 54, 98, 99
enjambment 111
entertain (writing to) 26
essays (writing) 65-77
evaluating texts 77
exaggeration 34, 55, 56
exclamation marks 1, 40
explain (writing to) 26, 58, 59

F

facts 36, 53, 58, 59, 155
fiction (types of) 25
figurative language 32-34, 48, 90
first-person narrators 37, 93, 98
flashbacks 92
flashforwards 92
fools 144
foreshadowing 92, 136, 147
form 97, 112
formal texts 31, 49, 50
free verse 112
full stops 1

G

gender roles 141, 143
generalisations 99

H

half-rhymes 108
heroes 142
histories 131
humour 29, 30, 35, 135
hyperbole 34
hyphens 8

I

imagery 33, 110, 135
imperative 40
impersonal language 98
inference 28, 90
informal texts 30, 49, 51, 98
inform (writing to) 26, 58
introductions 69
inverted commas 7, 72
irony 28, 35
its and it's 6

L

language
  and context 38
  for different audiences 26
  in fiction texts 90, 91
  in non-fiction texts 98, 99
  in Shakespeare 132
language techniques 32-36, 48, 52-54, 90, 99
layout 26, 27, 29
letters 49-51
lighting 124
linear structure 92
lists of three 36, 54

M

main clauses 2
metaphors 19, 32
metre 111
monologues 121, 134
mood 94
music 124

Index

EHS36